The Credibility

We rely on NGOs to monitor the ethical practices of governments and for-profit firms, and to undertake many humanitarian tasks that public and private actors will not do. While we are critical of public and private sector failures, we do not reflect enough on the credibility of the NGOs which take their place. Can we be sure that products NGOs label as child-labor free are in fact so, that the coffee labeled as "fair trade" is farmed in sustainable ways, or that the working conditions monitored by NGOs are safe and that the wages are reasonable? Can we know that humanitarian organizations are, in fact, using our donations to alleviate human suffering rather than pursuing other goals? This book explores the problems of establishing the credibility of NGO activities as they monitor working conditions, human rights, and elections, and provide finance through microcredit institutions, development aid, and emergency assistance.

PETER A. GOUREVITCH is Distinguished Professor of Political Science and founding Dean of the School of International Relations and Pacific Studies at the University of California, San Diego.

DAVID A. LAKE is Jerri-Ann and Gary E. Jacobs Professor of Social Sciences, Distinguished Professor of Political Science, and (Acting) Dean of Social Sciences at the University of California, San Diego.

JANICE GROSS STEIN is Belzberg Professor of Conflict Management in the Department of Political Science at the University of Toronto and the Director of the Munk School of Global Affairs at the University of Toronto.

The Credibility of Transnational NGOs

When Virtue Is Not Enough

Edited by

PETER A. GOUREVITCH

DAVID A. LAKE

JANICE GROSS STEIN

CAMBRIDGE
UNIVERSITY PRESS

CAMBRIDGE UNIVERSITY PRESS
Cambridge, New York, Melbourne, Madrid, Cape Town,
Singapore, São Paulo, Delhi, Tokyo, Mexico City

Cambridge University Press
The Edinburgh Building, Cambridge CB2 8RU, UK

Published in the United States of America by Cambridge University Press, New York

www.cambridge.org
Information on this title: www.cambridge.org/9781107651692

© Cambridge University Press 2012

First published 2012

Printed in the United Kingdom at the University Press, Cambridge

A catalogue record for this publication is available from the British Library

Library of Congress Cataloguing in Publication data
The credibility of transnational NGOs : when virtue is not enough / [edited by] Peter
A. Gourevitch, David A. Lake, Janice Gross Stein.
    p.   cm.
Includes bibliographical references and index.
ISBN 978-1-107-01804-4 (hbk.) – ISBN 978-1-107-65169-2 (pbk.)
    1. Non-governmental organizations–Moral and ethical aspects. I. Gourevitch,
Peter Alexis. II. Lake, David A., 1956– III. Stein, Janice Gross.
    IV. Title: Credibility of transnational non-governmental organizations.
JZ4841.C73 2012
172′.4–dc23
2011040407

ISBN 978-1-107-01804-4 Hardback
ISBN 978-1-107-65169-2 Paperback

Contents

     CRAIG MCINTOSH

     Conclusion   191

8   Credibility and compromises   193
     PETER A. GOUREVITCH AND DAVID A. LAKE

     References   208
     Index   222

Figures

Tables

Contributors

Michael Barnett is University Professor of Political Science and International Affairs at the George Washington University.

Carew Boulding is Assistant Professor of Political Science at the University of Colorado at Boulder.

Peter A. Gourevitch is Distinguished Professor of Political Science and founding Dean of the School of International Relations and Pacific Studies at the University of California, San Diego.

Susan D. Hyde is Assistant Professor of Political Science at Yale University.

David A. Lake is the Jerri-Ann and Gary E. Jacobs Professor of Social Sciences and Distinguished Professor of Political Science at the University of California, San Diego.

Craig McIntosh is Associate Professor of Economics in the School of International Relations and Pacific Studies at the University of California, San Diego.

Irfan Nooruddin is Associate Professor of Political Science at the Ohio State University.

Sarah Wilson Sokhey is Assistant Professor of Political Science at the University of Colorado at Boulder.

Janice Gross Stein is the Belzberg Professor of Conflict Management in the Department of Political Science and the Director of the Munk School of Global Affairs at the University of Toronto.

Laura Thaut is a Ph.D. Candidate in Political Science at the University of Minnesota.

Wendy H. Wong is Assistant Professor of Political Science at the University of Toronto.

Acknowledgments

This book arose from a shared commitment to the importance of norm enforcement. Governments and firms fail to do many important things, and non-governmental organizations around the world have stepped in to fill the breach. While the public and private sectors are subject to criticism, often withering, NGOs generally do not have to meet the same standards; evaluation is sympathetic and often uncritical. How do we really know that salmon is wild, that a soccer ball was made without child labor? How do we monitor the quality of production processes (invisible in the final product), rather than the use value of the final, visible output? These questions blend into a wider set of theoretical concerns in international relations and comparative political economy, including the impact of global supply chains, the challenges of norm enforcement, and the role of non-state actors.

The authors discovered they shared these concerns at a chance meeting over coffee at the 2008 International Studies Association meeting in San Francisco among Janice Gross Stein, Peter Gourevitch, Susan Hyde, Carew Boulding, and Wendy Wong. In making introductions, we became aware that we shared a common interest in an analysis of NGO efforts to monitor compliance with norms. The opportunity to collaborate was visible and compelling. Off we went, initially through the creative exchange of emails, memos, and drafts that modern technology makes possible. We quickly drew in David Lake at UC San Diego, where Hyde, Boulding, and Wong had recently finished doctorates on topics of importance to our themes. We then added Michael Barnett, working with Stein on Islamic charities, and his student Laura Thaut. We involved Irfan Nooruddin, whose work on child labor was familiar to several of us, and he drew in his student Sarah Sokhey.

In September 2008 we held a planning meeting at the Munk School of Global Affairs at the University of Toronto where we sketched ideas for further work. We held a larger workshop at UC San Diego in March 2009 to which we invited other colleagues, and a third, smaller workshop at the Munk School that overlapped with the Toronto 2009 meeting of the American Political Science Association. We decided to include Craig McIntosh's work on Kiva, presented at the UC San Diego workshop, because it provided a clear case of an NGO responding openly to criticism.

For help in funding the meetings, we thank the Munk School at the University of Toronto, the UC Institute on Global Conflict and Cooperation (IGCC), the Panta Rhea Foundation, and the UC San Diego Senate Research fund. Lynne Bush was, as ever, an admirable editor. Staff were wonderful to us at the School of International Relations and Pacific Studies at UC San Diego, IGCC, and the Munk School. The Munk School and IGCC provided financial assistance to help us prepare the manuscript for publication.

A number of colleagues read various drafts, attended one or more of the workshops, and discussed the ideas in different settings. We note particularly Nigel Bigger, Richard Carson, Mike Hiscox, Lane Jost, Margaret Levi, April Linton, Rick Locke, Kristin Parks, Michael Piore, Dale Squires, and Junjie Zhang. This book is immeasurably better as a result of their critical thinking.

In the process of working on this book, the team of editors discovered anew their shared interests and reinforced their long-standing friendships. Both of these were made easier because of the central importance of the topic: the sense among all three of us that virtue is not enough, that transnational organizations which monitor the public and the private sector themselves have to meet standards of transparency and performance if we are to believe the claims they make. We hope that this volume starts a conversation and stimulates others to continue the work on a subject that we believe will only grow in importance in a more tightly interconnected global system.

Introduction

1 | Beyond virtue: evaluating and enhancing the credibility of non-governmental organizations

PETER A. GOUREVITCH AND DAVID A. LAKE

Does being virtuous guarantee credibility for transnational non-governmental organizations (NGOs)? NGOs are increasingly important in monitoring the ethical behavior of others – certifying that products are made according to socially responsible standards or that elections are free and fair. Likewise, NGOs now deliver greater humanitarian aid around the world than ever before. In both the monitoring and humanitarian activities of NGOs, we rely largely on their own reports to verify performance. Do the products actually meet the desired standards? Does the aid help relieve human suffering? Usually, we are far away from the scene of production or assistance and cannot observe directly what NGOs are doing. Generally, we assume that they have carried out the responsibilities that we, as a society, entrust to them. Yet, sometimes we have reason to wonder about the virtue of NGOs, and we seek reassurances. This book is about that doubt and how it is managed and, possibly, manipulated. When are statements by NGOs credible and believable, when are they not?

Most NGOs are, indeed, virtuous. They pursue laudable goals, attract dedicated individuals who labor hard for little remuneration, and – in general – do good work. We find them credible, in turn, precisely because of their virtue. Recent surveys show that NGOs are

For comments on earlier drafts, we would like to thank Michael Barnett, Suzanne Berger, Carew Boulding, Celia Falicov, Susan Hyde, Miles Kahler, Kal Raustiala, Dan Posner, Michael Schudson, Janice Stein, Wendy Wong, and Dan Yankelovich; and for comments on talks to the Fellows at the Rockefeller Conference Center, Bellagio, Italy, April 23, 2008; the Global Fellows Seminar at UCLA in June 2008; the Law School at Duke University in February 2009; and an APSA panel, September 2009. We also acknowledge the generous financial support of UC San Diego and its Academic Senate, the Panta Rhea Foundation, the University of California Institute on Global Conflict and Cooperation, and the Rockefeller Foundation.

3

trusted to address pressing social problems more than governments
or businesses.[1] But is virtue sufficient? Whereas transnational NGOs
were once mostly small groups of committed activists, many now
are major organizations, and as such are subject to all the pathologies common to large bureaucracies. Reports of malfeasance by nonprofit corporations, increasing in the United States at least, threaten
to undermine confidence in the virtue of the entire NGO community
(Gibelman and Gelman 2004). Even in the absence of explicit wrongdoing, however, NGOs can be threatened with a loss of credibility.
Kiva, the leading peer-to-peer (P2P) microfinance NGO, for instance,
was heavily criticized for oversimplifying its lending procedures on
its website by friendly critics who feared that its misrepresentations
might undermine support for microfinance institutions as a group.
Kiva was forced to respond to preserve its credibility (see Chapter 7).
Similarly, Islamic Relief was challenged after September 2001 on its
charitable work in Islamic countries, especially by Western governments worried that it was channeling funds to possible terrorists. It
undertook a series of institutional reforms to show a now more skeptical audience that it was, in fact, acting in accordance with the practices of other similar NGOs (Chapter 6). When virtue is not sufficient,
NGOs turn to other mechanisms to enhance their credibility. They
are not passive actors who take their virtue for granted, but are active
shapers of how they are perceived by others. Our central question,
then, is when, why, how, and to whom do NGOs make themselves
credible when virtue alone is not enough?

In this volume we examine the issue of credibility from the perspective of NGOs as strategic actors within environments that they cannot fully control.[2] We explore how different audiences evaluate and
come to accept or doubt an organization's credibility. As we outline
in this chapter, NGOs are credible not only when they are virtuous
but also when they share common interests with an audience, send

[1] "Faith, Hope, and Charities," *The Economist*, November 13, 2010, 69–70.
At the same time, surveys indicate that the public systemically underestimates
the extent to which many NGOs accept government funding and are staffed
by professionals rather than volunteers.

[2] On NGOs as strategic actors, see the large literature in economics on
nonprofit organizations, especially Anheier and Ben-Ner 2003 for a review.
For discussions of transnational NGOs as strategic actors, see Barnett 2005;
Bob 2002b, 2005; Cooley and Ron 2002; Gugerty and Prakash 2010; Prakash
and Gugerty 2010a; and Sell and Prakash 2004.

costly signals, incur penalties for misrepresentation, and are subject to third-party verification. When their virtue is challenged, NGOs seek to enhance their credibility by adopting autonomous govern-ance structures, increasing transparency, professionalizing their staff and processes, and integrating into the community of NGOs. These conditions and strategies for credibility are then examined at greater length in Chapters 2–7. We find that NGOs are, indeed, extremely sensitive to the need for credibility, and increasingly aware that they cannot rely simply on their perceived virtue. At the behest of donors who rely on NGOs as their agents, and others who depend on the valuable information and services they provide, NGOs do undertake significant actions to establish and maintain their credibility. This is a valuable asset they strive to acquire and protect.

Indeed, the need to maintain credibility may lead NGOs to act in ways that potentially divert them from their core missions. As we dis-cuss in the concluding chapter, they may emphasize procedure at the expense of substance, shift their focus from the members of the local community with whom they are working "upwards" to their donors, direct resources toward immediate and more easily verifiable tasks and away from longer-term, more ambiguous ends, and become more "bureaucratized." We cannot say that these diversions decrease the effectiveness of NGOs, for without credibility their ability to bring about any social change would be diminished. It is unrealistic to measure real NGOs against a utopian standard where they are always credible on the basis of their virtue alone, and therefore free to devote all of their energies to their appointed tasks. But at the same time, minding their credibility is not without importance and sometimes with costly consequences for NGOs.

NGOs, social change, and the need for credibility

NGOs are engaged in many activities around the world today. In this book, we are concerned primarily with NGOs engaged in the pro-cess of transnational social change, especially NGOs that monitor the ethical behavior of others or provide humanitarian aid and devel-opment assistance to suffering populations.[3] These NGOs are central

---

[3] Other major categories of NGOs include transnational advocacy networks (TANs) (Keck and Sikkink 1998) and nonprofit health and human service providers, of which most of the latter are domestic in their activities. TANs work across the public and private standards division. To the extent that they

to enacting and enforcing ethical standards of third-party behavior, like human rights, honest elections, or goods produced without child labor. They are also bound only by their own standards of behavior when engaged in humanitarian work in other countries. Precisely because they are operating outside areas of established public law, and in areas where actions by all are hard to observe directly, the credibility of NGOs is essential to their success in bringing about social change. Because NGOs are ever more important in monitoring ethical behavior and in providing humanitarian aid, the problem of credibility is more acute today than in the past.

Ethical consumption, which features in several of the case studies below, is an increasingly popular means through which individuals by their purchasing power can seek to improve working conditions abroad, reduce environmental degradation, and in many other small ways improve human welfare. By their examples, individuals hope to encourage others to consume in a more ethical fashion, potentially setting off a "norms cascade" (Finnemore and Sikkink 1998). NGOs are integral to monitoring the production and sale of such ethically-produced goods. In 2008, TransFair USA, the leading fair trade organization in the United States, certified 90 million pounds of coffee produced by cooperatives that were paid a "fair," above-market price for their beans, yielding an additional $32 million for their members.[4] Rugmark similarly certified in that year that $52 million of hand-woven rugs were made without child labor.[5] Consumption of goods labeled antibiotic and pesticide free has grown considerably, and mass suppliers like WalMart are now sourcing organic broccoli from China.

Similarly, NGOs are also deeply involved in promoting and monitoring the ethical behavior of sovereign states, including free and fair elections and internationally recognized human rights practices.[6] Since 1989, for instance, the Carter Center has monitored eighty-

---

lobby for public standards (that is, law), credibility is less central since claims can be contested in established legal settings.

[4] Figures provided by TransFair USA, www.transfairusa.org/content/about/aboutus.php (accessed May 2, 2010).

[5] Constituting about 3.25 percent of the market for hand-woven rugs. Rugmark is now Goodweave. See the annual report at www.goodweave.org/uploads/2008%20Annual%20Report.pdf (accessed May 2, 2010).

[6] One of the first studies of NGOs as monitors of sovereign states is Raustiala 1997.

two elections in thirty-four countries, calling national leaders who engage in electoral fraud to account and sometimes, with the aid of mass demonstrations or foreign pressure, forcing them from office.[7] Amnesty International tracks human rights abuses around the world, issuing annual reports on every country and sending out "urgent action" notices to its members on specific cases of abuse. In all of these examples, NGOs have emerged as powerful monitors of the ethical practices of other private and public actors.

Likewise, NGOs are themselves ethical actors delivering humanitarian aid in crises and, increasingly, implementing long-term development projects that seek to promote human welfare and especially empower previously disadvantaged groups within societies. Humanitarian NGOs such as Save the Children, World Vision, and the International Rescue Committee provide tremendous amounts of aid to countries around the globe, often in alliance with local NGOs in the target countries. For example, CARE USA, one of the largest humanitarian NGOs, distributed in 2008 nearly $708 million in humanitarian aid in sixty-five countries.[8] Since its founding in 2005, the microlending charity Kiva has channeled over $191 million to more than 496,904 small borrowers in fifty-eight developing countries.[9] In contrast to the monitors, such humanitarian NGOs work directly to relieve human suffering. Funded by donations from individuals and corporations, and often under contract to particular governments or international organizations, humanitarian NGOs are on the front lines of relief and development efforts around the world today (Barnett 2005, 2009).

Ethical behavior is regulated in two ways: by public standards, typically enacted into law, and private standards, on which we focus here. The role of NGOs is different under the two types of standards. Where ethical behavior is mandated by law, NGOs often play the role of vigilantes, tracking down violations and pursuing legal remedies (Elliott and Freeman 2003). In such cases, the credibility of the NGO itself is not at issue, as its claims can be contested in a court of law under established rules of evidence. Although it may not be

---

[7] See Carter Center report at http://cartercenter.org/peace/democracy/observed. html (accessed February 9, 2011).

[8] See CARE USA's 2008 report at www.care.org/newsroom/publications/ annualreports/2008/AR_2008.pdf (accessed May 1, 2010).

[9] www.kiva.org/about/facts (accessed February 9, 2011).

common practice, NGOs can make biased claims to provoke popular support for legal action as long as some of their charges stand up
under scrutiny. When clear public standards exist, NGOs need not be
as concerned directly with their own credibility. Their role is to press
governments into enforcing the law, lobby for stronger laws, or urge
compliance with them.

Under private standards, NGOs both promote and enforce normative compliance. Private standards are likely to emerge when ethical
behavior lacks sufficient consensus to be enacted into law – in other
words, when the behavior is not yet widely shared as a norm or lacks
the political strength to become law.[10] Because of weak law, most
ethical consumption is guided by private standards, such as those
that determine the conditions for coffee to be sold under the Fair
Trade label (Daviron and Ponte 2005), the meaning of "child labor"
debated by the Fair Labor Association (FLA) and the Worker Rights
Consortium (WRC), how much recycled input is required for a product to be marketed as "made from recycled materials," and so on.[11]
What constitutes a free and fair election is determined not by any
international rule but by NGO observers themselves, and the standard has evolved considerably over time (Chapter 2, this volume; Hyde
2011b). And of the many international principles defined in the United
Nations human rights agreements, not all are equally the subject of
international pressure and sanction, and NGOs are central to setting
the agenda for which rights states shall be held to account (Chapter 4,
this volume). What constitutes appropriate delivery of humanitarian
aid is also defined by the NGOs themselves; what is an appropriate
share of administrative expenses, how much should be spent on fundraising, what kinds of development projects are worthy, and how aid
workers should conduct themselves in the field are not defined by any
public laws but are set by the NGOs individually and collectively as a
community of service providers.

---

[10] Due to this lack of consensus, there may also be competing private standards
in any given issue area, complicating the ability of audiences to assess the
statements of NGOs. On private standards in the global economy, see Abbott
and Snidal 2000; Baron 2001; Conroy 2007; Cutler *et al.* 1999; Hall and
Biersteker 2002; Hansen and Salskov-Iversen 2008; Haufler 2001; Held and
McGrew 2002; Kahler and Lake 2003; and Vogel 2005.
[11] The problem of determining the value of ethically produced goods blends
analytically with the problem of valuing the quality of "singular" goods such
as art. See Aspers 2006; Beckert and Aspers 2011; and Karpik 2007.

The credibility of NGOs matters deeply for bringing about successful social change under private standards. Without the backing of law, the ethical claims of NGOs either as monitors or service providers must stand the test of public opinion if they are to change social behavior. That is, their claims must themselves be credible if others are to act upon them. If an NGO's certification that a soccer ball is made without child labor is "meaningless," for instance, consumers will not condition their purchases on whether or not the ball bears an appropriate logo. If consumers are to bring their purchasing power to bear on those who exploit workers or employ children, they must believe that the products NGOs certify meet desired ethical standards.[12] Likewise, if promoters of democracy are to reward honest leaders in new democracies and punish corrupt autocrats who attempt to steal elections, they must trust the word of election monitors on which contests are "free and fair" and which are not. The same holds for those seeking to promote better human rights practices. In order for individuals and states to bring economic or political pressure to bear on those engaging in unethical behavior, monitors must be perceived as credible by those pursuing social change. Moreover, if a humanitarian NGO's assertion that it is relieving human suffering is not believable, donors will dry up and target countries may prohibit the organization from working within its borders. Since this is where the issue of credibility is most binding for NGOs, we focus our attention throughout this volume on the problem of private standards.[13]

The problem of credibility is prominent in private standards not just because they lack legal standing but also because ethical behavior is often impossible or very costly to observe directly. In ethical production, for instance, it is not possible to see how something is made simply by looking at the final product. Fair trade coffee looks and tastes identical to "unfair trade" coffee, with the primary difference

---

[12] Consumers appear to care about the values on the labels concerning ethical production standards, but it is not clear how much they care about the accuracy of the labels. See work by Hiscox and Smyth (2009) and the concluding chapter in this volume.

[13] NGOs are also involved in the setting of private standards. The setting of standards is analytically distinct from the task of monitoring whether there is compliance with the standards. The two do interact: it is easier to comply with weak standards than stringent ones, so monitoring a tough standard is costlier than a weak one, and audiences will differ on what they want. But once we have a standard, the various audiences want to know if it is being met.

being in how growers are organized and compensated; similarly, an ethically produced apparel item looks the same as one produced using child labor. Electoral fraud is by its very nature difficult to detect, especially if carried out subtly, and human rights abuses are typically hidden from public view. Whether humanitarian NGOs are providing aid in an effective manner or actually "developing" countries is also difficult to observe from afar. Unlike other activities where the qualities of a product or an outcome can be more readily assessed, the "ethical" part of behavior is typically hidden from view. NGO monitors arise for precisely this reason. They specialize in providing information to others that would otherwise be difficult to obtain. But it is for this same reason that the credibility of NGOs is most crucial. Since the behavior they are observing or performing is largely unobservable, others cannot independently verify the claims of NGOs that they are themselves acting ethically. We often have only their "word" for it, and thus others will condition their responses to NGOs – and thus, their efforts at social change – on whether their word is credible.

Sources of credibility

An NGO is credible when its statements are believable or accepted as truthful by one or more audiences.[14] Monitoring NGOs certify that this coffee is "fair trade" or that a particular election is "free and fair," in both cases attesting that the behavior of another meets certain standards. Humanitarian NGOs report that they have saved a number of lives that otherwise would have been lost in the aftermath of some natural disaster or that they have alleviated human suffering by vaccinating some number of children against disease. Both types of NGOs report that they have spent their resources in the service of these causes, and not on waste, corruption, or excessive pay of employees. In all such cases, we rely on their statements and must reach a judgment about their veracity. Their "word" is credible when we find it reasonably convincing or likely to be true, a continuous condition that varies from less to more. As we shall emphasize, a statement can also be more or less credible to different audiences. Credibility is not a singular fact, but is always variable and interpreted by the various listeners.

---

[14] In game theory, a statement is credible when it is in the self-interest of the speaker to carry out the promised action in the future. Our use here is considerably broader and relates to past behavior as well.

Table 1.1. *Sources of NGO credibility*

Internal	External	
		Strategies for increasing credibility
Virtue Rests on the internal or personal qualities of NGOs as perceived by audience	*Common interests* NGO claims more credible when an audience perceives that it possesses common interests with the NGO	*Promoting bonds around shared values* *Adopting autonomous governance structures*
	Costly effort NGOs more credible when their claims are backed by observable costly effort	*Adopting autonomous governance structures* *Professionalizing* *Expending costly effort in other fields*
	Penalties for misrepresentation NGOs more credible if they suffer penalties for lying or otherwise misrepresenting information.	*Increasing transparency*
	External verification NGOs more credible if claims are subject to the possibility of external verification	*Increasing transparency* *Integrating into the community of NGOs*

Sources of NGO credibility, both internal and external, are summarized in Table 1.1 and discussed in further detail in the next sections.

Virtue: internal sources of credibility

Virtue is one foundation of credibility. Virtue rests on the internal or personal qualities of a speaker – in our case, NGOs – as perceived by an audience. As Aristotle noted long ago, "We believe good men more fully and more readily than others" (quoted in Lupia and McCubbins 1998: 41). We believe virtuous individuals or organizations because they are inherently and intrinsically "good," although what that might mean in different contexts remains open.[15] Importantly, people or organizations need not actually be virtuous to be credible, but they must be perceived as virtuous by relevant audiences if they are to be credible on this basis alone. Organizations that are virtuous often refer to themselves as "legitimate," a synonym preferred by Thaut, Barnett, and Stein (Chapter 6, this volume) for that reason.[16] NGOs have traditionally relied to some large extent on virtue – or legitimacy – for their credibility.

Many NGOs are indeed virtuous, and comprised of individuals who are themselves virtuous. They are deeply committed to their cause and are perceived as such by various audiences. This image of virtue is often confirmed and possibly promoted by NGOs taking principled stands on issues that are unpopular with one or more audiences – the act of "speaking truth to power," as it is sometimes called. Virtue is also communicated by "right" conduct in public, as with environmentalists who live "green" to publicly demonstrate their character.

Although virtue alone can produce credibility, it may be a fragile foundation. Right conduct is difficult to maintain – if it were not, we would not need norms to promote it. We all have moral lapses. Even the most committed activists may find it hard to live up to their principles in daily life. In turn, critics are quick to identify hypocrisy by NGOs and their leaders. Climate change skeptics were delighted to point out the size of environmentalist Al Gore's carbon footprint as he traveled to give presentations on the dangers of CO_2 emissions, prompting the former vice president to begin making carbon offset payments out of his lecture fees.[17] To criticize someone's virtue is, in this way, to undermine their credibility.

As NGOs develop, moreover, they acquire interests as organizations that may deflect them from their ultimate cause (Bob 2005; Cooley

---

[15] In book II of *Rhetoric*, Aristotle posited that three things "inspire confidence" in an orator's character: "good sense, excellence, and good will" (Lupia and McCubbins 1998: 41).

[16] The discussion of virtue and credibility resonates with the analysis of trust. See Habyarimana *et al.* 2009 and Ostrom and Walker 2003.

[17] For an explicit link between hypocrisy and credibility in Gore's carbon footprint, see www.usatoday.com/news/opinion/editorials/2006–08–09-gore-green_x.htm (accessed November 1, 2010).

and Ron 2002; Kennedy 2004). When founded, NGOs are often small and comprised only of deeply principled individuals. As they grow in size and activities, NGOs must sustain themselves as organizations in ways that may put them at tension with their various "publics." To survive as organizations, they must pay their employees, publicize their activities to recruit donors, compete for funding against other NGOs, and so on. As they grow further, NGOs may also come to rely on a professional cadre of managers and fundraisers, not all of whom may share the original founder's or the activists' commitment to social change. Reports of high-paid executives and the rare financial scandal in the nonprofit sector threaten all NGOs because they undermine the public's perception of their virtue (Gibelman and Gelman 2004; O'Neill 2009). Finally, NGOs may develop specific organizational interests and cultures, sometimes referred to as pathologies, which can lead them away from their ethical principles.[18] Barnett and Finnemore (2004) have shown how organizational cultures bias and constrain the operations of international organizations like the World Bank and IMF. NGOs have similar organizational pathologies, especially as they grow very large. In a perhaps extreme view, Kennedy (2004: 26–29) declares that "the human rights bureaucracy is itself part of the problem" in professionalizing the humanitarian impulse and excluding non-lawyers "who might otherwise play a more central role in emancipatory efforts," promoting bad faith by extending human rights principles to new topics, and turning those who the professionals are ostensibly protecting into "victims." Although it is easy to justify organizationally-driven actions as proximate means toward a long-term goal, organizational interests may entail compromises that undermine the perceived "goodness" of NGOs and, thus, their credibility (Naidoo 2004; Simmons 1998).

Beyond virtue: external conditions for credibility

If virtue is often insufficient for credibility, when are NGOs likely to be believed by various audiences? Are there conditions that do not depend on assessments of the internal characteristics or "goodness"

---

[18] Organizational theorists have long studied how complex social organizations survive qua organizations, and how organizational structures, cultures, and processes distort practice and efficacy. An early classic is Simon 1976. For an application to international relations, see Allison 1971.

of an NGO that make it more or less believable to different audiences? Drawing on theories of reasoned choice, learning, and persuasion, we identify four conditions for credibility (Lupia and McCubbins 1998).[19] Along with virtue, these four conditions are each in theory sufficient for credibility (i.e., any single condition if met is enough for the NGO to persuade an audience). Shortfalls on any condition, however, can be supplemented by progress in one or more of the others, although it is not clear how much more on one dimension is necessary to offset fully failings on another. This suggests that, in an imperfect world, NGOs that make efforts to meet more of these conditions are likely to be more credible than NGOs that make efforts to meet fewer. We discuss the strategies NGOs can use to meet these conditions in the next section.

Common interests
Claims are more likely to be credible when an audience perceives that it possesses common interests with the NGO. This requires a judgment by the audience that the NGO shares its values. Muslims in Western countries believe that Islamic Relief is likely to share their political and social preferences, and thus they are more likely to find its claims credible and to support the organization than other agencies doing similar work in Islamic countries. Conversely, other Western communities with different preferences are likely to be more skeptical about the organization, especially after the terrorist attacks of 9/11 (Chapter 6, this volume). In similar ways, human rights supporters will find reports from Amnesty International, which is dedicated to promoting human rights, more credible than the US Department of State's human rights reports, which may allow "politics" to trump ideals. When it perceives that it shares common values with an organization, an audience can infer that the NGO will act as it would act were it to carry out the task of certifying others or delivering aid itself.

---

[19] Lupia and McCubbins 1998 demonstrate theoretically that each condition is sufficient for persuasion and empirically that all can affect the ability of a speaker to persuade an audience. See also Lupia 1994. For an application to international organizations, see Lake and McCubbins 2006.

Common interests are related to but somewhat different from virtue. As above, virtue is attributed to the speaker herself. Common interests are a perceived tie or relationship between the speaker and the relevant audience – the notion that they share values. One can believe a speaker because she is virtuous – inherently "good" – but skeptics will find her less credible when they have opposed interests and more credible when they perceive shared interests. Conversely, one might know a speaker is less than virtuous – a lawyer paid to argue a case, for instance – but find him credible because you perceive that you share his interests. Virtue and common interests together form an especially strong foundation for credibility. If an audience both perceives an NGO as virtuous and shares its values, it is very likely to accept its statements as truthful. In other words, the audience is likely to defer to the NGO unless it has good reason to doubt its virtue or commonality of interests.

Problems arise, however, when NGOs develop organizational interests separate from their normative goals. As with virtue above, different audiences may share common values with an NGO but not its organizational interests, undermining its credibility. Problems also arise when an NGO faces different audiences who diverge in their assessments of their interests. For consumers of ethical products, industry-funded NGO monitors will always be less credible than independently-funded organizations (see Chapter 3, this volume). Election monitors from quasi-democratic states, perceived as seeking to lower the bar on "free and fair" elections, will likewise be less credible to promoters of democracy than those from more democratic states (see Chapter 2, this volume). In these cases, the common interests that may make an NGO credible to one audience actually undermine its credibility to another – a point we develop further below. Only when an NGO's interests are perfectly congruent with all relevant audiences can it be credible on the basis of common interests alone – a highly unlikely possibility.

Costly effort

NGOs are likely to be perceived as credible when their claims are backed by observable costly effort. In essence, visible costly effort serves as a signal of the NGO's "type," or unobservable preferences. Ideally, the signal is sufficiently costly that only an NGO truly committed to social change would be willing to pay it. Thus, the greater the cost of the effort, the more credible the NGO is likely to be.

For NGOs, visible costly signals can take many forms. One common signal is the willingness of leaders (and staff) to work for significantly lower compensation than they could receive in comparable employment. If leaders are paid "too much," they signal that they are in the job only "for the money," and therefore might be too willing to compromise on principles to enhance their budget and salary. This ostensible compromise on remuneration extends to many other dimensions of NGO practice, including office space (the shabbier, the more credible) and perks (the fewer, the more credible). Yet, as above, signaling to multiple audiences can be difficult. Spartan offices may persuade some donors that the NGO is using their money appropriately, but may suggest a lack of competence to other groups. This is particularly problematic, as Boulding suggests in Chapter 5, for developing country NGOs who must navigate between the poor communities they are intended to assist and their developed country counterparts who are looking for "competent" local partners.

Another costly signal is the NGO's willingness to risk alienating donors to defend a claim, potentially losing resources. By standing up for principles in the face of potential opposition from others, the NGO signals that it is willing to pay substantial costs for speaking truth to power. Visible costs can also be incurred in lengthy or expensive investigations, such as frequent and cumbersome inspections of production facilities or large election monitoring missions carried out over many months before the election. Finally, costs are incurred in admitting failure or otherwise criticizing one's own organization in public, which also risks alienating donors. Although NGOs are typically reluctant to engage in public discussion of their shortcomings, their willingness to admit mistakes can be a persuasive sign of their sincerity and commitment to social change. All of these signals help persuade audiences that the NGO is committed to the cause of social change over its narrow organizational interests and survival.

Penalties for misrepresentation

NGOs will be more credible if they would suffer penalties for lying or otherwise misrepresenting information. For most NGOs, the primary penalty for misrepresentation is to their reputation as a virtuous agent.[20] If found to be distorting the truth in ways favorable to its interests, the NGO may suffer a loss of donors, access, acceptance in the community of other NGOs, and so on. The case of Kiva noted above is instructive. McIntosh, in Chapter 7, demonstrates that though P2P networks appear to link directly individual lenders with specific borrowers, they actually work through local microfinance institutions that repeat transactions and thus acquire reputations. In practice, 95 percent of the individuals shown on the Kiva website as potential borrowers have already been funded by the microfinance institution, which in turn uses the newly committed financing to fund other borrowers. Thus, the P2P lending network draws in donors based in part on misinformation. Once this misrepresentation was revealed by a sympathetic but concerned blogger and picked up by others, Kiva was quick to change its description of its process to preserve its reputation, most visibly altering diagrams on its web portal to more accurately reflect the flow of funds. It appears likely that Kiva would not have enjoyed its explosive success without its personalization of the relationship between lender and borrower, but this personal connection, at least as originally described, was more myth than reality. Ironically, endowed or self-funded NGOs dependent on only a few loyal donors may be more autonomous and able to dedicate themselves to a cause, but they may simultaneously be less credible because they would suffer fewer penalties if caught misrepresenting the truth.

External verification

Finally, NGOs are more likely to be credible if their claims are subject to the possibility of external verification. The case of Kiva is again instructive, as it was a blogger who publicized its misrepresentation of its lending practices. At a most general level, this suggests that NGOs headquartered and operating in democratic societies with a free press are more credible because their claims are potentially open to scrutiny by a number of external verifiers. This may be one reason for the disproportionate number of NGOs headquartered in wealthy democracies, not because they necessarily want to be scrutinized more thoroughly but because only in such countries are they sufficiently credible

---

[20] On "branding" of transnational NGOs, important for establishing reputations, see Quelch and Laidler-Kylander 2006.

that individuals are willing to donate enough for them to survive and succeed. This is, as Boulding (Chapter 5) shows, an issue with the growing number of NGOs in non-democratic developing countries who have to work harder in other ways to demonstrate their credibility. Overall, NGOs that are more transparent in their procedures and budgets and make it easier for outsiders to verify their practices are more likely to be perceived as credible.

Strategies for increasing credibility

NGOs are not passive actors constrained by the conditions above to be credible or not. Indeed, they are active shapers of their own images, reputations, structures and, thus, credibility. To understand when NGOs are credible, we must also examine what they do to make themselves credible. Credibility is not a static quality of an organization, but a dynamic attribute that can change over time at least in part through the NGO's efforts. The greater the challenges to the NGO's credibility, in turn, the more effort the organization can be expected to devote to enhancing its veracity. Although we cannot assess the challenges and effort systematically, given the limited range of cases in this volume, the strategies NGOs adopt to enhance credibility do reflect their beliefs about what is necessary to establish credibility within the competitive world of NGOs. It appears that there are at least six strategies that NGOs use to demonstrate or enhance their credibility.[21]

Promoting bonds around shared values

NGOs often aim to promote a bond with audiences around shared values. The common interests between NGOs and audiences are not entirely exogenous, but are manufactured, in part, by the NGOs themselves. This is reflected in how organizations represent themselves to the public and other audiences in advertisements, solicitations, and websites. These often emotional framings are intended to communicate a commitment to social change by the organization to others who are similarly committed but not yet mobilized. Many NGOs are

---

[21] Gugerty (2009) and Prakash and Gugerty's (2010b) concept of voluntary regulation programs overlaps with strategies two through four below.

also membership organizations that, though dues may comprise only a small portion of their overall revenues, seek to deepen the identification of individuals with the cause. Bumper stickers or window decals with the NGO logo allow members to declare "who they are" to others. Eco-tourism, community groups, and letter-writing campaigns all serve to further bind people to the organization. Personal bonding to the people being helped can also be hugely important in making connections around shared values: thus Kiva provides details on the specific individuals it funds (through local financial intermediaries), fair trade organizations on the farmers benefiting from the higher prices charged for beans, human rights groups on the people who are abused, and so on. These community-building exercises may be a substantial drain on the organization's resources but are intended to not only produce more funds over the long run but equally important, in our view, to enhance the credibility of the NGO with the participating audience. These efforts also create their own vulnerabilities, as already noted in the case of Kiva.

Adopting autonomous governance structures

NGOs also create and defend autonomous governance structures designed to ensure that they can pursue their ethical goals without undue conflicts of interest. This deepens the sense of common interest with audiences that share their normative views. Formal institutions appear to matter considerably in evaluating credibility. Most successful NGO monitoring and humanitarian organizations are nonprofit corporations for a reason; profit and ethics are not necessarily antonyms (as reflected in the "triple bottom line" movement), but there is certainly a tension between the two that leads most NGOs to constitute themselves as public charities.[22] Likewise, if the NGO is dependent on financing from its target audience, it will try to establish an independent board and populate it with social activists visibly committed to its own or other ethical causes. This is not necessarily the "green-washing" of an otherwise compromised NGO, but possibly evidence that, despite its ties to the target, it is sufficiently autonomous that well-known advocates of social change are willing to lend their names and devote time to the organization.

[22] On public perceptions of nonprofit organizations, see Schlesinger *et al.* 2004.

Targets that sincerely want to reform will support such efforts at autonomy. Since at least the Nike controversy over shoe production in the Third World, for instance, it is taken for granted in the activist community that firms cannot be the judges of their own ethical behavior. When Nike hired Andrew Young to report on its plants, the analysis was criticized over its lack of objectivity. Nike then needed to find an organization sufficiently far removed from its direct control to reassure consumers. The Fair Labor Association (FLA) came into being with Nike's support to provide this necessary measure of objectivity (see Elliott and Freeman 2003; Locke and Romis 2007). In turn, critics continue to charge that the FLA's objectivity is compromised by the presence of the manufacturers on its governing board. This allows them to influence the setting of standards and the inspection process in ways that make it easier for abuses to be covered up. Critics of the FLA therefore created the Worker Rights Consortium (WRC) as an alternative monitor with an explicitly more autonomous organizational structure. Dominated by university bookstores, the WRC is funded by fees charged on campus apparel rather than by fees paid by manufacturers.[23]

Increasing transparency

Another, somewhat related, way to increase credibility is for the NGO to stress process transparency by publishing important data, including their sources of funds, tax returns, and other financial information. By literally "opening their books," NGOs make external verification of their claims easier to monitor. As part of this increase in transparency, NGOs will also adopt more quantitative indicators of success that can be more readily tracked over time and, perhaps, compared across organizations. Indeed, other, second-order monitoring agents like Charity Navigator actually impose common metrics on NGOs. These quantitative indicators, of course, may have little to do with actual success in field, or may be easily manipulated by shifting budget categories (in the vaunted "administrative expenses" category that is important in some ratings schemes). Nonetheless, as

---

[23] Other firms, however, continue to do their own monitoring. They are likely betting on differentiating among audiences: the highly conscious activists will know, while the average consumer will not.

part of efforts to increase transparency, NGOs will be increasingly drawn to such seemingly unambiguous metrics.

Increasingly, major donors are also insisting upon impact studies, especially for humanitarian agencies. Several (but not all) NGOs are visibly trying to get out in front of this trend and scientifically evaluating their programs through randomized field experiments. Although we are not yet at this point, there may come a time when the failure to design impact analyses into new activities will be taken as evidence that the NGO itself does not believe its programs work. Overall, though, NGOs worried about their credibility will make greater efforts to invite scrutiny from skeptical audiences.

Professionalizing

NGOs can demonstrate credibility by becoming more "professional" organizations, especially in internal processes and procedures. A form of costly signaling, a professional staff and operating procedures signal to outsiders that the organization has the capacity to deliver on its promises, whether this be monitoring others or carrying out humanitarian missions. As Thaut, Barnett, and Stein show in the case of Islamic Relief, developing standard operating procedures which follow well-known norms in the various professions such as accounting and evaluation has been essential in the organization's efforts to demonstrate its credibility after 9/11. Similarly, Boulding shows that local humanitarian NGOs in Bolivia must be professional if their international NGO partners are to have confidence in their abilities to carry out programs. Although it leads to a "rich get richer" problem of working with the same NGOs over time rather than fulfilling their stated goals of developing local capacity, having successfully received and implemented one grant, Boulding shows, is nearly a prerequisite for receiving new grants.

Integrating into the community of NGOs

As implied above, NGOs can enhance their credibility by becoming part of the community of NGOs working in related areas. NGOs exist within a community of cooperation, in which organizations come together to promote joint campaigns, and competition, when they compete for grants or other limited funds. Because unethical behavior by one NGO can affect audience perceptions of all NGOs, acceptance into the community is a signal that other professional organizations judge the NGO as adhering to industry standards and as sufficiently credible so as to put their own reputations at least partially on the line. Thus, NGOs can seek to increase their credibility by actively networking with other NGOs, serving on joint campaign planning boards, co-sponsoring events and activities, and so on. The key here is for the organization to be visibly and publicly associated with a shared movement not just to bring about more effective mobilization for social change but also to assure audiences that it is acceptable to other trusted organizations. This reinforces the perception of common interests with audiences that share the organization's values but need reassurance that other organizations believe the NGO to be sufficiently credible to be invited into the "club" (Gugerty and Prakash 2010). Indeed, many of the meetings between NGOs that otherwise appear to accomplish little may have great importance in validating the participants in each other's eyes and those of other communities. Islamic Relief also pursued this approach after its virtue was challenged in the West after 9/11.

Expending costly effort in other fields

Finally, NGOs can engage in costly visible actions unrelated to their main activities. Rugmark, for example, which was created initially to monitor the use of child labor, now highlights its building of schools in communities where children are employed; although this may have the effect of keeping children out of the labor force, it also is a concrete (literally) accomplishment that is both more visible to the target community and other audiences than occasional factory inspections. TransFair and other fair trade organizations similarly publicize the building of schools by producer groups who have been aided by their activities. This approach is similar to philanthropy by corporations. It does not mean the "alleged" bad behavior has been altered, nor does it necessarily mean that "good" is being done. Rather, by engaging in more visible costly action the NGO hopes to compensate for the lack of proof of ethical action and build goodwill for the organization as a whole.

These six strategies are not the same as direct verification of ethical behavior by NGOs. Nor do they provide direct evidence of any

NGO's virtue. What they do, however, is limit criticism by mobilizing advocates of social change and increasing autonomy, permit costly visible actions that demonstrate commitment to their respective causes and the capacity to fulfill their promises, and facilitate external verification through transparency and acceptance by related organizations who may be best equipped to judge each other's credibility. Alone or in tandem, NGOs at least appear to believe that these strategies can enhance their credibility with important audiences. We find all of them at play in the cases and chapters that follow.

Credible to whom? The multiple audiences for NGOs

NGOs operate in a complex strategic environment populated by diverse audiences they seek to persuade and for whom they "perform." It is to these different audiences that NGOs must be credible. Many problems of credibility arise when there is tension among the demands of the different audiences, where what is necessary for an NGO to be credible to one audience conflicts with what it needs to do to be credible to another.[24] NGOs must therefore balance the demands of their various audiences. The chapters that follow explore the relevant audiences for NGOs in their specific issue areas. Here, we examine five generic types of audiences for whom the credibility of NGOs nearly always matter.

Targets

All monitoring and humanitarian NGOs are centrally concerned with "targets," the actors whose behavior they hope to change. In ethical consumption, targets are the producers who, it is hoped, will stop using child labor or will grow food organically. In election monitoring, targets are the incumbent governments who, likewise, will stop stealing elections through fraud. In humanitarian aid, the target is the population receiving aid and, in the longer run, the government that has created or failed to rectify the conditions that allow humanitarian crises to occur. In short, targets are the objects of social change.

---

[24] On the complex relations between foreign donors and local NGOs in Russia, see Henderson 2003. For a similar treatment of the relations between NGOs and local rebel groups, see Bob 2005.

Although it is sometimes assumed that targets and NGOs have opposing interests – the polluter and the NGO trying to stop it – this need not always be the case. Indeed, targets may want to comply with ethical standards. Some political leaders, for instance, may sincerely want to compete in truly democratic elections, but others may doubt their ability to resist electoral manipulation (see Chapter 2, this volume). Some firms are ethical, or may want to reform after protests against their unethical behavior. In a world of incomplete information and potential opportunism, targets that sincerely want to conform to ethical standards need monitors to certify that they are, in fact, adhering to accepted practice. As with Nike, discussed above, they come to "need" the NGOs or some other monitor. In similar ways, states often welcome humanitarian aid from the international community as a form of generalized social insurance to help cope with natural disasters beyond the normal scale. One should not assume that the targets of ethical action are necessarily unethical.

While targets are not always opposed to social change, they are the objects of skepticism by many other audiences. While some producers or incumbents want to demonstrate that they are fully meeting ethical standards, others hope to appear to conform while really cheating in more subtle ways and keeping their costs down at the risk of compromising standards. This possibility fuels the skepticism of other audiences and implies that even real reformers need independent verification of their actions. As Hyde (2011b) again argues, it is precisely this dynamic of sincere targets wanting to demonstrate their commitment that can generate a "race to the top" in ethical behavior and monitoring. Nonetheless, it is rare that the interests of targets and NGOs are perfectly aligned. Even when targets committed to ethical standards exist, there may be differences of opinion with NGOs over how ethical they need to be and at what cost. Thus, there is usually some tension between NGOs promoting social change and targets who are the objects of their campaigns.

Regardless of their common interests, or not, NGOs often need to maintain viable working relationships with targets, thereby making them vulnerable to criticisms of co-optation or collaboration. Both monitoring and humanitarian NGOs typically need access to the target to carry out their activities. Humanitarian NGOs cannot deliver aid against the wishes of a sovereign state, as was made clear when Myanmar refused to allow humanitarian aid into the country after Cyclone Nargis hit in 2008. Election monitors likewise must be invited by the incumbent government both out of respect for the sovereignty of the state and to protect the safety of individuals who are doing the monitoring, which can be dangerous enough even with the formal assent of the incumbent government. NGOs monitoring private actors also need access. To certify that rugs or soccer balls are not being made with child labor, NGOs need regular inspections of the factories and even the homes of workers when production is out-sourced. To verify that the coffee sold under the Fair Trade label is in fact produced by cooperatives, NGOs must monitor the entire pro-duction chain from farms to roasters to distributors to stores. Even when current access has been given, and thus we might expect NGOs to speak freely, they may be inhibited by the continuing need for future access, limiting their ability to challenge targets and reinfor-cing perceptions of collaboration.

Not all targets are able to control access, however, and thus the NGOs have greater independence. In human rights monitoring, for instance, NGOs have developed effective networks of local observers, opposition leaders, domestic and foreign journalists, victims, and other informants to reveal and document cases of abuse even though the organization itself may not have direct access to the country. Since governments that abuse their citizens are unlikely to permit monitors to observe directly these events, the NGOs have had to develop other mechanisms for gathering and verifying information. In such cases, the NGO is not limited by the target and is free to speak against it to other audiences.

The costs to NGOs to develop independent sources of information without access to countries is, in some ways, a measure of the outer bounds of control that targets may exercise over the activities of the NGOs. Were election monitors, for instance, to be prohibited from visiting the country during campaigns they could, like the human rights organizations, create an alternative "in-country" network of informants to provide information on events. The costs of setting up such a network define the limit of how much the NGOs will com-promise with targets to get direct access. The need for access poses a tradeoff for NGOs between sharing power with the target to get cooperation and maintaining distance so as to signal objectivity.

Donors

NGOs have an important second audience external to the organization – their set of donors or, drawing on principal–agent theory, which we shall sometimes call on throughout this volume, principals.[25] Donors have a fiduciary relationship with NGOs, in essence hiring and firing them by their funding decisions. Without funding, NGOs cannot carry out their monitoring or humanitarian missions, and if funding is withdrawn they will likely have to end their activities. The Ford Foundation can fail to fund Fair Trade USA. The members of the board of the FLA can end the contract with the managers or fail to fund the organization. Thus, donors are like the shareholders of a corporation who "own" an organization. They are the principals to whom the NGO, as their agent, must be ultimately responsible.

Donors can be highly concentrated in a single or perhaps small group of wealthy individuals, as in the case of Bill and Melinda Gates in the Gates Foundation, now active in funding many NGO-led programs in the fields of global health and education. Donors can also be highly diffuse, with many individuals each paying small annual dues or making small contributions. There may also be a range between these extremes and mixed sets of donors, including organizations with boards comprised of a few large contributors and large membership bases.[26]

Concentrated donors exercise more control over an NGO, often exerting influence on the day-to-day operations of the staff and the hiring and firing of specific employees. The more control these concentrated donors exert, the more credible the NGO will be to *them*, as its activities are more likely to reflect their preferences and priorities. Diffuse donors exercise less control. If an individual resigns her membership in protest over some action, as many did when the Sierra Club came out in favor of tighter immigration laws in the mid 1990s, they can be replaced by new members who may favor the new course. Even if the NGO has a regular convention of members or some representative assembly, the executives of the NGO typically set the agenda

---

[25] For a direct application of the principal–agent model from corporate governance to NGOs, see Prakash and Gugerty 2010a and 2010b. On principal–agent theory in politics, see Epstein and O'Halloran 1999; Kiewiet and McCubbins 1991; and McNollgast 1987.

[26] On multiple and collective principals, see Lyne *et al.* 2006.

for the conclave; members are seldom able to coordinate in advance to push their own proposals. Similarly, a humanitarian NGO may have multiple contracts with multiple governments simultaneously. Each grantor is a principal, in essence, but having multiple sources of funding means that no single government can control the NGO entirely. In NGOs with diffuse donors, the organization will have greater autonomy – even though it must remain credible to a large enough group of members to fund its activities.

In some cases, targets may both regulate access and have a direct fiduciary relationship with the NGO. In the area of ethical consumption, for instance, many producers typically purchase or otherwise pay for the required certification from the NGO monitor. In the case of child labor for instance, described by Nooruddin and Sokhey in Chapter 3, rug manufacturers pay Rugmark directly for the right to display its symbol on their products. The same is true for Fair Trade coffee, where the cooperatives in coffee-producing countries pay FLOCERT (the certification arm of FLO-International, of which Fair Trade USA is the American member) for the right to market coffee under the Fair Trade label. In such cases, the NGO is effectively responsible to the producers through both the latter's control over access and their control over the purse strings. When targets are donors, NGOs may be forced to compromise their principles to gain access and receive funding. This creates a real conflict of interest between the target and NGO, and between the NGO and other audiences who do not support such compromises. That targets may be donors that control NGOs in part is a major challenge to the credibility of those organizations with other audiences.

The public

A third audience is the public that NGOs hope to harness to their campaigns for social change through their purchases, votes, or volunteer effort. In ethical consumption, consumers may want to buy products made without child labor, degrading the environment, or exploiting peasants, but unless the NGO's certification is credible the public will not be willing to pay the higher prices usually entailed. The goals of the NGOs and perhaps a set of concentrated donors may not be widely shared or at least not at a price consumers are willing to pay. But the credibility of the NGO's claim that certain goods were ethically produced is necessary for yoking the broad mass of consumers to the goal of social change. Similarly, monitors of state behavior, as in human rights, or humanitarian NGOs that seek to change practices of target governments must also mobilize the broad mass of voters and activist volunteers in foreign countries to encourage their governments to press target governments for change. This is the "boomerang effect" discussed by Margaret Keck and Kathryn Sikkink (1998). Critically, though, for the boomerang to fly, the information provided by the NGOs to foreign publics must be credible to a large number of people if they are to expend the costly effort of lobbying their own governments to challenge the unethical behavior of some target government.

Other NGOs

A fourth audience for whom NGOs must be credible is the community of other NGOs. As above, acceptance into the community of NGOs can be a strategy for any single NGO to increase its credibility with other audiences. Thus, the community of NGOs itself is another audience for whom an NGO must perform and be attentive.

External verifiers

The fifth and final audience is what can be called the external verifiers, independent parties that can assess for accuracy claims made by NGOs. Most countries have laws governing basic practices by all organizations, including NGOs. Home country governments can be external verifiers by holding the activities of NGOs up to public scrutiny and minimal standards of law, documenting that they have not breeched their status as nonprofit corporations, diverted funds to illegal activities, engaged in libel or gross misrepresentations, and so on. More specifically, NGOs can also be brought before legislative committees to testify about their reports and activities under oath. Either in public legislative hearings or courts of law, governments can hold NGOs to account for their statements and behaviors.

The media is another important external verifier. NGOs often need the media to disseminate their claims to other audiences, especially the public. At the same time, the media can investigate their claims and reveal problems and inconsistencies between principles and practice. Disgruntled employees or other insiders from the NGO can also take evidence of the organization's deviations from stated ideals to the press or the blogosphere, which can then choose to investigate and publicize these deviations or not. In principle, the media is always looking over the shoulders of NGOs, although it is likely to monitor actively only when some form of malfeasance is initially brought to its attention. But in a variety of ways, external verifiers can hold NGOs to account and, in a phrase, help keep them honest.

Conclusion

All NGOs that we actually observe in the world today likely have some minimal level of credibility with at least one and usually more audiences.[27] If credibility is necessary for NGOs to survive and effect social change, as we have argued, then NGOs that survive past some initial founding period must be at least somewhat credible to at least one audience – most likely their donors.[28] What does vary across observed NGOs are the conditions for credibility, the challenges these conditions create for different organizations, and the strategies each adopts for responding to these challenges.

Although speculative, two general patterns appear likely based on the framework of conditions and strategies for credibility outlined above. First, smaller, more issue-oriented, volunteer-based NGOs with specific agendas for social change are more likely to earn credibility through their perceived virtue or by attracting supporters who share common interests. Such NGOs will pay a high price for misrepresentation and seek to promote shared bonds around common

---

[27] Some NGOs may be promoted as "mouthpieces" for particular governments or interest groups and lack credibility with other audiences, but even here the NGOs will have to be credible to at least their funders.

[28] This is a larger methodological problem of selection bias found in any study of existing NGOs. Ideally, as researchers, we would want to compare the NGOs that do exist to a sample of NGOs that *might* have existed if only they had been able to solve their credibility problems, an obviously impossible task. In practice, even while recognizing that we are truncating the dependent variable it is still possible to gain some analytic leverage by studying NGOs of varying credibility. More explicitly in some than others, all of the chapters below compare NGOs that are more credible to those than are deemed less credible. We also gain additional leverage by examining what NGOs do to make themselves credible to different audiences given the above conditions.

values, but they will be less concerned with transparency and other conditions that promote external verification, autonomous governance structures, and professionalization. Indeed, these NGOs may develop an "us versus them" view in which insiders are skeptical and even hostile to outsiders who are seen as questioning their deeply held virtues. In similar ways, NGOs with simpler messages about social change that communicate readily to smaller audiences with common interests – or that are concerned with fewer audiences overall – will be more credible or, at least, will be more likely to rely on perceptions of their virtue for credibility.

Second, as they grow larger and tackle more issues of social change, NGOs will devote more effort to sending costly signals of commitment and, especially, to increasing transparency, a pattern strongly confirmed in the cases below. Still promoting bonds around shared values, these successful NGOs will adopt more formal and autonomous governance structures, professionalize their staff and procedures, and integrate themselves further into the community of NGOs – with the largest and most successful often taking a leadership role in the community that sets standards for others to follow. Undertaking costly efforts in other, more visible domains may also create a centripetal force that further enlarges the NGO's purview. The increasing centralization of the NGO community, in which eight organizations dominate humanitarian aid, two organizations dominate human rights monitoring, and so on (Simmons 1998), may be a product of this dynamic, in which increasingly bureaucratic organizations take on new issues and more visible activities to enhance their credibility. This may produce a race to the top among competing organizations as they seek to demonstrate their credibility to multiple audiences, but it may equally produce a form of organizational hegemony that produces a lowest common denominator that squeezes out smaller and potentially even more credible NGOs.

The chapters that follow assess the conditions and strategies for credibility in different issue areas. The case studies were not chosen randomly, but from a convenience sample drawn from ongoing work of an already networked group of scholars interested in similar questions. While valid on their own terms, the conclusions from the cases may not be generalizable to broader populations. They are, however, interesting and provocative plausibility probes of the problem of credibility in NGOs.

The chapters in Part I focus on the conditions and strategies for credibility in NGOs as monitors of the ethical behavior of others. Susan Hyde looks at the case of election monitors in Chapter 2. In a crowded field of many overlapping and sometimes competing organizations, there has been, she argues, a race to the top in best practices by election monitors. In tandem with true democrats who sincerely want to demonstrate their commitment to free and fair elections, NGO monitors have over time fielded larger and more professionalized missions, a form of costly effort, and have themselves become more clearly independent and transparent, adopting governance structures more likely to generate credibility with donors and other audiences committed to democratic reform. Multiple monitoring organizations and an active media, which serves as an external verifier, along with high penalties for misrepresentation, serve to reveal and limit biased or overtly political reports by non-credible NGOs.

In Chapter 3, Irfan Nooruddin and Sarah Sokhey examine the cases of child labor in the hand-woven rug and soccer ball industries. Comparing the organizations of Rugmark and Kaleen in the former and the Foul Ball campaign in the latter (all of which certify that products are child labor free), Nooruddin and Sokhey argue that credibility is dependent on demonstrating a measure of autonomy from the monitored industry. Although in all cases the manufacturers pay for the certification, Rugmark as a relatively independent NGO is both more credible and successful than Kaleen, which is sponsored by the Indian Ministry of Textiles and more closely tied to the industry. Similarly, the Foul Ball campaign is closely connected to the soccer ball industry, lacks the ability to extensively monitor practices, and, with nearly all the major stakeholders involved, lacks any real external verifiers; in turn, it has been comparatively unsuccessful in establishing credibility. Nooruddin and Sokhey caution, however, that in the area of ethical consumption the threshold for credibility may be quite low, with consumers appearing to be swayed by the mere presence of a symbol than by any real knowledge of the NGO behind it. Given the need for independence and stronger standards, they conclude that only more formal government-based regulation is likely to have any significant effect on child labor conditions in these industries.

NGOs have long been central to the international human rights regime as monitors of state behavior. From their inceptions, Amnesty International (AI) and Human Rights Watch (HRW) have been serving as "witnesses" to state abuses as key elements of their strategies for promoting social change. In Chapter 4, Wendy Wong examines how these two NGOs have established their credibility through their respective organizational structures, and how other human rights organizations, such as the International League of Human Rights, have suffered because of their different organizational models. Although both AI and HRW are highly credible organizations, Wong argues, Amnesty is slightly more constrained and therefore more credible because of its large membership base. Both organizations, in turn, have central research units that emphasize accuracy in their reporting and set the agenda for the NGO as a whole. Both also eschew government funding. These features enable AI and HRW to be more credible – and visible – than other human rights organizations.

The chapters in Part II examine the credibility of humanitarian NGOs as direct service providers. In these cases, it is not the NGOs' reports on other actors that must be credible, but their own statements about their efforts to reduce human misery. Carew Boulding in Chapter 5 probes the problem that foreign aid donors face in selecting local grassroots NGOs as development partners. Drawing on extensive fieldwork in Bolivia, she argues that donor organizations and granting agencies assess the credibility of the promises of local humanitarian NGOs primarily by tangible signals of "quality," including professional offices, websites, and glossy reports. These easily observed indicators of professionalism, however, may not reflect accurately the ability of the NGO to actually deliver services to remote locales. Indeed, Boulding suggests, recognizing the importance of the superficial indicators of quality used by the donor agencies, local NGOs consciously adapt and focus resources on these indicators, often at the expense of real performance in the field.

In Chapter 6, Laura Thaut, Michael Barnett, and Janice Gross Stein examine the difficult case of "moral suspects," NGOs that cannot appeal to specific audiences on the basis of their inherent virtue or legitimacy. Specifically, Islamic Relief, headquartered in Great Britain and directing aid to Islamic societies, looks like many other humanitarian NGOs. Yet, after 9/11 it faced a more hostile public and, especially, foreign governments that suspected it was funneling money to possible radicals in the Middle East. With its virtue called into question and subject to greater scrutiny, Islamic Relief undertook new efforts to increase its credibility by enhancing transparency, especially in financial accounting, and associating more frequently with other Western aid agencies. By promoting its credibility with Western audiences, however, Islamic Relief risked its credibility with Islamic targets, precisely the communities it was aiming to assist. This compelling case illustrates clearly the tensions created by the need to establish credibility with multiple audiences with different and possibly conflicting preferences.

Recent years have seen an explosion in the use of peer-to-peer (P2P) lending, in which websites such as Kiva and Microplace offer individuals the ability to make loans to small borrowers across the developing world. Credibility lies at the heart of these organizations, both for borrowers, who pledge to repay the loans, and for lenders, who rely on the P2P organizations to get their funds to borrowers. Such sites offer a fascinating new example of a multi-tiered monitoring device in which microfinance institutions (MFIs) maintain dynamic relationships with local borrowers and P2P NGOs maintain dynamic relationships with MFIs. This system enables private parties to lend to clients whom they have never met and for whom credit histories are not available. In Chapter 7, Craig McIntosh examines the case of Kiva in some detail, especially its response to online criticism that identified certain misrepresentations on its website regarding its relationship with individual borrowers. The organization responded swiftly to this threat to its credibility and increased its already high level of transparency. Yet, McIntosh demonstrates that key mechanisms in microfinance are still obscured. Most borrowers presented on Kiva's website have already been funded and would likely have received funding even without the donation. The donation is, in any event, actually to the local MFI, which has an incentive to pay back the loan even if the borrower defaults. Full disclosure on these practices and results may undermine the common interests between lenders, Kiva, and the MFIs, threatening to reduce both credibility and new donations.

After summarizing the findings of the chapters above, and re-evaluating the criteria for credibility developed in this chapter, Chapter 8 examines how actions taken by NGOs to establish and bolster their credibility affect their ability to bring about social change. Drawing on the case studies below, it appears that the need for credibility:

(1) leads to an emphasis on procedure at the expense of substance;
(2) favors numerical and other tangible criteria of success, especially financial accounting, over program evaluation;

(3) places a priority on short-term responses rather than long-term programs;
(4) leads to excessive bureaucratization and a loss of flexibility;
(5) prioritizes the donors of the organization over the local populations they are designed to help or the other entities they are intended to monitor; and
(6) diverts attention to ancillary programs.

Together, as Boulding emphasizes in Chapter 5, these compromises produce a tendency for the "rich to get richer," or for NGOs that have established their credibility to grow and expand even though they may not be the "best" or most effective organizations in their area.

Finally, in the conclusion we reflect on the implications of our findings about NGOs for the task of social change in the international arena. NGOs will have limits on their ability to function as some idealists would like. Some improvements can be made within NGOs about transparency, autonomy, and other sources of credibility. Hopefully, our analysis will contribute to such improvements. At the same time, it may be necessary to have more government regulation and to encourage a greater reliance on the profit-making sector to challenge some assumptions in the NGO community. New thinking is needed on how governments, for-profit, and voluntary associations interact.

PART I

Monitoring and NGOs

2 | Why believe international election monitors?

SUSAN D. HYDE

When are international election observers – including NGOs such as the Asian Network for Free Elections, Carter Center, the International Republic Institute, the National Democratic Institute, and the Electoral Institute of Southern Africa – credible sources of information on the quality of elections in sovereign states? Following Chapter 1, I show that election observers are more likely to be credible when there is a perception of common interests between the audience and the monitor, observable costly effort by the monitor or the target, penalties on the monitor for misrepresentation, or external verification of the monitor's reports. Each of these variables is discussed in greater detail below. I also outline how election observation organizations employ various strategies to increase their credibility and how the absence of such strategies can reduce credibility. These strategies include integration with the community of other election observer organizations, promoting shared values among these organizations related to best practices, professionalizing election observation, adopting governance structures that signal their independence from states that invite election observation, and increasing transparency in the governance, funding, and methods of election observation.

Before discussing how and why some international election observers have become credible judges of election quality, I first introduce international election observation in the context of this edited volume, explaining the demand among democracy promoting actors for improved information on elections, and outlining why leaders now invite foreign election observers even when their elections are likely to be criticized. I then discuss variation in the credibility of election observers and the correlates of credible election observation. A number of more general empirical implications are outlined, but the central evidence is based on a case study of the Carter Center and its efforts to maintain credibility, and the comparison of this book's theoretical framework to existing findings on international election observation.

Democracy promotion and the rise of election observation

It has become more difficult for international and domestic actors to evaluate whether a given country is committed to democratization, particularly since the early 1990s. Individuals, states, non-governmental organizations (NGOs), and international organizations work to encourage the development of democratic political institutions in other countries. The motivations of democracy promoters range from the moral to the self-interested, but they are united by an objective of facilitating the spread of democratic political institutions. Especially since 1990, the diffusion of democracy promotion has increased the amount of democracy-contingent benefits available to governments that are not already democracies. The combination of democracy-contingent benefits and imperfect information about which governments are actually democratizing gives a subset of governments the incentive to falsely claim to be moving toward democracy (Hyde 2011a, 2011b). In fact, there are currently few regimes that do not claim to be democratic or democratizing (McFaul 2004). If incentives exist for some governments to "fake" democracy, it is more difficult for democracy promoters to evaluate whether a state is truly democratizing. It is similarly difficult for democracy promoters to accurately target their support. From the perspective of states that are truly moving toward greater political liberalization and democratization, the existence of pseudo-democratic regimes makes it more difficult for them to demonstrate their commitment to democracy to international and domestic audiences.

This dilemma helps explain the growth of international election monitoring. Although competitive elections are one essential component of democracy, many politicians have the incentive to rig elections or otherwise bias them in their favor. International election monitors are invited by the host government to observe and report on the quality of the electoral process, and are now present at more than 80 percent of elections for national office held in the developing world (Hyde 2011b; Kelley 2008). This chapter is motivated by the fact that since the mid 1990s, following an election, international news reports typically highlight the reports of foreign observers, usually without controversy or qualification, as credible sources of information about the quality of the electoral process.

Other sources of information on the quality of elections exist, including accounts of election quality from political parties, the central election commission, or non-partisan domestic observers, and these alternative sources are also sometimes viewed as credible. Nevertheless, even though international election observers are voluntarily invited by the host government, they are frequently invited to fraudulent elections. When they document and condemn election fraud, they can discredit an election to the domestic population and to the broader international community.

There are many reasons why one might expect that reports on elections from foreign election observers would not be credible. Measures of whether a given election is democratic are subjective and inherently difficult, particularly given the clandestine nature of many forms of election manipulation. A delegation of foreigners rarely has an understanding of politics in the target country that equals that of political parties or non-partisan domestic observers (Carothers 1997; Geisler 1993). Additionally, other actors often have a vested interest in whether the election is deemed credible or not, and work to bias the information available to international observers and their judgment of election quality.

Given these challenges, why are the reports of international election observers ever credible? Why do the international news media and many pro-democracy actors consider international observation missions valid sources of information about election quality? Why have other election monitoring organizations not developed such reputations, and are instead viewed as "rubber stamp" groups whose reports are perceived as biased among many domestic and international audiences? How have some organizations improved their reputations over time? How do pro-democracy actors ensure that elections are actually democratic given the difficulty in judging the quality of elections in sovereign states?

In the remainder of this chapter, I examine election monitoring as a case in which a subset of international NGOs have successfully developed reputations as credible observers of election quality. I evaluate credibility of election monitoring organizations and discuss the implications of Gourevitch and Lake's theoretical framework in light of variation among international observers and the degree to which they are perceived as credible sources of information about the quality of elections.

Credible monitors and election quality

The central questions raised by this volume focus on the credibility of "virtuous" international actors. The substantive chapters focus on issue areas that vary in the types of actions that must be considered credible for NGOs to be effective. In the field of election observation, the credibility of election monitors influences the degree to which other actors (the audiences) perceive observer reports on elections to be accurate. Accurate reports allow democracy promoters to target international benefits more accurately, and therefore should encourage democratization.

There are many organizations that sponsor international election monitoring missions, including international NGOs and intergovernmental organizations. They vary in quality, professionalization, and credibility. Past international observation missions have included relatively informal missions like those from the Latin American Studies Association, as well as professionalized groups from intergovernmental organizations like the OSCE's Office for Democratic Institutions and Human Rights (OSCE/ODIHR) and the European Union. A few organizations send international observers even when they are blatantly uninterested in democracy promotion, such as observation missions sponsored by the Shanghai Cooperation Organization and the Commonwealth of Independent States. Still other organizations sponsor election observation missions that are harder to generalize in terms of their credibility, such as the African Union, the Southern African Development Community, or *La Francophonie*.

Even among the groups that are most respected in the field of election observation, detecting and criticizing election fraud is an imperfect science, and decisions to condemn elections are frequently influenced by political variables (Kelley 2009). Most of the time, international observers point out some problems in the electoral process and highlight areas for future improvement, but give their general endorsement to elections. When domestic groups concur, elections are viewed as democratic.[1] When there is suspicion of election

---

[1] It is possible that fraud still exists even when both domestic groups and international observers endorse the election, but losing political parties should have a strong incentive not to accept the results of an election they perceive to be rigged.

manipulation, international election monitors play a visible role by either condemning the election outright, or by arguing that irregularities are not serious or widespread enough to influence the outcome of the election. International election monitoring became a globally accepted practice in the mid 1990s. Since that time, criticism by foreign observers is rarely questioned by international actors, and many domestic audiences such as opposition political parties cite observer reports as credible evaluations of the quality of elections.

As outlined in Gourevitch and Lake's introductory chapter, the *principals* in election observation are donors interested in promoting democracy. Representing a diverse set of actors, democracy promoters include individuals, non-governmental organizations, international organizations, and states. The *targets* of democracy promoters are states that are not already widely perceived to be consolidated democracies.[2] Democracy promoters wish to encourage democratization in target states by supporting them, both financially and with technical assistance. Yet because genuine democratization is difficult to observe directly, and most governments claim to be democratic or moving toward democracy, a government's actual commitment to democratization cannot be inferred from its rhetoric. Further complicating the issue of democracy promotion is that when democracy-contingent benefits exist and judging a government's commitment to democracy is difficult, some states have the incentive to introduce hollow forms of political liberalization and attempt to imitate the behavior of democratizing states without risking their hold on power through genuine democratization.

Just as consumers may pay more for fair trade coffee or goods produced with better labor standards (Hiscox and Smyth 2009), or wish to avoid soccer balls produced with child labor (Chapter 3, this volume), democracy promoters promise rewards or punishments in part based on whether target governments hold passably democratic elections. Some international organizations (IGOs) have formalized these commitments by making democracy or periodic democratic elections a condition of membership. IGO pressure on governments to hold democratic elections may exist, and may influence the behavior of

---

[2] Since the 2000 elections in the United States, and in response to charges of hypocrisy, a number of developed democracies have also held internationally monitored elections, particularly in the OSCE region.

member states. However, the difficulties of international enforcement make such standards analogous to the private standards outlined in Chapter 1. By offering democracy-contingent benefits to target states, and by withdrawing international benefits from states that fail to democratize or that experience democratic reversals, democracy promoting states have created a diffuse private standard for governments to hold democratic elections, and to engage in other behaviors that are perceived as democratic.

If democracy promoters were to use the strictest observable standards for democratic elections, they should reward only those governments that experience consecutive peaceful alterations in power. Although this standard is observable and credible, it should not be preferred by democratizing states, as most parties in power wish to have some chance of remaining in power. The "turnover test" makes sense as a restrictive standard: it is possible for democratically elected leaders to be reelected without resorting to fraud. Therefore, alteration in power is a credible but extreme signal of democratization, as many democratic elections do not result in turnover in power.

Despite the difficulty in judging a government's commitment to democracy and democratic elections, all else held equal, democracy promoters prefer to withhold support from targets that are holding rigged elections. As a subtype of "virtuous" or goal-driven actors, democracy promoters wish to accurately target their support because if they do not, their efforts will arguably encourage less democratization. In general, democracy promoters prefer to avoid supporting target governments when they hold fraudulent elections.

Yet when the possibility exists that pseudo-democrats who allow multi-party elections can fool democracy promoters, the incentives change for "true democrat" target states. In this scenario, states cannot credibly self-report their regime type, even if they are genuinely committed to democratization. In a world in which most governments hold elections, it is easy for pseudo-democratic governments to proclaim a (false) commitment to democracy. In order to maximize their share of international benefits and distinguish themselves from pseudo-democracies, democratizing regimes must identify a credible (costly) signal of the quality of their elections.

In theory, if election monitors are not costly for pseudo-democratic governments, they should not be credible, and they should not lead to any change in the rewards or punishments allocated by democracy promoters. Credible election monitors should be more costly for governments holding fraudulent elections than for governments holding democratic elections. If monitors are credible, inviting them causes (pseudo-democratic) governments to risk a negative report and a subsequent reduction in international support. Receiving a positive report from a credible election monitor leads to increased rewards or decreased punishment from democracy promoting states.

Monitoring the monitors and the diverse audience problem

To whom might election monitors be credible? Who are the likely audiences for international observers? These questions are difficult to answer with precision because the reports of international election observers are public and widely reported. Numerous domestic and international audiences cite them, and the relevant audiences vary by election. The public nature of the reports means that there are multiple audiences for every report, creating important variation in whether all audiences view a monitor's report as credible, as well as which actions observers can take to increase their credibility.

Gourevitch and Lake highlight a variety of potential audiences, including the targets of monitoring, donors, the public, other NGOs, and external verifiers. This generalized list applies relatively well to the case of election monitoring: audiences for election monitors include other governments holding elections (potential targets); donors or sponsors of election observation missions (donors); citizens within the target state or the sponsor states (the public); domestic election observers and other international observers (other NGOs); the international media, the domestic media, and parties and election officials within the target state (external verifiers). I return to the multiple audiences question below. For now, it is sufficient to highlight that the existence of multiple audiences for election monitoring creates numerous problems for the credibility of election observation groups. Actions that might increase credibility to one audience may decrease credibility to another audience. This section discusses the conditions under which an audience is more likely to believe that an election observation mission's report is credible.

As a point of departure, I focus on comparing other observer organizations to a more detailed description of the Carter Center, which is one of the more credible international non-governmental organizations involved in election observation. The Carter Center, based in Atlanta, Georgia, was founded by former US president Jimmy Carter and his wife, Rosalynn Carter. The organization works in a number of issue areas, including the eradication of diseases like guinea worm and river blindness, conflict resolution, the promotion of human rights, and strengthening of democracy. Election observation is one of many activities conducted by the Carter Center, although it attracts a disproportionate amount of media attention, both in the United States and in the countries where the organization works. By their own count, as of the end of 2010, the Carter Center had observed eighty-two elections in thirty-four countries, many of which have been high-profile elections in countries transitioning to democracy.

The Carter Center is particularly interesting as a case of election monitoring because it is an independent international NGO that has monitored a number of controversial elections. Governments that invite the Carter Center to monitor their elections are under no obligation to do so, not even under the weak international legal obligations which are now conditions of membership in some international organizations such as the Organization for Security and Cooperation in Europe or the Organization of American States. One may expect that election monitoring NGOs are invited only to elections that are already likely to be democratic. Empirical evidence contradicts this expectation, as Figure 2.1 illustrates that the Carter Center has criticized a number of elections for being fraudulent or illegitimate. Along with similar organizations, the organization has also maintained a relatively good reputation as an impartial third-party observer whose judgments of elections are generally cited by international and domestic news media without qualification. For example, following the 2006 elections in the Democratic Republic of Congo, the *International Herald Tribune* reported that "The Carter Center has given the presidential runoff in Congo its stamp of approval, saying that despite sporadic violence and isolated reports of voter fraud, the election had been disciplined, peaceful, free, and fair."[3]

[3] Jeffrey Gettleman, "Congo Vote Called Success," *International Herald Tribune*, November 3, 2006.

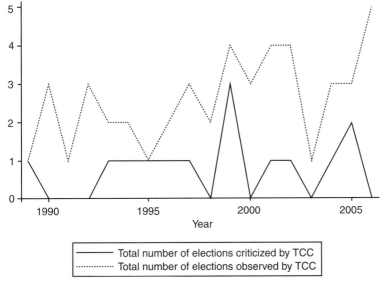

Figure 2.1 Carter Center election observation and criticism

Similarly, an international news wire report following the 2000 elections in Zimbabwe makes the Carter Center's credibility clear in relaying the content of their report:

The Carter Center, the internationally renowned elections monitor, Friday condemned Zimbabwe's elections two weeks ago, concluding that "by no means could they be called free and fair." … The Carter Center was … one of a long series of respected observer groups, including those from the European Union and the Commonwealth, to denounce the violence in the run-up to the election.[4]

Credibility-enhancing variables

How have election monitors like the Carter Center, the European Union, the Organization of American States, the Organization for Security and Cooperation in Europe, and the Commonwealth developed reputations as credible observers of election quality? Why have other organizations failed to do so? I now evaluate the

[4] "Carter Center Says Zimbabwe Elections Were Not Free or Fair," Deutsche Presse-Agentur, July 7, 2000.

credibility-enhancing variables discussed by Gourevitch and Lake in relation to the case of election observation, including a perception of common interests between the audience and the monitor, observable costly effort by the monitor or the target, penalties on the monitor for misrepresentation, and external verification of the monitor's reports.

Common interests

First, as Gourevitch and Lake argue, perception of common interests between the monitor and a given audience should make the monitor more credible to that audience. When the donors behind election observation promote democracy above all other objectives, this argument is straightforward. A democracy promoting state should be more likely to view the reports of monitors as credible when they view the monitoring organization as one that shares its interests. In contrast, a perception of common interest between the target of election monitoring and the monitoring organization should undermine the credibility of election monitors. If the principals supporting election observation missions have goals that conflict with support for democracy, a perception of common interests between the monitor and the audience should make those observers less credible to democracy promoters. Similarly, if an election observation mission is closely aligned with the target of monitoring, the monitor's report should not be credible to democracy promoters. At the extreme, if a state is both the target of the monitoring and the donor of the election monitor effort, the reports of the monitor should not be credible.

There have been instances of target-funded election monitoring, including the 2004 elections in Cameroon.[5] These missions are much harder to document systematically because they are less professionalized and tend to attract less media attention (another indicator of their lack of credibility). Some international observer missions are created for specific elections, but are not supported by a permanent organization. They typically conceal their donors, and their biases are open to speculation. For example, the 2008 elections in Pakistan were observed by an organization called the "Center for Media and Democracy in

---

[5] Ken Silverstein, "Democracy, or an Exercise in Fraud? Some Criticize the '04 Cameroon Vote. Several on a Regime-funded U.S. Team Call it Free and Fair," *Los Angeles Times*, February 14, 2005.

Pakistan." The mission was called an election observation mission but was also composed of domestic observers. It received little media attention outside of two pieces in the *Washington Times* written by the delegation's leader and one web report in a Pakistani paper quoting the delegation that the elections were "the best ever."[6] Their presence in the field was reportedly not visible, but the organization set up a table and passed out glossy brochures in the Islamabad Marriott, a hotel that hosted major press conferences about the election and that was frequented by foreign journalists, diplomats, prominent elected officials from other countries, and other election observers.

In general, observers are more credible when they are more independent from the target of the monitoring, when they do not have motives that can conflict with promoting democracy, and when they are more closely aligned with a variety of democracy promoting donors. The dozens of organizations that have sponsored or deployed election monitoring missions vary widely in the degree to which election monitors are effective agents of democracy promoters, or the degree to which democracy promoters and election monitors have common interests. When election monitors are partially funded or governed by states that are the targets of election monitoring, they should be less credible. Additionally, if they are funded by organizations or states with policy priorities that may conflict with or override democracy promotion, they should also be less credible.

Even if the accuracy of a monitoring organization's reports is identical across countries, perceptions of common interests between the donor and the target undermine the credibility of some missions. For example, the United States funds several democracy promoting NGOs, including the National Democratic Institute (NDI), the International Republican Institute (IRI), and the International Foundation for Electoral Systems (IFES). In countries in which US objectives are believed to be focused on democracy promotion rather than other strategic objectives, the reports of IRI and NDI are relatively more credible. In countries in which US efforts to promote democracy are questioned as illegitimate, however, such as post-2003

---

[6] Thomas Houlahan, "Pakistan's Pleasant Surprise," *Washington Times*, April 28, 2008; Thomas Houlahan, "Musharraf Makes Stability a Priority," *Washington Times* (Islamabad), March 10, 2008; "Pakistan: Foreign Observers Term 18 February Polls as 'Best Elections Ever'," *The News* website (Islamabad), February 28, 2008.

Iraq or Venezuela under Hugo Chavez, reports from the US-funded organizations are more likely to be questioned.

The Carter Center has both endorsed elections in which anti-US candidates have won legitimately (such as the 2006 elections in the Palestinian Territories), and even more controversially, the Carter Center has been supportive of elections in which a rising anti-US dictator held plausibly democratic elections (such as various elections in Venezuela under Hugo Chavez). In light of concerns about credibility, these cases are unsurprising. A perception (even if inaccurate) of a strong link between the US government and the Carter Center would undermine their credibility in some countries. Issuing reports that are explicitly contrary to US policy has the effect of distancing the organization from the United States, even if reports are based entirely on how the Carter Center views election quality.

Evaluating the independence of election monitors and the degree to which their motivations are primarily to promote democracy requires greater transparency in their governance structure and funding sources.

Observable costly effort and the race to the top

Costly effort on the part of international election monitoring groups can also increase the credibility of monitors' reports on election quality by improving the methods used by election observers. More comprehensive election observation missions signal to domestic and international audiences that observers are more likely to detect manipulation in various parts of the electoral process. These more comprehensive delegations now include media monitoring, voter registration audits, numerous long-term election observers deployed months in advance of an election, and coordination with and support for non-partisan domestic election observers.

These increases in observable costly effort can be initiated by election observers or by the targets of monitoring. Once initiated, other monitors and other target governments have the incentive to invite such similar forms of observable costly effort, generating a dynamic that might be called a "race to the top." Election monitors can send more extensive delegations and improve their methods in order to improve the credibility of the signal. The targets of monitoring can also invite increasingly costly signals – such as a larger number of election observers, extending the invitation well in advance of the election, allowing observers to access all aspects of the electoral process, and inviting groups that are more likely to criticize election fraud. Monitors that engage in more costly or more comprehensive monitoring should be more credible than those that engage in less costly or less comprehensive monitoring.[7] For targets seeking a credible signal of their commitment to democracy, inviting all of the best available election monitors is a common strategy.

Is it really costly for governments to invite observers, and can inviting international election monitors be viewed as observable costly effort by target governments? I have treated this issue in greater detail in other research, and have shown that election observers can reduce election fraud, lead governments to choose less direct and more costly forms of election manipulation, and increase the risk that their elections will be discredited (Hyde 2007). In order to make election monitoring more credible, both the supply side of election monitoring (the monitors) and the demand side (the target regimes which invite them) must engage in observable costly effort. Jointly, regimes seeking a credible signal of their commitment to democratization and democracy promoters attempting to evaluate the quality of elections have made election monitoring more effective and more costly (Hyde 2011b).

The cost of inviting election monitors is not uniform across countries. From the perspective of target governments, the cost should be greater for a government holding fraudulent elections, and negligible for governments holding democratic elections.

Particularly for governments that are likely to orchestrate widespread election manipulation, a clear tension exists between the fact that governments must invite monitors in order for them to come, and the possibility that these monitors will criticize their election. Since at least the mid 1990s, the perception is widespread that in order to effectively monitor an election, observers must be officially credentialed by the host government, and must be allowed access to all components of the electoral process. In some countries (such as the United States) government invitations to international observers and official

---

[7] Similar issues have been discussed by other scholars with respect to establishing a credible monitoring regime in applying global environmental standards to forestry (Auld *et al.* 2008; Gleditsch 2002).

credentials do not guarantee that individual polling station officials respect the credentials of observers and allow them to enter polling stations. This makes it much more difficult for observers to accomplish their objectives and should make their reports less informative. The evolving standards surrounding monitored elections, however, mean that government efforts to limit observer access are usually interpreted as a sign that the government is hiding something, and usually result in criticism of the election.

Observer organizations also take a number of steps to enhance their credibility, which can be interpreted as observable costly action. Nearly all delegations of reputable international observers are multinational. Many delegations include pairs of short-term observers that are composed of individuals from two different countries. Thus, in part to demonstrate their impartiality even at the local level, voters who encounter international observers on election day are more likely to encounter representatives from multiple countries, rather than, for example, a team of observers who are both from the United States.

In terms of their findings, organizations like the Carter Center, the OSCE/ODIHR, the European Union, and the Organization of American States also release detailed information about how they reached their judgment in the form of a final report. These reports typically include an overview of the electoral process, information about who served on the delegation, what elements of the pre-election process were observed, the techniques used to monitor the election, and so on, in addition to detailed information about the quality of the electoral process across a number of dimensions. Organizations like the Commonwealth of Independent States (both the IGO and the NGO of that name) and the Shanghai Cooperation Organization make such reports difficult to access or unavailable, if they are released at all. Their reports are not viewed as credible by Western democracy promoting audiences, and it is not clear that they are credible to any audience. Rather than attempting to establish their own credibility, it is possible that such missions are intended to undermine the credibility of Western organizations, creating some (usually minimal) diversion from credible evaluations of elections, material for state-run media, or a diversion of resources to countering the false claims made by anti-democracy groups.

For example, following the 2004 parliamentary elections in Kazakhstan, the Russian news agency reported that observers from the Shanghai Cooperation Organization met with journalists and reported that "they had visited 10 polling stations in [a southern city] and did not find a single case of violation by either representatives of the electoral commission or voters."[8] Under normal circumstances, such a minuscule observer mission would not have attracted any media attention, as a mere ten polling stations is not typically viewed as sufficient to be called an election observation mission.

Regimes seeking a credible signal of their commitment to democratic elections help boost the quality of election monitors by inviting them well in advance of elections, facilitating their access to all parts of the electoral process, responding to their concerns, and allowing local government officials to cooperate with long- and short-term observers. Although such actions are observable across all types of governments, they should be more costly for governments engaging in election manipulation.

Not all regimes are interested in increasing the credibility of monitors through observable costly effort. Governments sometimes invite observers and then challenge their credibility, working to limit their access or expel them from the country. Eric Bjornlund (2004) cites the 1989 Panamanian election as crucial in establishing the Carter Center's independence, and President Carter successfully protested against Manuel Noriega's efforts to clamp down on the Carter Center's work after he had invited them to monitor the election. By threatening to refuse to monitor an election or withdraw a mission – and thus by threatening to condemn the election before it happens – election monitors have some ability to negotiate with a government, even after they have accepted an invitation to monitor and are deployed within the country.

Implicitly, one long-term effect of the existence of international election monitoring is that it gives a subset of governments the incentive to manipulate elections in different ways. Some forms of election manipulation are easy to spot: when there is only one candidate on the ballot for a given national office; when pre-marked and bundled ballots are visible inside ballot boxes; when ballot boxes are abducted from polling stations; when vote buying takes place in the open; when

---

[8] "Observers See No Violation in Southern Kazakh Polling Stations," *Kazinform, Astana,* September 19, 2004, reprinted in *BBC Summary of World Broadcasts.*

opposition party supporters or candidates are unjustifiably attacked by the police; or when vote totals are mathematically impossible (more than 100 percent turnout, for example).

Nevertheless, by inviting professionalized election observers, target governments open their regimes to several risks, including that their elections will be criticized, that observers will deter fraud directly and therefore make it more expensive to cheat, or that the government must pay the cost of increasingly sophisticated methods of manipulation. Combined, these potential costs make it much riskier for cheating governments to invite international election monitoring (Gandhi and Przeworski 2009). Inviting or deploying observer missions that have previously criticized elections in other countries, and who are permitted to observe well in advance of the election, with both long- and short-term observers, represents observable costly effort.

Penalties for misrepresentation

Another source of credibility for international election monitors stems from the penalties for misrepresentation that an organization would suffer if it inaccurately judged the quality of an election. In general, election observers should be less credible if they misrepresent the quality of an election. Misrepresenting the quality of an election involves criticizing an election that was actually democratic, or more commonly, failing to condemn an election that was actually fraudulent. Therefore, an organization that criticizes elections should be more credible than one that does not. Conversely (and much more rarely), an organization that criticizes elections that are known to be democratic should also be less credible. This dynamic is amplified if the organization monitoring the election would suffer larger reputational costs for engaging in misrepresentation.

Measuring the degree to which a given election monitoring organization would suffer penalties for getting a report "wrong" are difficult to judge, as the consequences are likely to be reputational. However, if the organizations that sponsor election observation missions also engage in other programmatic activities in target countries, they should be more insulated from the reputational costs of getting a report wrong than those organizations that exist only to conduct election observation, and for whom lying would impose severe punishments if revealed.

Also influencing the penalties for misrepresentation is the commitment of the donors (sponsors of election observation) to democracy promotion. Election monitors that report to many democracy promoting donors, or very committed democracy promoters, should suffer greater reputational cost from endorsing fraudulent elections or otherwise engaging in misrepresentation. Election monitors that report to fewer democracy promoters suffer less reputational cost from lying. The Shanghai Cooperation Organization is an extreme example. Although it has sponsored several election observation missions, the principals are not committed to democracy promotion. In fact, the opposite is probably true, and SCO election monitors may be rewarded for inaccurate reporting on elections so long as their reports are consistent with the foreign policy goals of member states (China, Kazakhstan, Kyrgyzstan, Russia, Tajikistan, and Uzbekistan).

Significant costs to observers of inaccurately judging an election may also increase their credibility. Being "wrong" in election monitoring involves misjudging election quality, either by endorsing a fraudulent election or falsely criticizing a democratic election. Professionalized election monitors tend to be somewhat reluctant to condemn elections unless they are certain that the elections were intentionally manipulated, and they are therefore much more likely to endorse a manipulated election than to falsely criticize a democratic election. All elections have some flaws, and there is no bright line between democratic elections and ones that are not.

Thus in general, the costs of being wrong are equal to the costs of endorsing an election that was actually stolen. Yet somewhat counter-intuitively, the chance that observers will endorse a fraudulent election is a central reason why they are invited to fraudulent elections at all. The fact that credible observers sometimes validate fraudulent elections means that governments holding problematic elections are more likely to invite them, and they are therefore invited to more lower-quality elections and more likely to observe elections that warrant international criticism. Together, this means that accounting for dynamics over time, somewhat imperfect election monitors are more likely to be useful to democracy promoters.

Another effect of observer reluctance to criticize is that when a group like the Carter Center does criticize an election, few dispute their criticism. When a credible observer organization does get it wrong, an autocratic regime may gain some undeserved democratic credentials, and the organization may suffer some reputational cost. Those election monitoring groups that always endorse elections or that endorse elections based on who wins rather than the quality of the process suffer reputational costs and their reports receive less attention from democracy promoters and in the international news media.

External verification

A final source of credibility for election monitoring organizations pertains to whether the reports of election observers are subject to external verification. Monitors that are based in a country with a free press that is able to verify their statements should be more credible and more common than those that originate in a country without a free press, although I do not evaluate this condition in depth here.

Strategies for increasing credibility

The variables that influence credibility are distinct from strategies that can increase credibility. Gourevitch and Lake outline six strategies for increasing the credibility of NGOs. I evaluate them relative to the case of election observation. They are rephrased and reordered for this case.

To increase credibility, election observing organizations promote high-quality election observation and a commitment to democracy promotion among other election observing organizations and among donors (*1. promoting bonds around shared values*), increase professionalization of their organizations and adhere to recognized standards for election observation (*2. professionalization*), and coordinate with other NGOs and IGOs that conduct election observation (*3. integrating into the community of NGOs*).

Reflecting the first three strategies outlined above, and in one of the biggest cooperative ventures in election observation to date, more than twenty organizations have signed onto two documents intended to standardize some practices within election observation. The documents, which include the Declaration of Principles for International Election Observation and a Code of Conduct for International Election Observers, were signed at a 2005 meeting hosted by the United Nations. The UN, the Carter Center, and NDI convened the project, and the documents were introduced at a Ceremony of Endorsement presided over by UN Secretary General Kofi Annan, former US President Jimmy Carter, and former US Secretary of State and NDI Chair Madeleine Albright (Carter Center 2006). The documents were produced over a series of four meetings held between 2003 and 2006, which were attended by more than a dozen monitoring organizations. As of June 1, 2006, twenty-five organizations had endorsed the Declaration and Code of Conduct (Carter Center 2006). The declaration included agreement on the scope and purpose of election observation activities, how to prohibit conflicts of interest between monitors and the target of monitoring, guidelines for reporting on election quality, recommendations for cooperation with other international election observation missions, standards for when not to observe an election, prerequisites for organizing a mission to a country, how to train observers, how to encourage support for partisan and non-partisan domestic observers, and a recommendation for transparency in the methods employed to observe an election.

Several governments now request that all individual observers sign a code of conduct before they can be granted a visa to observe an election. Since the document was signed in 2005, the participating groups have continued to meet annually in order to discuss challenges facing international election observation and democracy promotion more generally.

Individual election observing organizations can also increase credibility by adopting governance structures that signal their independence from the targets of election monitoring and from the geopolitical biases of donors (*4. governance structures*).

For groups like the Carter Center, the separation between the governments subject to election monitoring and the governance of the NGO is quite clear. The Carter Center's twenty-one-member board of trustees is fully transparent and composed primarily of business and community leaders. No leaders of countries being monitored serve on the board, nor does anyone who represents them. Thus, in this sense, the targets of the monitoring are clearly separated from the governance of the organization.

Any perceived link between the international monitoring organization and the target government would likely be viewed as a sign of corruption. A sure way to discredit an election monitoring organization would be to accuse it of being funded by the government holding

the election. As mentioned above, target-funded international monitoring has been attempted by some regimes in the past. Several electoral autocracies also fund or send election monitors. The Russian
government funds several election monitoring groups (an IGO and
an NGO) that exist primarily to contradict the reports of the more
reputable OSCE/ODIHR election monitoring missions. The Russian-
dominated Commonwealth of Independent States is an international
organization composed of former Soviet states, and has deployed a
number of election monitoring missions within member states. The
CIS and the OSCE monitor many of the same elections in former
Soviet states, and the CIS predictably reaches the opposite conclusion
of the OSCE.[9] For example, if the OSCE criticizes elections in Belarus
or Uzbekistan, the CIS endorses them as democratic. Even more
implausible was the report following the 2010 elections in Myanmar
(Burma) that although international observers were prohibited, the
election was reportedly "witnessed" by diplomats from North Korea,
Vietnam, India, and China.[10]

The Organization of American States was the first international
organization to accept an invitation to monitor elections in a sovereign state, and represents an intermediate case in terms of independence from the targets of monitoring. Democratic elections are
a condition of membership in the organization, and states which are
monitored by the OAS are also members of the international organization. More importantly, funding is allocated separately for each
observer mission by the OAS General Assembly. The funding sources
are transparent in that they are detailed in the final election observation reports. Yet resources are scarce, and because the OAS must
secure funding for each election monitoring mission from other member states, geopolitics can play a large role in determining whether an
election monitoring mission is funded or not. For example, the OAS
has never monitored an election in Brazil. Perhaps more importantly,
the OAS response to Alberto Fujimori's clearly fraudulent elections
in 2000 was tempered (or hamstrung) by the fact that Peru was a
member state of the organization, and some of Peru's allies worked

[9] Roman Kupchinsky, "CIS: Monitoring the Election Monitors," Radio Free
     Europe, April 2, 2005.
[10] Mark MacKinnon, "Early Results in Heavily Criticized Myanmar Elections
     Favor Junta-Backed Party," *Globe and Mail* (Toronto), November 7, 2010.

to stop the OAS from intervening more directly (Cooper and Legler 2006).

In contrast to the OAS, some intergovernmental organizations intentionally structure their election monitoring organizations such that they appear more independent from the organization. The OSCE, which monitors elections in many of its fifty-five member states, tasked a quasi-autonomous branch of the organization with election monitoring, and located the branch (the ODIHR) in Warsaw rather than in Vienna where the OSCE Secretariat is based. Additionally, its funding sources are allocated annually rather than on a mission-by-mission basis, and individual member states have limited ability to influence which missions are funded. As an alternative structure that also decreases the influence of member states, the European Union is engaged in election monitoring throughout the developing world but does not observe elections within its own member states.

A fifth strategy used by international observers to increase credibility is to increase transparency in their governance, funding, and methods of election observation (*5. increasing transparency*). Among NGOs, funding also influences the credibility of monitors to both democracy promoters and within the population of the target state. The Carter Center receives funding transparently and from many sources, and maintains an endowment that helps fund missions to regimes that attract less donor interest. The Carter Center's funding sources for election monitoring include official development assistance from countries like the United States, the United Kingdom, and Ireland; private donors; and money given to the Carter Center foundation that is later channeled to election monitoring. These funding sources are compiled in an annual report that is made available online and is mailed to all contributors and supporters of the Carter Center.[11] In addition to its annual reports, the Carter Center also posts its IRS filings on its website. This transparency in funding applies across all areas of the Carter Center, including election monitoring. They are therefore more financially independent in deciding where to accept invitations to monitor, and this independence is made publicly available to all relevant audiences.

NGOs like NDI and IRI are primarily funded by the US government and are somewhat less independent from their principals. They

---

[11] See www.cartercenter.org/news/publications/annual_reports.html.

are therefore sometimes perceived as less credible by target states (or targets try to discredit them by alleging they are biased toward pro-Western candidates or pro-US interests). Although NDI and IRI are formally independent from the US government and receive funding separately from the National Endowment for Democracy (funded by the US Congress), USAID, and the State Department, they are likely to be allocated more funding for missions in countries that are important to the United States.

For specific election monitoring missions, international organizations like the EU and the OSCE, and NGOs like the Carter Center are particularly proactive in working against potential claims of bias. In order to counter impressions among target-state audiences that they are biased, they take a number of actions to try to make it clear that they are independent from sponsor governments, and that their relevant interests favor democracy. Although the central offices of the Carter Center are based in the United States (in Atlanta), each of its election monitoring mission accepts no more than one-third of its funding from USAID, despite the fact that some missions could be entirely funded from US assistance.

This does not make the Carter Center immune to charges that it is biased toward pro-US candidates. Particularly in very polarized countries or when the United States has been heavily involved, it is difficult for NGOs to maintain credibility as a non-partisan observer group. To illustrate, during the 2004 recall referendum in Venezuela, supporters of the opposition were convinced that if they did not win, the election must have been stolen by the incumbent president Hugo Chavez. Supporters of Chavez held the opposite position, and were convinced that if the Carter Center criticized the election, it must be because the organization is biased, a tool of US foreign policy, and determined to bring down the Chavez government. Either way, partisans within Venezuela tied the credibility of the Carter Center to the content of their report, and supporters of Chavez perceived that if the report was critical of the elections, it would be due to US influence rather than any actual problems with the election.

Overall, greater transparency in governance and funding help reveal the degree to which election monitors are aligned with pro-democracy actors and the degree to which they may have ulterior motives.

The final strategy outlined by Gourevitch and Lake suggests that observers can increase their credibility by taking observable costly action in other fields (6. *costly actions in other fields*). Out of the six strategies outlined by Gourevitch and Lake, this is least clearly linked to the case of election observation. It is true that most of the well-established election monitoring organizations discussed in this chapter also conduct other activities in the countries in which they operate. These activities most commonly include giving foreign aid, supporting economic development programs, or supporting other elements of democracy promotion programs. What is less clear is whether these activities – which might be labeled observable costly effort – also result in increased credibility for these organizations. Counterfactually, if these organizations were not to pursue other activities, they might be less well known or well established before beginning an election monitoring effort. Such development work may help monitoring NGOs establish a relationship with relevant stakeholders in the country, but it is not clear whether this work increases their credibility.

Conclusion

Because most governments are now under pressure to invite election monitors, and those that do not are believed to be holding fraudulent elections, election monitoring has become a widespread practice, and one that is likely to continue so long as international actors are interested in judging whether other regimes are committed to democratization. As Gourevitch and Lake argue in this volume, "in a world of incomplete information and potential opportunism, targets that sincerely want to conform need monitors to certify that they are, in fact, adhering to accepted practice" (p. 24). The existence of a variety of monitoring groups means that the professionalized organizations coordinate on best practice, share information, invest in efforts to improve election monitoring, and make it more difficult for leaders to invite observers and get away with election manipulation. International election monitoring is a diverse field, and the competitive aspect of election monitoring (or the fact that multiple groups deploy election monitors to the same elections) can be characterized as a "race to the top."

However, there are also low-quality monitoring organizations that endorse elections if their favorite party wins, regardless of an election's quality. It is difficult to list the "green-washing" election monitoring organizations comprehensively, because some organizations that began as low-quality election monitors have improved over time. Organizations like the Commonwealth Secretariat used to engage in very superficial election monitoring, regularly announced their findings from the airport before election day was over, and would depart the country before the counting of votes or the winner had been announced (Geisler 1993). Today, they engage in much more comprehensive election monitoring, and have criticized a number of elections (Sives 2001).

Competence and professionalization are important sources of variation among election monitoring groups, yet most election monitors have developed these reputations over time, and nearly all organizations have been criticized for failing to condemn problematic elections. The first election monitoring missions were composed of a few prominent individuals visiting the capital city on election day. It was not until the 1980s that observers were invited to clearly fraudulent elections, and many advances in observation techniques can be linked to this period. Similarly, individual observers and organization staff gained experience over time, which allowed them to learn which observing techniques were most effective, how both government and opposition parties manipulated elections and sometimes attempted to manipulate the monitors, and how to deal with governments that are intent on limiting their ability to engage in effective election observation.

Election monitoring illustrates that in the field of judging elections, as in other areas of NGO work, reputations as credible sources of information are enhanced by perceptions of common interest between "ethical" audiences and the NGO, observable costly effort, penalties for misrepresenting the quality of an election, and external verification of monitoring techniques. Conflicts of interest, when they exist, are a challenge to credible election monitoring. NGOs and some of the target states – namely those who are actually committed to democratization – can work to enhance the credibility of election monitors. NGOs benefit from a credible reputation by increasing funding and positive publicity for their organization. Democratic targets of monitoring benefit from credible monitoring when they are distinguished from pseudo-democracies and supported by pro-democracy international and domestic audiences.

Both sets of actors employ a variety of strategies to improve monitors' credibility. Monitors can increase credibility by promoting shared values in election observation, integration into the community of election observers, and professionalization. Individual organizations can improve credibility through governance structures which demonstrate independence, increasing transparency, and potentially by taking costly actions in other fields. Overall, the case of election monitoring illustrates how NGOs can pursue successful strategies to become credible monitors, as well as some of the dynamics of the process of maintaining such a reputation.

3 Credible certification of child labor free production

IRFAN NOORUDDIN AND SARAH WILSON
SOKHEY

Introduction

In the early 1990s, reports surfaced of the prevalence of child labor in many industries, including rugs and soccer balls. In the rug and carpet industry, critics alleged, children as young as four years old were being sold into bonded labor, their families receiving the equivalent of about $50 in return for several years of labor by the child. Children were expected to work weaving carpets for twelve or more hours a day while living in deplorable conditions.[1] Some estimates were that as many as 1 million children were forced to work fifteen to eighteen hours a day weaving carpets across the countries of South Asia.[2] Around the same time, allegations surfaced that the soccer balls sold by major sports companies including Umbro, Reebok, Adidas, and Mitre – which provides balls for Britain's Football Association and Premier League – were being stitched together by Pakistani children, some of whom had been sold into bonded labor by their parents. The reports indicated that children as young as six years old were being paid 10 pence for a single football that would later sell for 50 pounds.[3]

Reports of the prevalence of child labor in the making of rugs and soccer balls were part of a larger global awareness about exploitative working conditions by multi-national corporations. This era of "stateless regulation" (Seidman 2005, 2007) – in which exploitative

We would like to thank all of the authors in this volume for their comments and suggestions and, in particular, Peter Gourevitch, David Lake, and Janice Stein for their advice. Comments by Mark Anner, and audience feedback at the 2009 Annual Meeting of the American Political Science Association, Toronto, Canada, were extremely valuable. All errors are our own.

[1] "Bound to Looms by Poverty and Fear, Boys in India Make a Few Men Rich," *New York Times*, July 9, 1992.
[2] "Children Protest Slave Labor," *The Gazette*, February 23, 1993.
[3] "Scandal of Football's Child Slavery," *Sunday Times* (London), May 14, 1995.

working conditions proliferated as corporations took advantage of governments' reluctance and inability to enforce labor regulations when faced with the threat posed by mobile capital – resulted in the growing involvement of non-governmental organizations (NGOs) in monitoring corporations. NGOs have used the threat of "naming and shaming" corporations they deem to fall below minimum thresholds of "ethical behavior" to influence consumer behavior in the belief or hope that consumers will be unwilling to tolerate and support such businesses. Businesses, in turn, wishing to protect the value of their brand seek to avoid such embarrassment and so respond to NGO demands by either offering their own codes of conduct to which they promise to adhere or by agreeing to be monitored by the NGO in exchange for certification of good behavior which they can tout to discerning consumers as evidence of their ethical behavior (Conroy 2007; Seidman 2007).

Such certification allows businesses to target an important niche market in ethically-produced products, and, presumably, gives consumers the information they require to make ethical consumption choices. It is a virtuous self-reinforcing circle that should lead to a "race to the top" (Spar 1998). However, while consumers and the retailers who supply them might often be willing to pay more for more socially responsible goods, there is no tangible difference between products made with or without child labor, making it hard to know at the point of consumption which products meet these higher social standards. Therefore, the focus has shifted to assessing whether the production process conforms to social norms, and NGOs have sought to reduce the informational asymmetry between consumers and producers by certifying the production process. This raises the question that is the focus of this chapter: *when and why is NGO certification credible?*

To address this question, we organize this chapter around a comparison of the rug and carpet sector versus the soccer ball industry. The rug industry is especially useful since it permits a comparison of two competing labels, Rugmark and Kaleen, where the former has achieved a measure of credibility that the latter has not, allowing us to isolate the determinants of certification credibility while holding the industry specifics constant. Further, for all the limitations of the two main rug labeling schemes, the fact is that both have been more successful than the "Foul Ball" campaign in the soccer industry, a fact which we leverage in an industry-level comparison. Using these within- and across-industry cases, we assess progress on the four conditions for credibility laid out by Gourevitch and Lake in Chapter 1 – common interests of the audience and the NGO, costly effort by the NGO, penalties for misrepresentation, and external verification. While Rugmark and Kaleen have some serious shortcomings in meeting the criteria for credibility, they fare much better than the Foul Ball campaign which – while somewhat increasing awareness of the presence of child labor – has failed to provide credible information to consumers about whether children were involved in production of particular soccer balls. In all of these cases, many factors, including public sector education and the structure of the economy, could help explain why child labor is more prevalent in some places than others. Our focus, however, is on NGO credibility rather than the eradication of child labor. As such, we will focus on the characteristics of NGOs rather than the countries or economies in which they operate.

Our cases suggest three important points. First, on the basis of the criteria laid out in Chapter 1, some NGOs are indeed more credible than others in establishing that a product was made without the use of child labor. We are skeptical, though, that consumers and retailers will engage in a systematic consideration of which NGOs meet these four criteria or not. Regarding labels, for instance, we suspect that many consumers struggle to differentiate between labels claiming that a product is free of child labor. Second, although some NGOs may be more credible than others for the discerning consumer or retailer, all suffer from a lack of external monitoring. We conclude that the most credible signal that a product was made without child labor would come from mandatory government initiatives that are industry-wide. Indeed, Gay Seidman (2010) notes that the carpet industry in India was decentralized precisely to avoid government regulation of working conditions. Likewise, the use of NGOs as certifiers is a way for businesses to avoid a more credible effort by the government to monitor the use of child labor. We argue in favor of moving beyond relying wholly on the virtue of NGOs, which are better suited to being watchdogs than credible certifiers, toward a central role for states in the monitoring and regulation of child labor so that consumers and retailers can be confident about how their merchandise has been produced.

In developing our two main arguments, we seek to offer a stronger theoretical foundation for future empirical tests regarding the perception of credibility to consumers and retailers. Specifically, building on work like that of Michael Broukhim and Michael Hiscox (2009) we advocate more empirical research on what enhances perceptions of credibility to consumers and retailers and on whether credible signals can be linked to actual reductions in the use of child labor. Finally, we put forth a clear policy prescription regarding child labor, notably that credibility in monitoring and certification – according to the criteria laid out by Gourevitch and Lake – can be best assured by bringing the state back in, rather than relying on NGOs to accomplish a task for which they are at a comparative disadvantage.

Credible certification: rugs versus soccer balls

In establishing credibility of child labor free production, Rugmark fares better than Kaleen (McClintock 2001), and both rug-industry labels fare better than the Foul Ball campaign in the soccer industry. Table 3.1 summarizes our characterization of Rugmark, Kaleen, and the Foul Ball campaign in relation to four conditions for credibility.

The success of Rugmark versus the Foul Ball campaign is especially surprising given that both were reactions to publicity about the use of child labor in the same era – the early to mid 1990s – and both campaigns included some of the same advocates and organizations backing them. Despite their similar origins, Rugmark established credibility with consumers and retailers, while the Foul Ball campaign failed to create a system by which to convey credible information that its suppliers were not using child labor in production. Explaining this variation in perceived credibility is the goal of this chapter, and, therefore, we turn to a closer examination of the background and implementation of means to certify child labor free production in the rug and soccer ball industries.

The rug and carpet industry: a relative success in certifying child labor free production

Rugmark and Kaleen are the two largest organized efforts to combat the use of child labor in the South Asian rug industry and both label rugs to provide an assurance that children were not involved in their

Table 3.1. *Conditions for credibility in Rugmark/Goodweave, Kaleen, and the Foul Ball campaign*

Criterion	Rugmark	Kaleen	Foul Ball campaign	Bringing the state back in: mandatory government regulation with NGOs as watchdogs
Common interests of organization and consumers	Yes; because Rugmark is an NGO with the express purpose of monitoring and eliminating child labor	Only partial common interests because Kaleen is quasi-governmental and the government has an interest in not finding cases of child labor	Largely not common interests because it was initiated by the industry rather than an NGO. While Save the Children has become involved, it does not spearhead the effort	Yes; NGO watchdogs would have common interests with consumers and retailers wishing to discourage child labor

Costly effort	Yes; producers pay to join Rugmark, but actual costs are low since Rugmark has very few monitors to conduct inspections	No; funded partially by the government via a tax on export sales, making the costs for producers lower. Also, Kaleen, like Rugmark, has very few monitors to conduct inspections	Some costs in efforts in Sialkot, but minimal continuing costs as it is largely a publicity campaign today	Yes; government initiatives should be mandatory and industry-wide, requiring a significant investment of resources; NGOs may commit significant resources too
Penalty for misrepresentation	Yes; because Rugmark would lose credibility in its very reason for existence	Limited; the Kaleen label would lose credibility, but overall impact is limited since the CEPC's mandate is greater than simply certification	Minimal; because no label and they do not purport to certify officially that production is child labor free	High; costs of a boycott are significant if abuses are found, and in more democratic countries bad publicity can hurt electoral chances
External verification	No	No	No	Yes; NGOs would verify government initiatives

making.[4] Rugmark is an entirely private organization, while Kaleen is quasi-governmental; this difference between the two plays a critical role in making Rugmark more credible.

Rugmark (Goodweave[5])

The Indian government has long taken the official stance of condemning child labor although its laws have frequently not been enforced. Article 24 of the Indian Constitution, passed in 1949, forbids the employment of children in hazardous industries and, unlike the United States, India is also a signatory to the 1989 Convention on the Rights of a Child and passed a comprehensive Child Labor Prohibition and Regulation Act in 1986 and a National Policy on Child Labour Act in 1987 (Chowdry and Beeman 2001; Sharma 2002–2003).

Nonetheless, the use of child labor in India was and, in some cases, continues to be, widespread in a number of hazardous industries (Weiner 1991). In the 1980s and early 1990s, the use of child labor in the carpet industry caught the interest of the international community and generated a great deal of negative press and threats of boycotts. In the summer of 1993, in response to the threat of an international boycott, the Indian government issued an order that the use of child labor in weaving rugs should be ended within three months with the threat from the textiles minister of "stringent legal action."[6] Estimates indicated that this was not a problem on the margins, but that millions of child laborers formed the backbone of the carpet and

---

[4] STEP and Care and Fair are two smaller organizations that certify a company's commitment to avoiding the use of child labor but do not certify that child labor has not been used in production. As such, STEP and Care and Fair offer awareness and signal that companies with their label do not openly support the use of child labor (Bachman 2000). Compared to Rugmark and Kaleen, these two organizations are small in scale. We exclude STEP and Care and Fair from our discussion here as they are not NGOs, but company-sponsored initiatives intended to announce a commitment to eradicating child labor rather than any assurance that it is not being used. Future research could incorporate the extent to which such efforts improve a company's reputation.

[5] Rugmark was renamed Goodweave in 2009 (www.rugmark.net/news/339). For clarity and consistency with previous scholarship, we use the name Rugmark throughout this chapter.

[6] "Carpet Traders Ordered to Free Child Slaves," *The Times*, July 27, 1993.

rug industry, with some reports alleging that as many as 75 percent of those employed in the carpet industry were children (Burra 1995).[7]

Because the carpet industry is one of the most profitable Indian export industries, the government had a strong incentive to be seen as taking action countering the use of child labor given the threat of international attention. At a minimum, the Indian government had a strong incentive to cooperate with NGOs working to combat the use of child labor in order to avoid the negative press that could hamper one of its most lucrative export industries. Several NGOs worked on child labor in the rug industry prior to the creation of Rugmark. One of these was the Bonded Labor Liberation Front (BLLF), which engineered raids to rescue bonded children in the mid 1980s, included a high-profile rescue of thirty children in the spring of 1984. Building on this, the South Asian Coalition of Child Servitude (SACCS) was founded in 1986 and included the BLLF and sixty-four other South Asian organizations (Chowdry and Beeman 2001). Both organizations were highly effective in raising public and international awareness about the widespread use of child labor in the Indian carpet industry.

Publicity of child slave labor in the Indian carpet industry further spread to other Western countries including Sweden, Holland, the United Kingdom, and the United States. The Indian government and domestic carpet associations began to fear a boycott, and so, two major carpet industry associations – the All India Carpet Manufacturers Association (AICMA) and the Carpet Export Promotion Council (CEPC) – began discussing the issue with SACCS. However, members of AICMA were split as to whether child labor was justified and whether they were even willing to acknowledge its prevalence, and little came of this industry effort to get out in front of the bad publicity.[8] A new organization arose, Carpet Manufacturers Without Child Labor (CMAWCL), which expressed greater commitment to the abolition of child labor in the carpet industry (Chowdry and Beeman 2001), but, again, little tangible progress was made.

---

[7] "Children Protest Slave Labor," *The Gazette*, February 23, 1993.
[8] "Experts Cannot Agree on How to End Child Labor in India," Deutsche-Presse Agentur, April 8, 1998.

Because Germany had a particularly high demand for Indian rugs, labor activist Kailash Satyarthi, who was a prominent player in the BLLF and SACCS, targeted his efforts on promoting consumer awareness in Germany and on developing NGO programs which would work to eliminate the use of children in rug weaving. His strategy succeeded: organizations like Bread for the World, Terre des Hommes, and Misreror worked together in creating the Campaign Against Child Labor, while other groups such as the Federal Association of Oriental Carpet Importers, the German Trade Association, and the Association for the Protection of Children helped promote public awareness about the problem (Chowdry and Beeman 2001; Ravi 2001). In 1991, after a speech a year earlier by Satyarthi at the United Nations Human Rights Commission subgroup on modern slavery, the United Nations accepted a resolution suggesting that a label be created for carpets to indicate that child labor had not been used in their production (McDonagh 2002). Ultimately, the Indo-German Export Promotion Council backed the foundation of Rugmark in 1994 to do just that.

Rugmark is an independent labor monitoring program financed by the dues of member companies. It certifies and labels rugs for which production is child labor free, and assists with rescuing and rehabilitating children in part by providing access to educational resources. After its founding, Rugmark quickly expanded to include as members businesses in other Western countries, including the United States (Compa and Hinchcliffe-Darricarrère 1995).

Today Rugmark has expanded its business to Nepal and Pakistan. Licensed importers can be found in the Netherlands, Belgium, Luxembourg, Sweden, Switzerland, the United States, and the United Kingdom. Rugmark has been widely praised as a success. The label's recognition is increasingly widespread and has even resulted in collaboration with major corporations, such as the 2009 initiative to begin working with Macy's. While there are limitations in verifying the number of child laborers in the carpet industry before and after Rugmark, some scholars have been able to verify independently a reduction in the number of children in the industry (Ravi 2001).

Rugmark has been able to finance its social assistance programs because it passes on the costs of certification to businesses. For extra fees, companies can also gain access to additional reports and case studies on the Rugmark website as well as being included in promotional projects such as its 2006 "Most Beautiful Rug" campaign intended to increase consumer awareness. Representatives of Rugmark are quick to emphasize that the initiative is led by retailers without whose fees none of the educational or social assistance programs would be possible.[9]

The relative success of Rugmark and the implications for credibility

Rugmark meets two of the four conditions for credibility (common interests and a penalty for misrepresentation), but is characterized by problems in making a costly effort and securing external verification of its efforts. On the positive side, some experts have concluded that "Rugmark appears to be more independent, credible, and better equipped to capture the spirit of public cooperation" than other programs such as Kaleen and STEP (McClintock 2001: 904).

Experts have reached this conclusion in large part because Rugmark's credibility is bolstered by several factors. First, Rugmark shares common interests with consumers and retailers seeking child labor free products. While Rugmark was backed by the German and Indian governments, it is a private NGO and an independent certifier whose sole purpose is to monitor the use of child labor in the textile industry. Customers seeking reassurance that their products are child labor free are better served by Rugmark than by a business, which may have ulterior motives. Rugmark's credibility is further enhanced by the somewhat costly effort required for certification as its member companies pay dues for certification, although problems with the extent to which their certification is truly costly will be discussed below.

Rugmark would suffer a penalty for misrepresenting its certification process as its reputation would be ruined if it were discovered that rugs with its label were made with the work of children. Because it is an independent NGO, Rugmark's very existence as an organization rests on its ability to convince consumers and retailers that it can monitor effectively. If rugs with the Rugmark label were discovered to have been made by children, its existence as an organization would be questioned. This also means that Rugmark does have an incentive

---

[9] "Responsible Trading: Mark of Progress," *Carpet and Floorcoverings Review*, May 18, 2007.

to find violators and exclude them from their labeling scheme whereas business initiatives might have incentives not to find offenders.

The underlying question is why Rugmark is successful in meeting some of the criteria for credibility. Certifying child labor free products is credible to the extent it is because of the label and its initiation primarily by an NGO, independent of companies and governments, which shares interests with consumers and retailers. This is also critical for there to be a penalty for misrepresentation. This suggests that NGOs can play a critical role in credible certification when their motives are not tainted by association with ulterior industry and government motivations.

Despite its relative success, Rugmark has faced some serious criticism that its certification is not entirely credible (Seidman 2009). Even with an operating budget of more than $1 million a year, Rugmark employs only eighteen monitors who often are unable to check any single loom more than once every three years. The small number of inspectors suggests that Rugmark is not making a very costly effort to monitor and that its label does not ensure that child labor was not used. For instance, in a 1995 interview, Ram Achal Maury reported that his brother, the president of Rugmark, could not confirm that his company's carpets were child labor free. Others have accused Rugmark inspectors of being corrupt and taking bribes, although documented cases of this have not been reported.[10] Activists in India have referred to Rugmark as "misleading" and "misguided" and UNICEF cut its involvement with the initiative in the late 1990s (Seidman 2010).

Rugmark also lacks any external verification of its organization or monitors. Consumers are in the position of taking their word for it that they monitor randomly and do not find instances of child labor. Kaleen, another monitoring organization which will be discussed next, may inspect some of the same looms that Rugmark inspectors do, but one has no reliable way of knowing.

Kaleen's efforts to monitor the use of child labor

The initial success of Rugmark was alarming to Indian carpet producers. While their early efforts to have industry lead the certification process failed, Rugmark's existence provided a new impetus. The

---

[10] "India Battles Illegal Child Labor," *Christian Science Monitor*, November 8, 1995 (accessed through LexisNexis Academic).

Carpet Export Promotion Council (CEPC), which falls under the auspices of the Indian Ministry of Textiles, formed a quasi-governmental program called Kaleen. The CEPC oversees the mandatory registration of all Indian carpet exporters and issues export licenses; the Kaleen labeling scheme was added to these tasks. Kaleen was thus established a year after the creation of Rugmark and modeled on its efforts, although as a response from within industry it differs explicitly in its origins. The CEPC effort has faced serious criticism, particularly regarding corruption and unreliability in the monitoring of looms. One carpet weaver indicated that it was easy to bribe government inspectors, stating that "If they get money, the inspectors say there was no child labor. If there is no money, even if the boy is 18, they write that he is only 14."[11] Such anecdotal accounts, and the lack of funding for adequate inspection of members' looms, suggest that the Kaleen label has been rendered meaningless by corruption.[12]

Kaleen does not fare well on the four conditions for credibility and highlights the importance of certification efforts being led by an independent NGO that has common interests with consumers rather than with government or industry. First, because Kaleen is a quasi-governmental initiative, it has fewer shared common interests with socially-conscious consumers. The rug export industry is a powerful lobbying group domestically, and the Indian government has an incentive not to discover the use of child labor and face political repercussions as a result. Additionally, the government has an interest in protecting the industry from bad press that could lead to boycotts and hamper the development of the industry. Thus, while the government, and, by extension, Kaleen, does have an incentive to convince consumers that child labor is being fought in the rug industry, it faces a conflict of interest because of its intimate relationship with the exporters it aims to police.

Second, the penalty for misrepresentation is arguably higher for Rugmark, a private organization whose very existence would be threatened by reports of falsified monitoring, while the Government of India as a whole does not necessarily lose credibility if Kaleen proves to be

---

[11] *Ibid.*

[12] Other accounts indicate that the Kaleen label only means that the companies have signed on to an agreement to follow guidelines intended to lead to the eradication of child labor in the rug industry (Bachman 2000), although the announcement of Kaleen does not indicate this to be the case.

a poorly functioning program. Furthermore, Kaleen can be framed as part of a long-term, ongoing effort which, while it has problems, is a step in the right direction. Indeed, an annual government report of the Indian textile industry in 1995–1996 said that Kaleen was just one of a number of measures taken to combat child labor in this industry.[13] Framing Kaleen as one of several steps is in keeping with the commitment model of corporate social responsibility by which businesses, NGOs, and the government must collaborate rather than having monitors serve as whistleblowers that encourage businesses to cover up any violations (Locke *et al.* 2009). Being a private initiative, Rugmark would have more difficulty framing itself as part of a long-term, overarching government commitment to countering child labor. Based on the penalty for misrepresentation, the discerning customer should find Rugmark more credible than Kaleen even if there are accusations of corruption and limited monitoring for both.

Kaleen is also a less costly effort because it is subsidized by the Indian government. Its operations are not financed by dues from member companies, but rather by a small tax on export sales.[14] Finally, as with the other NGO initiatives covered in this chapter, Kaleen lacks external verification. Kaleen could act as an external verifier of Rugmark or vice versa, but this is not currently the case.

Our comparison of the two major initiatives to certify child labor free production in the export rug industry in India suggests that, while Kaleen, like its private counterpart Rugmark, provides an official label, for the discerning customer it should be a much less credible source of certification because its interests are more diffuse and it faces fewer costs for making mistakes. However, in a low-information environment, and given the inherent difficulty in observing child labor, the introduction of additional labels through programs like Kaleen also runs the risk of confusing consumers and decreases their credibility (Sharma 2002–2003). Although Rugmark labels do, in principle, allow consumers to track the rug through the entire production process, there is no indication that most purchasers do so, nor is there a guarantee that an inspector saw a specific loom. Research

---

[13] "Indian Textile Exports Cross 9 Billion Dollars in Fiscal 1995–1996," Deutsche Presse-Agentur, August 7, 1996.
[14] "India Battles Illegal Child Labor."

suggests that a label alone is credible as consumers look for quick information shortcuts to allow them to buy what they think may be more socially responsible products (Broukhim and Hiscox 2009) and that we should be skeptical about the long-term positive gains from labeling initiatives (Basu *et al.* 2006).

Our concern – which we hope will be empirically tested in future work – is that consumers will either take all labels as equivalent indicators of credibility or that they may dismiss them altogether. The surge in the use of labels through multiple sources confuses consumers, leading them to conflate more and less credible labels. And, if consumers are aware of the labels, then they may unjustly penalize companies if the chances of getting a label are low even when a producer qualifies, as would be the case if bribes are required to get positive reports (Baland and Duprez 2009). As consumers, we should remain skeptical about what information these labels actually provide. While the ultimate impact of labels is not our focus here, problems with credibility suggest that labels are not likely to have the intended effect of creating incentives for producers to avoid employing children, but rather that labels create perverse incentives and mask the extent of the continuing problem.

Soccer balls: a lack of credibility in the Foul Ball campaign and Sialkot Project

Child labor violations in the stitching of footballs were publicized in the mid 1990s, around the same time that violations in the carpet industry were coming to public attention. In 1995, reports surfaced that the footballs sold by major sports companies, including Umbro, Reebok, Adidas, and Mitre (which provides balls for Britain's Football Association and Premier League), were being stitched together by Pakistani children, some of whom had been sold into bonded labor by their parents. This flurry of media attention included a CBS documentary aired in April of 1995, which presented disturbing images of children stitching soccer balls in dark rooms with no windows (CBS 1995) and a *Life* magazine exposé highlighting the disparity between the conditions of American children playing with soccer balls and the Pakistani children making them (Schanberg and Dorigny 1996). Reports indicated that children as young as six years old were being paid 10 pence for a single football that would sell for as much as

50 pounds.[15] Outrage emerged that children were being exploited to produce the soccer balls used in the World Cup, European competitions, and the FA Cup final. Many companies took defensive action, promising to cancel contracts with any suppliers using child labor. Reebok, for instance, announced that it had cancelled current contracts with its suppliers.[16]

The Bachpan Bachao Andolan (BBA), also founded by social activist Kailash Satyarthi (a prominent player in the creation of Rugmark), was the first organization to lobby to put an end to the use of child labor in soccer ball stitching during the 1996 European championship (Zutshi 2008). Because these efforts to combat child labor in the soccer ball industry were led by some of the same activists and organizations, it is all the more surprising that efforts to provide credible certification of the absence of child labor in production has been more successful for carpets than soccer balls. Understanding this variation is useful for identifying the conditions that enhance the credibility of certification.

The Fédération Internationale de Football Association (FIFA) and the International Labor Organization (ILO) responded to these charges by creating the Foul Ball campaign and adopting mandates for labor standards, including that children under the age of fifteen should not be employed in making footballs (Zutshi 2008). Efforts to highlight the use of child labor in the football industry have been echoed in more recent efforts like the 2006 event "Red Card to Child Labor."[17] These efforts have amounted to little more than public awareness campaigns and have not produced credible monitoring of the use of child labor. The Foul Ball campaign never achieved a "tipping point" in which businesses needed to sign on to certify child labor free production to be competitive.

The main result of the campaign to end child labor in soccer ball production was the Sialkot Child Labor Elimination Project, announced

---

[15] "Scandal of Football's Child Slavery," *The Sunday Times* (London), May 14, 1995.

[16] "Balls Made by Child Laborers," *USA Today*, April 7, 2005.

[17] For more information on the "Give a Red Card to Child Labor" events, see www.ilo.org/ipec/Campaignandadvocacy/RedCardtoChildLabour/lang – en/index.htm.

as part of the Atlanta Agreement in 1997.[18] The town of Sialkot in Pakistan is a significant case: reports estimate that it produces 60 to 80 percent of the world's footballs (Siegman 2008). The Atlanta Agreement was adopted in consultation with the Save the Children Foundation, the ILO, and UNICEF. Ultimately, the Pakistani government and local NGOs were also involved in the implementation of the initiative (Husselbee 2000; Siegman 2008).

While previously soccer balls were often assembled in village homes, the Sialkot Project involved the creation of stitching centers that could be monitored by the ILO. Social assistance programs similar to those run by Rugmark were also planned to help families send children to school while replacing the lost income. Some reviews of the efforts to curb the use of child labor in Sialkot have been very positive and, because such a high percentage of soccer balls are made in this town, argue they have had a big impact on the industry as a whole. Two years after the program's implementation, former US President Bill Clinton announced that the program was a success in which "the industry, the ILO, and UNICEF joined together to remove children from the production of soccer balls and give them a chance to go to school, and to monitor the results" (Clinton 1999 in Boje and Khan 2009).

NGOs played a secondary role in combating child labor in the soccer ball industry. While several international organizations became involved (including Save the Children, the ILO, and UNICEF), there was no single NGO that was created for the sole purpose of monitoring or certifying child labor free production that was comparable to Rugmark in the rug industry. David Husselbee (2000) indicates that Save the Children was a relative success in Sialkot because it operated from a position of trust within the partnership, so that businesses did not fear an adverse effect on their commercial relations based on the findings. In other words, the initiative was led by business rather than an independent NGO. Among the successes achieved in Sialkot, Husselbee notes that fifty-three manufacturers in Sialkot were monitored by the ILO. Social assistance has been provided, including 104 government primary schools and 150 non-formal education centers (although it is unclear what constitutes a "non-formal education

---

[18] A copy of the Atlanta Agreement can be obtained at www.imacpak.org/atlanta.htm (accessed August 2009).

center"). It appears that the inclusion of NGOs has been important for obtaining the access to facilities and other logistical prerequisites necessary to monitor the use of child labor.

The main shortcoming of the project is that it is limited to the one town of Sialkot. Similar procedures have not been set up throughout the football industry. The ILO reported in 2004 that 95 percent of soccer ball production was being monitored and in 2007 reported that only 3 percent of producers were "performing badly" (IMAC 2004, 2007). However, there continue to be reports of pervasive use of child labor in the production of footballs (Zutshi 2008). For instance, in 2008 the International Labor Rights Forum (ILRF) found that the use of child labor continued to be pervasive in Pakistan and India.[19] Notably, while some minimal efforts have been made to monitor and reduce the use of child labor in the football industry, there is no labeling campaign comparable to Rugmark. There is no way for consumers to know whether the football they are purchasing was produced with child labor, and there is little indication that companies have credible information about their own supply chain. Finally, while this chapter focuses principally on the determinants of credibility rather than eventual social outcomes, it is important to note accusations that the efforts to eradicate the use of child labor in Sialkot have done little to address the underlying social issues such as the improvement of wages or conditions (Khan *et al.* 2007).

The Foul Ball campaign and the Sialkot Project and the implications for credibility

Even if the efforts in Sialkot have reduced the use of child labor in one town, they have failed to convey credible information to consumers about whether child labor has been used. We cannot, for instance, know whether our soccer balls were made in Sialkot or not, which, allegedly, would mean that it was less likely child labor was used.[20] The Foul Ball campaign and the Sialkot Project did not do well on any of the four

---

[19] See the ILRF repot at www.laborrights.org/stop-child-labor/foulball-campaign (accessed August 2009).

[20] Although news reports indicate that most soccer balls are made in Sialkot, there is typically no label indicating exactly where the ball was made. For instance, information on Umbro soccer balls indicates "Made In: Imported" without actually specifying a location. An example of this can be found at www.soccer.com/IWCatProductPage.process?Merchant_Id=1andN=4294 960224+331andProduct_Id=523623. In 1996, Reebok announced it would

conditions for credibility. The campaign does not share common interests with consumers, its efforts are not costly, there are low penalties for misrepresentation, and there is no system of external verification.

First, because the Foul Ball campaign was established and is maintained by the industry rather than an independent NGO, it does not share common interests with its consumers. Although Save the Children, the ILO, and UNICEF were involved, these organizations did not take the lead. Because these NGOs were acting under the directive of the industry rather than independently, their credibility as certifiers was damaged.

Furthermore, Save the Children concluded that stitching footballs was not especially dangerous or exploitative work for children and provided needed financial assistance for families (Husselbee 2000). This contradicts previous research from the ILRF, which indicates that children suffer serious vision and back problems from working long hours hunched over in poor lighting and that needles used to sew balls together often puncture children's hands.[21] Disagreement among NGOs about whether child labor was even a significant problem further undermined their credibility.

Second, efforts in the soccer ball industry were not very costly in the long term. While there was an initial cost involved in establishing the stitching centers, there appear to be minimal continuing costs. The cost of social assistance is also limited to a single town. While companies claim that the majority of their soccer balls are made in Sialkot, there is no label that indicates where a ball was made. Furthermore, companies do not pay membership fees to be part of a monitoring organization as they do with Rugmark, making the ongoing costs low.

Third, while there was some penalty for misrepresentation since the industry would lose face and, possibly, customers, if the initiative could not claim to have produced any results, the penalty for misrepresentation was much lower because there was no label. If violations were found, companies could claim to have been unaware of them and point to their continuing efforts to eliminate child labor. Even if some soccer ball stitching continues in village homes, the Sialkot

start putting a label on its soccer balls indicating that they were not made with child labor, but such labels were never created.
[21] See the ILRF report at www.laborrights.org/stop-child-labor/foulball-campaign (accessed August 2009).

Project is likely to face serious criticism if child labor is found in the stitching center itself. Otherwise, the companies can simply point to the reticence of workers to commute to a central location and the difficulty of eradicating child labor if it is concealed in the home. In other words, even in light of continuing child labor in making soccer balls, companies like Umbro and Reebok can make the claim that they are doing all they can.

Finally, the efforts of the Foul Ball campaign, including the Sialkot Project, lacked any external verification. ILO monitors did observe stitching centers, but as part of the original initiative, this does not constitute truly external verification. Additionally, there was no monitoring of soccer ball production that was not done in Sialkot. There was no effort by external NGOs or the Pakistani government to monitor the consequences of the Sialkot Project. In short, despite the positive reviews of its success, we really just have the word of the industry, which has a vested interest in maintaining a positive public appearance.

The underlying question is why the Foul Ball campaign failed to meet the basic criteria to establish credibility with consumers and retailers. One of the primary reasons is that Foul Ball (like Kaleen in the rug industry) was initiated and maintained by the industry rather than being led by an NGO, whose conflicts of interests might be fewer. The source of initiatives to certify child free labor is, therefore, a key underlying explanation for when efforts will be credible. Although NGOs serve as collaborators in this case, they were not the initiating organizations and do not function independently. Without an independent NGO leading the cause, the Sialkot Project appears to be simply a one-time effort in a single location. The industry also had no incentive to create labels if it could sufficiently improve its image without investing in a costly effort. A perfect illustration is that, although Reebok announced in 1996 after the initial outcry that it planned to begin labeling its balls as "child labor free," no such labels were ever created.[22] Reebok very likely calculated that the increased possibility of a tarnished reputation – if it was discovered that labels were erroneously placed on balls that were in fact made with child labor – was not worth the risk.

[22] "Reebok International to Label Soccer Balls with 'Made Without Child Labor' Guarantee," PR Newswire, November 16, 1996 (accessed through LexisNexis Academic).

There is no indication that negative press hurt sales of soccer balls or that the efforts of the Foul Ball campaign led to a resurgence in soccer ball purchases by consumers previously concerned about the use of child labor. This case pessimistically suggests that any negative consequences suffered by the companies as a result of bad press were countered by a one-time, non-credible effort in a single town.

Conclusion: implications for NGO credibility in monitoring and certification

Credible certification is an important first step in promoting social change. While Rugmark has successfully promoted awareness and provided what consumers and retailers are willing to accept as a credible signal, Foul Ball has failed to reach even this important first step of promoting awareness and providing what is at least perceived as credible information. There is no way for a consumer to know whether the soccer ball she purchases has been made with the use of child labor.

The cases also suggest that, although some NGO efforts may be more credible than others, NGOs are limited in the extent to which they can offer truly credible signals of child labor free production. One example of this can be found in labels. Labels provided by NGOs are inherently problematic, in part due to the proliferation and diversity of what different labels represent. What consumers take as credible signals may convey little actual information (Broukhim and Hiscox 2009). Gay Seidman (2009) notes that the growth of labeling initiatives in the carpet industry actually provides "credible" information to consumers but makes the labels less meaningful as it is not clear what each denotes. Alakh Sharma (2002–2003) indicates that Rugmark and other initiatives in the carpet industry have been mostly successful in raising awareness. Our concern, therefore, is that less discerning consumers will not pay attention to all four of the criteria that should promote credibility – meaning that they should favor a Rugmark label over one from Kaleen – but rather will pacify their desire to be socially conscious by purchasing any labeled product.

Labels are only one part of the larger problem of NGO credibility, as all NGOs face inherent limitations in certifying child labor free production. The cases in this chapter suggest that external verification is a problem of particular concern for NGOs that are attempting to monitor and certify labor standards. Other NGOs may act as whistle-blowers, but it is uncertain that they would have a clear incentive to invest their time and energy in doing so most of the time.[23] In cases where multiple, even competing, NGOs exist, they could possibly serve as external verification for each other. However, Rugmark and Kaleen also lacked any external verification despite the fact that they might be able to provide this check for each other. There is no whistle-blower for any of the NGOs discussed in this chapter. Realistically, larger international organizations like the ILO or UNICEF may be able to provide verification that smaller, issue-specific NGOs are reliable and credible monitors. However, the incentive for international organizations to engage in such external verification is unclear.

Rather than relying on other NGOs and international organizations, governments can and should play a central role in regulating the use of child labor. Furthermore, for the government to be most effective, it should establish a universal and compulsory monitoring system of its own, which could establish systems of verification as are done with many public programs (i.e., some type of ombudsman). In short, governments can provide the most credible signal of all. For one-time efforts like the Sialkot Project, the government is unlikely to conduct an extensive review of whether the program is doing what it says it does. Furthermore, programs to monitor and certify labor standards are sometimes in countries that lack the capacity or incentive to monitor NGO activity. In fact, if an NGO can improve the image of the industry in a country with little to no cost to the government, the government has no motivation to intervene to discredit the organization's work. This means that external monitoring of NGOs is, empirically, unlikely to occur. NGOs can help fill the gap in an era of "stateless regulation," but as we think about the large goal of effecting actual social change, it may be necessary for governments to

---

[23] Some for-profit organizations like ForeignAid Ratings, LLC do provide lists of credible NGOs (see Chapter 5, this volume). The earthquake in Haiti in January of 2010 prompted a demand for lists of worthy NGOs to which individuals should feel comfortable donating. For example, Charity Navigator has provided a list of ten credible NGOs in Haiti (www.charitynavigator.org/index.cfm?bay=content.viewandcpid=1004). This suggests that when there is a major crisis or event, there will be demand for NGOs providing external verification of other NGOs, but in long-term practice most individuals are unlikely to look at these, particularly if they are not considering making a donation. Most importantly, these rankings do not give us any information about whether NGOs can credibly certify labor standards.

spearhead widespread efforts to regulate, monitor, and penalize those who do not comply.

NGOs face an inherently difficult time in serving as credible and effective monitors of child labor use in global supply chains for at least two related reasons. First, NGOs do not have adequate financial resources for an undertaking of this sort, and so are required to generate funds. In Rugmark's case, start-up capital provided by the German government proved invaluable, and subsequently Rugmark charges the businesses it monitors a fee in exchange for certification. But taking funds from the same companies one is monitoring creates conflicts of interest that can easily undermine the monitor's credibility. This lack of resources is witnessed again in the persistent difficulty of gathering the information required to render a credible assessment of the businesses' practices. Second, even when NGOs appear to have gained some credibility – as Rugmark arguably has – their broader impacts are very limited and face problems of scaling up. A recent Rugmark self-assessment suggests that there are still 300,000 children working in the carpet industry in South Asia (Rugmark 2008). How does a certification program that accounts for less than 8 percent of the total market for the goods being certified tackle a problem of that scale? More generally, certification programs typically focus on specific industries, while the problems they tackle are general. So even if Rugmark succeeds in eradicating child labor in the carpet industry, what guarantee is there that their former employees will not simply find jobs stitching footballs? To the extent that we hope NGOs can effect broader social change, our analysis suggests a pessimistic outlook.

The pessimism expressed here should be hardly surprising to anyone familiar with the history of successful regulatory movements in the developed world. The role NGOs are being asked to play as monitors and enforcers of anti-child-labor codes of conduct lie well beyond their comparative advantage. In fact, arguably, asking them to play this role reflects an apolitical perspective and an ahistorical *naïveté*. In most developed countries, the regulatory function is fulfilled by states, which can utilize their vaster resources and their unique position to influence the behavior of even the largest corporations. Indeed, in both India and Pakistan, child labor is illegal and has been so for decades (Weiner 1991). The problem is that governments do not enforce the laws that are on the books, and politicians and bureaucrats turn a blind eye to their violation. Faced with such a pusillanimous and craven state, the solution has been to turn to civil society to

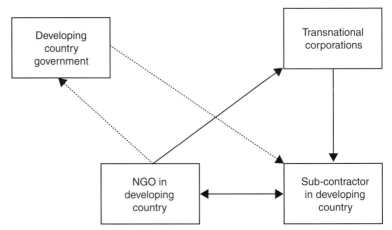

Figure 3.1 Bringing the state back in – state as regulator and NGO as whistleblower

fill the gaps, but in so doing, we have both asked these NGOs to reach well beyond their grasp and have let the state off the hook.

Figure 3.1 presents the current role of NGOs in monitoring child labor (with solid lines) versus our alternative proposal for bringing the state back in (with dotted lines).

The key actors are three: transnational corporations (typically headquartered in the West), a sub-contractor in a developing country, and an NGO in the same developing country. In the current scenario, the NGO plays the role of monitor, conveys information about alleged violations to the transnational corporation either through public shaming or private channels, and the transnational corporation exerts pressure on the sub-contractor to amend its ways. The state is left out of the picture.

In contrast, we argue that NGOs must make the state the focus of their activity, as suggested by inherent problems with the credibility of NGOs in the rug and soccer ball industries demonstrated here. In this formulation, the NGO should play two roles simultaneously. First, with respect to local factories and businesses, the NGO should assume an adversarial position, seeking to identify and publicize violations of the law. Second, with respect to the state, the NGO should use its position in civil society to build public awareness and mobilize public opinion against the state. In Table 3.1, we have included a column assessing our proposal in relation to the four criteria for credibility. Our model of the state as regulator and the NGO as watchdog provides the most credible system of monitoring. NGOs have a common interest with consumers and retailers who want to avoid child labor; the effort should be mandatory and industry-wide, constituting a significant investment of government resources and substantial costs for NGO watchdogs; the penalty for misrepresentation would be high both economically and politically (particularly for politicians relying on competitive elections to stay in power); finally, NGO watchdogs would serve as external monitors of the government. Although the state may have an incentive to misrepresent the existence of child labor and officials can be bribed – which we argue is part of the problem with the continuing prevalence of child labor in India – NGOs acting as watchdogs should make it more likely that government deception will be revealed, thereby providing an increased incentive for honest government monitoring. The key is to encourage the state to take on the role as the primary entity responsible for monitoring and certifying whether child labor has been used.

The twin tasks of whistleblower and mobilizer lie within the comparative advantage of NGOs, and constitute roles they can play credibly and effectively. The parallel to the human rights regime is apt: one would not think of seeking to defend human rights by excluding the state, even if the violators of such rights are extra-state. Rather what human rights NGOs do, with Amnesty International as a prime example (Wong 2009), is utilize their grassroots networks to elicit information about the facts on the ground, and publicize this information broadly in an effort to pressure the state either to enforce its own laws or to make new ones. In our pursuit of labor rights for workers employed at the bottom of global supply chains, we have all too often forgotten the state, and relied entirely – and mistakenly – on NGOs. Moving beyond the virtue of NGOs and incorporating a central role for the state will go a long way toward helping the working children of the world.

4 Becoming a household name: how human rights NGOs establish credibility through organizational structure

WENDY H. WONG

Why should we believe the word of non-governmental organizations (NGOs) working on human rights? They are, after all, actors with interests and values, pursuing political agendas. Contrary to what some have argued, their positions are not apolitical (Wilson 1997; Winston 2001); they do not adopt views in an idealistic vacuum. While human rights NGOs can be considered virtuous because the nature of their work is characterized as "good" by most, like other NGOs and other political actors, NGOs also have distinct agendas. They make tradeoffs on the issues and cases they choose to advocate. Knowing this, under what conditions should we believe human rights NGOs? Should we always find them credible because they do good work protecting people from oppressive regimes, exposing violations of international law? Should we accept their monitoring as credible because they tend to be accurate? As it will become clear below, the "we" (i.e. the audience) that evaluates NGOs actually matters quite a bit. Knowing that credibility is in the eye of the beholder, human rights NGOs also attempt to position themselves such that they are more credible to certain audiences. The credibility of two of the most important human rights NGOs, Amnesty International and Human Rights Watch (HRW), is achieved through different organizational structure choices,

I would like to thank the participants of the Beyond Virtue meeting at UC San Diego, in particular Peter Gourevitch, Michael Hiscox, David Lake, April Linton, Irfan Nooruddin, and Janice Stein, Michael Barnett, and two anonymous reviewers for comments on earlier drafts. Thanks to the human rights activists from Human Rights Watch and Amnesty International who generously lent their knowledge, experiences, and time to this chapter.

which I argue is one critical method by which audiences can evaluate NGO credibility.[1]

Human rights NGOs often stress the accuracy of their reporting to demonstrate their trustworthiness as a strategy to establish or augment their credibility.[2] First, human rights NGOs fundamentally have to be accurate – their accounts that states are abusing human rights need to be true, or else it undermines their ability to engage in transnational politics: information, symbolic, leverage, accountability (Keck and Sikkink 1998). However, accuracy of information is a function of the perception of NGOs as trustworthy organizations themselves. NGOs are taken seriously when their reports turn out to be true; they become credible as political actors and informants as they establish their reputations for accurately revealing abuses on individuals. Accuracy leads to credibility. However, the credibility of an actor can also lead to the perception of that actor's words as accurate. In other words, at some point, the assumption that an actor is credible leads to the perception (real or not) that the information she shares is accurate. Accuracy can therefore be seen as part of a definition of credibility, but not its entirety.

Organizational structure, defined as the formal and informal rules that govern NGOs, provides a metric by which to evaluate the credibility of multiple NGOs beyond "accuracy." NGOs can attempt to gain or increase their credibility through modifying internal characteristics through tactics such as professionalization (Chapter 5, this volume) or creating standards (Chapter 3, this volume). Another way to create credibility is to build ways of increasing credibility into the very organizational structure of the NGO. Following the logic introduced in Chapter 1, organizational structure is an important, verifiable way for NGOs to signal credibility beyond virtue, and appeal to different audiences. Organizational structure informs us as to which audience(s) an NGO finds relevant to its work and thus helps explain how they react to challenges to their virtue. Three aspects of organizational structure – membership, funding sources, and the distribution

---

[1] Studies have shown the centrality of both of these organizations in the human rights network (see Brewington *et al.* 2009).
[2] See for example: www.amnesty.org/en/who-we-are/faq#is-ai-effective (accessed July 28, 2009); www.hrw.org/en/node/75136 (accessed July 28, 2009); physiciansforhumanrights.org/about/mission.html (accessed July 28, 2009).

of agenda-setting powers – are examined here as choices for how human rights NGOs might establish and increase their credibility.

First, the organizational structure of the NGO is key for understanding what the NGO stands for, who it represents, and how it goes about achieving its goals beyond "human rights." How are various branches of the NGO structured vis-à-vis a center, where does the NGO get its funding, which parts of the NGO execute the campaigns and programs, who determines strategies and tactics? The structure of an NGO also dictates to what extent it engages with grassroots populations. The organizational structure also is critical for how others evaluate its credibility because it shapes the NGO's values and interests. Because audiences for human rights NGOs might vary – charitable foundations, governments, individuals – the reasons that make HRW credible are not going to be the same as the reasons that Amnesty is credible. Both NGOs centralize agenda-setting powers, but they differ in their funding sources and their view of membership, two key factors that might create credibility for some audiences but not others. Organizational structure provides an objective basis by which to understand claims of NGO (non-)credibility.

The chapter proceeds in four parts. The first section discusses credibility in NGOs, drawing on the theoretical framework from the introduction. In the second section I develop a theory about credibility in NGOs. Third, I use the theory of credibility to evaluate HRW and Amnesty along three dimensions of organizational structure that reflect NGO concerns with establishing common interests, taking on costly behaviors to demonstrate their credibility, and ensuring their allegations are externally verifiable. I provide a point of contrast through a brief discussion of an alternative human rights NGO that did not take off, the International League of Human Rights. I conclude in the fourth section.

Credibility

The first question is why we should even consider the credibility of human rights NGOs. After all, their nonprofit status, and the fact that they work on something as moral as protecting the rights of others should make them credible by default. Moreover, the language of volunteerism and donations permeate the nonprofit world, thereby distinguishing them from the commercial concerns of profit margins and employment (Hansmann 1980). Beyond non-profit status, human rights NGOs have no official international or domestic mandate, so their legitimacy as political actors exists only if they are credible. Many NGOs are not accountable to the populations on whose behalf they speak out, or to the governments whose territories they cross into in order to monitor and report on human rights (Stein 2009). A huge emphasis is placed on the accuracy of human rights NGO reporting and the correctness of their actions (Neier 2003), as NGOs can often pay in terms of reputational costs when they are found to have falsely reported on a human rights concern.

The evaluation of the accuracy of information by states is fickle: states often question accurate information when it does not serve an immediate political goal. States are incredibly fickle about the accuracy of reporting, based on their own security and economic interests. Take, for example, cases from Helsinki Watch in the 1980s. Helsinki Watch reporting on the mistreatment of dissidents in the USSR was seen as credible to the United States and the West more generally. In fact, Helsinki Watch leaders maintained good relations with the Assistant Secretary of Human Rights Elliot Abrams, even securing visas for Hungarian dissidents (Laber 2002: 159–60). When it moved to report on Turkey, a key ally in the Middle East, the US government dismissed such claims very publicly, with Abrams calling human rights NGOs like Helsinki Watch "myopic" (Laber 2002: 212–27).

The Turkey example illustrates the need to decouple an NGO's credibility from its accuracy. Helsinki Watch may have correctly reported that 120,000 political dissidents had been arbitrarily arrested and tortured, but the US government would not move to recognize the brutality of the Turkish regime because it was a key ally in the Cold War. The interest of the NGO, to stop human rights abuses in the Soviet Union through accurate reporting, did not help its credibility as a critic. The US government continued to ignore calls for human rights protections through the Kirkpatrick doctrine and other such methods, and in some cases, directly questioned the NGO's credibility as a monitor.

Since accuracy is not sufficient for establishing credibility, we can look to the criteria set forth in this volume for ways to assess the credibility of NGOs. Chapter 1 introduced a framework by which to assess the credibility of monitoring organizations by thinking about how organizations position themselves for different audiences. For NGOs, credibility is first and foremost a function of the audience, whether that is the "target" (in this case, an abusive or influential state), the donors (the principals), and the public (supporters). NGOs can be more or less credible to these audiences, depending on a number of factors. It is important for human rights NGOs to establish credibility in as many ways as practical because they must appeal to both violator states and states or actors that can "do something" about human rights abuses. NGOs can primarily do so using three of the four credibility mechanisms outlined in the introduction: establishing common interests, taking on costly behaviors to demonstrate their credibility, and ensuring their allegations are externally verifiable. Human rights NGOs control their advocacy agendas to create common interests with their audiences, at times taking on controversial statements or adopting risky and costly strategies, and of course, their accusations are often (if not easily) externally verifiable by an alternative source that wishes to replicate or discount an NGO's findings. On the whole, however, human rights NGOs tend to not pay noticeable penalties for misrepresentation (the fourth criteria) for two reasons. First, by the nature of what they do, NGO reporting will always generate naysayers and denials of their factual validity. Second, our knowledge of human rights conditions in the world today comes largely from the two NGOs examined in this chapter. As discussed below, there are very few "independent" human rights resources other than Amnesty and HRW reports.

Focusing on organizational structure can help us evaluate the efforts NGOs take to generate credibility. NGOs can vary in the degree to which their leadership is held accountable. Most international NGOs have a staff that is accountable to an elected or designated board. International NGOs can also be composed of various independent national sections, or be controlled via one central office, with outposts in different countries. NGOs also often differ as to whether or not they are membership-driven. Although the term "membership" can be stretched to apply to many different things, here I refer to "members" as non-professional supporters of NGOs that support its functions. NGOs vary in the degree to which they allow members, rather than staff and formal leadership, to be the primary voice in organizational choices. NGOs also have different funding structures. Some argue that independence of the agenda can only truly be achieved if they do not take state funding, relying on voluntary contributions from individuals and foundations. Others find ways to spread the funding, so as not to allow a few donors to contribute most of the budget.

Finally, the structure of human rights NGOs affects the way that information travels internally, which in turn has implications for the type and content of the advocacy. Some NGOs grant a large degree of autonomy to the various national sections or divisions within the organization, whereas others have tightly-controlled, centralized agendas that apply across the NGO, regardless of location. In other words, there can be single or multiple agenda-setters about a number of factors that affect the way the NGO is perceived: the operational rules, the advocacy priorities, and the strategic and tactical emphasis placed on various countries and regions of the world. The organizational structure, beyond flow charts and lines of authority, translates into how an NGO makes advocacy decisions and pursues its goals. These internal factors translate into the external credibility of the NGO.

The attention to organizational structure also gets us away from the circular discussion about accuracy and political "impartiality," which is another central claim to human rights NGO advocacy (Neier 2003). The emphasis on not seeming to favor one kind of state (Western, US-allied) over another (Soviet, global South) is seen as necessary to gain credibility and lend credence to their reports. That is, NGOs should promote shared values (human rights based on international conventions) rather than adopt an obviously biased position that political bodies, such as political parties, would take. This kind of logic finds a counterpart in studies of conflict mediation, where impartial third party mediators were assumed to be the most effective (Fisher 1995; Young 1967), but others have found biased mediators to be equally, if not more, up to the task (Kydd 2003; Myers 1998; Walter 1997, 2002). We can sidestep the lack of resolution on the "best" type of monitor based on accuracy or impartiality, concentrating on the less-controversial elements of NGO work by examining organizational structure.

Having an overt political or moral bias does not discredit an NGO as a monitor of human rights. More importantly, NGOs are rarely consistently "credible." The work of human rights monitors is used by all kinds of states to fulfill their interests; and at certain points in time the same NGO was embraced as a credible, virtuous enforcer of human rights, and then vilified by the very same government as a group with shaky credibility.[3]

Structure, interests, and values: credibility for NGOs

An NGO's organizational structure has two aspects: formal and informal. The formal part is the one that those involved in an organization often point to and is easily found in the NGO bylaws, statutes, and memoranda of understanding. These documents indicate whether an NGO is a volunteer-based NGO, one of professionalized staffers (some with very specialized expertise in law or medicine) or a hybrid form. Formal rules also dictate how the various parts of NGOs link together, whether one part has responsibility for certain tasks (publicity, research), and where final decisions are made. Do national sections, for example, delegate authority to a center that makes strategic and tactical decisions? Does the center then delegate duties to national sections in terms of executing campaigns, lobbying home governments on behalf of the rest of the NGO, or pursue other campaign tactics, such as organizing rallies or signing petitions? Who decides the course of action for the NGO? Is there a representative body with regular meetings, or are decisions taken at an executive level?

Informal rules, on the other hand, often reveal the answers to other types of questions: where does the money come from – small donors, corporations, foundations, or governments? What are the primary activist techniques and strategies adopted by the NGO? Do they write reports, do they run programs on the ground with local groups, are they involved in campaigning against governments or intergovernmental organizations, and do they mobilize in a grassroots fashion? What types of issues does the NGO stand for?

Following the logic outlined in the previous section, it would seem that there are various structural determinants of credibility. First, having an active membership that participates in some aspect of the

---

[3] This actually happened to Americas Watch when it became openly critical of the Reagan administration (detailed in Laber 2002; Neier 2003).

policymaking holds leaders accountable.[4] Statements made by NGOs with active memberships should be considered more credible because they represent the views of individuals in more than one country rallying for a human rights cause, a more diverse view than one which originates from the offices and boardrooms of a headquarters located in a Western capital. More importantly, membership creates maintenance costs for an NGO to keep members engaged. Membership can also increase the visibility of campaigns through public lobbying, which may contribute to the perception that a group is indeed credible if so many of its members are willing to go out and campaign on its behalf.

Membership also alters the nature of governance in NGOs, as discussed below. It can also change the nature of the "product." Amnesty kept a short list of rights as a function of organizational structure in two ways. First, decision-making rules allowed those who did not want to expand the mandate to block changes. Second, engaging a global membership in letter-writing campaigns meant that general reports were less useful than hard-hitting individual cases that could elicit sympathy. That is, the type of information that Amnesty produces for its membership's consumption is not the same as the reports that HRW publishes for an entirely different crowd – political elites. Amnesty's structure is built to target broader audiences than HRW's. This simultaneously limits its capacity to produce generalized reports and expand the scope of its activities. HRW, by contrast, responds to the decisions of its leadership and the pressing concerns of researchers, as well as key donors such as the Ford Foundation and the Open Society Institute.[5]

Closely related to membership is funding. The sources of funding for an NGO can reveal the influences it responds to, which explains why many NGOs elect not to take government funding so as to avoid being seen as co-opted by one government or another.[6] The

---

[4] "Active" meaning not merely donor-members, but members who participate in some aspect of advocacy, decision-making, or other type of activity beyond monetary contributions.

[5] A recent $100 million grant by George Soros has put a new emphasis on HRW growth beyond OECD countries, giving further impetus to a 2008 strategic decision.

[6] See physiciansforhumanrights.org/about/ (accessed July 30, 2009), www.hrw.org/en/node/75138#8 (accessed July 30, 2009), www.amnesty.org/en/who-we-are/faq#who-finances-ai (accessed July 30, 2009), www.humanrightsfirst.org/about_us/charter.aspx (accessed July 30, 2009), www.msf.org/msfinternational/invoke.cfm?objectid=130CB2BA-E018–0C72–097046C7C4

more funders, or principals, the less likely that co-optation by any one party will happen. However, given the discussion in the previous section, the need to appear untied to any government may be less relevant today than historically during the Cold War. Part of the reason why human rights NGOs have been known to claim that they are apolitical rests on the fact that if they are to advocate human rights on behalf of everyone, they should come from a universal position, not some politically-biased agenda.[7] This problem extends to service-providing organizations as well. Nonetheless, the sources of funding send a signal of NGO intent and positioning.

Finally, having a central agenda-setter contributes to the credibility of an NGO. Having multiple points of veto and proposal in an international organization can quickly devolve into publicized disputes at worst, and confusion of advocacy message at best. Having a central office to which various parts of the NGO look for adjudicating deadlocks and disagreements and expanding or contracting the scope of human rights work is key. Not only does the centralization of these functions help coordinate the economies of scale, it also allows for a coherence of strategy and advocacy message. Centralization makes it easier for outsiders to understand what an organization stands for. Having a single set of advocacy issues makes some human rights NGOs more credible than those who have contradictory internal agendas or whose factions split off and make statements only on behalf of part of the organization. In fact, making sure that information passes through a central point in the NGO can also make reporting more accurate. It creates accountability for getting the facts straight and ensures that statements made contain the same core information. Centralization creates consistency of message, and it also ensures systematic fact-checking.

There are two alternative explanations for NGO credibility that I seek to link to organizational structure. The first is the notion of the "product" human rights NGOs produce: the type of information provided. The second is how organizational structure constrains the content of the information. Some might argue that the type and content

---

2A8573&component=toolkit.indexArticle&method=full_html (accessed July 30, 2009).

[7] For example, Amnesty in its early days was often seen as a tool of the UK government, because its headquarters is located in London.

of information that an NGO produces can make it more or less credible. General country or topical reports will be harder to verify than narrower claims about individual cases.

Some NGOs highly value appearing to be run by their members as an important aspect of human rights work. Thus, the relevant audience for a membership organization such as Amnesty is not only the state and IGO officials it is trying to convince with its reporting, but everyday individuals, whose labors are used in activist efforts. Amnesty meets its monetary needs through small contributions. For other organizations, maintaining a professional face, with an emphasis on expertise (legal, medical, policy) is the primary concern, and their relevant audiences are much more truncated – political leaders, major news media, and other persons of influence. HRW seeks large foundational donors and the contributions of the well-heeled in major cities. Accordingly, the audiences with which each respective NGO attempts to achieve credibility will differ, depending on organizational structure.

As stated at the outset, credibility is relational, and thus reliant upon an external comparison: credible according to whom, and relative to whom? The perception of the evaluator, whether that is a state, funder, or beneficiary of human rights advocacy, is key to whether an NGO is a credible monitor. Of course, the targets of human rights NGOs' advocacy need to find them credible as accusers. But organizational structure is a way to evaluate how an NGO has taken on constraints to its future behavior to ensure observers it is credible. At the same time, organizational structure is a generalized picture of credibility for a particular NGO that does not rely on case-by-case evaluations of its reporting.

Thinking about credibility through Amnesty International and Human Rights Watch

Comparing Amnesty (founded 1961) and HRW (which began as Helsinki Watch in 1978) is, in some ways, cheating. They are two of the most oft-cited and credible international human rights NGOs today. However, using the two cases to walk through some of the theoretical criteria outlined above is helpful for conceptualizing how minute differences between NGOs might be significant in changing an evaluation from credible to not, and vice versa. Because HRW and Amnesty have pursued different organizational structures, the comparison shows the multiple pathways to credibility. But there are also minimal bounds that must be met – the International League of Human Rights (ILHR), for instance, does not meet the bar in the organizational sense of credibility.[8]

Both Amnesty and HRW have reputations for accurate reporting, and both have had an acknowledged role in pushing and sustaining the human rights agenda to its current prominence in international politics (Bob 2002a; Neier 2003; Rosenau 2002). HRW researcher Alison Des Forges wrote the authoritative report on Rwanda, and was one of the first in the West to demand that the genocide be declared as one in 1994 (Des Forges 1999; Power 2001). Amnesty's reporting is often used as a metric by scholars (Cingranelli and Richards 2001; Gibney and Dalton 1996; Hafner-Burton 2008; Ron *et al.* 2005) and a continued fascination with its political effects (Clark 2001) and internal politics (Hopgood 2006) contributes to the NGO's credibility. In Steven Poe *et al.*'s (2001) study of bias in US State Department reports, they assess US State Department reports against the credibly impartial Amnesty metric.

While Amnesty and HRW are household names in the practice of international human rights, there were other groups before these that were credible in their work as well. The first transnational campaign to protect the rights of human beings predates the modern human rights instruments we have today: the anti-slavery campaign of the mid-1800s. Abolitionists were successful both in stopping the trade of slaves between Africa and England, as well as the use of chattel slavery in the Americas. There were others that were less credible, such as the Anarchist Red Cross, founded in 1907, that served smaller audiences (Rabben 2002).

One of the early human rights NGOs was the ILHR, which was founded in the United States in 1942 by Roger Baldwin. Baldwin had, two decades earlier, founded the American Civil Liberties Union (ACLU), but unlike the ACLU, the ILHR did not become a dominant and credible source for human rights in the same way the ACLU would come to play such roles in US politics. A large part of the

---

[8] Until the 1970s, it was known as the International League for the Rights of Man.

reason for this comes from its organizational structure, which in theory linked it to an international alliance of like-minded human rights and civil rights organizations. In practice, the ILHR maintained a removed presence in human rights, mostly lobbying at the UN level, and only occasionally seeking the help of its international partners. The ILHR pursued an elite-oriented politics that was, by and large, ad hoc and not driven by an overarching mandate.

There are two formal leadership organs within the ILHR: the International Board of Directors, made up of US members, and the International Advisory Committee, with an international composition (Ray and Taylor 1977). However, power lies with the Board of Directors. The motivation behind the different compositions is obviously to mitigate the effect of US dominance, forging an international network of affiliates with a common purpose. In the event of disagreement between the board and advisory committee, the board decides. The board also approves the membership of national-level affiliates (Wiseberg and Scoble 1977: 296). National-level affiliate groups can fund ILHR projects on an ad hoc basis. For the most part, however, the ILHR works rather informally, gathering money when it needs it, or holding fundraising dinners. One of its marquee actions is to grant a human rights award – past recipients have been ex-Presidents Mary Robinson and Chen Shui-bian – but the ILHR has very much shied away from disseminating reports and information in the same ways that others have.

Thus, even though the ILHR took on tough issues, such as decolonization (Clark 1981), it was not successful in bringing those topics to the forefront of international politics. This was not because anything the ILHR said was wrong. Rather, the ILHR's organizational structure prevented it from ever being credible because of its elitist approach to human rights politics. It was very much premised on techniques that did not involve many collaborators. Affiliates to the ILHR were seen as benefitting from the association with it, rather than the other way around; this was true in spite of the fact that national affiliates funded ILHR projects. The ILHR, furthermore, did not seek a broad-based audience, even at the state official level (Wiseberg and Scoble 1977). The NGO focused its efforts on very high targets and pursued issues and cases sporadically. At some point, it took on political prisoners, modeled in a fashion after Amnesty's work, but it lacked resources (staffing, funding) to carry out such a large task.

It is therefore no surprise that the ILHR built up very little credibility (or visibility, for that matter) over the years because it has not
attempted to build up support around its advocacy, and its limited
work has not been particularly costly because it is not distributed
widely. Finally, its organizational structure provides very little space
for accountability. The dominance of the board makes it easy for it
to control its agenda; inconsistent funding structures mean that it can
find willing donors of all stripes when necessary. There are organizational choices that, as we see below in the cases of Amnesty and
HRW, have created an opportunity for both NGOs to establish themselves as credible monitors of rights.

Basic comparison of HRW and Amnesty

To compare HRW and Amnesty, I use a combination of several
sources. From February 2009–February 2010, I gathered a series of
forty in-depth, semi-structured interviews that ranged from thirty to
ninety minutes each. The interviewees were former or current senior
staffers at HRW or Amnesty. For the sake of anonymity, all identities
have been withheld. I also made ample use of secondary sources where
available, and consulted various archival sources on Amnesty from
their London office and archives held at the International Institute
for Social History in Amsterdam. The great majority of the data
presented here are drawn from the interviews, which reveal structural characteristics that are not easily discernible from examining
documents.

In 1961, as the story goes, Amnesty founder Peter Benenson came up
with the idea after reading about two Portuguese students who were
arrested because they toasted freedom under a dictatorial regime. This
perceived injustice led Benenson to write the London *Observer* article
on May 28 about the "Forgotten Prisoners" as part of the launching
for a year-long campaign called "Appeal for Amnesty, 1961." The
article quickly caught fire, and what was a small campaign grew very
quickly into an international phenomenon, with participants all over
Europe eagerly responding to adopt these so-called "prisoners of conscience." Very soon thereafter the International Secretariat (IS) was
established in London. The origins of HRW are no less interesting:
eager to support dissidents in Russia and the rest of the Soviet Union
in holding the government accountable to the Helsinki Accords signed

in 1975, Random House publisher Bob Bernstein founded the first of the regional Watch groups, Helsinki Watch, in New York, as a support group for the indigenous Watch groups in the USSR. Over time, however, the tactics of Eastern European governments and Moscow dispersed many of the dissident groups based in the Soviet Union. Helsinki Watch expanded into Americas Watch (1981), Asia Watch (1985), Africa Watch (1988), and Middle East Watch (1989), adopting the name Human Rights Watch in 1988.

There are many general similarities between Amnesty and HRW. Amnesty and Helsinki Watch initially focused on particular prisoners. Both groups wrote letters in support of political dissidents, raised issues about their treatment, and formed groups around the world to advocate on behalf of those fighting in repressive countries. While Amnesty groups adopted prisoners distributed in the pattern of Threes (one from the First, Second, and Third worlds, in Cold War parlance), Helsinki Watch formed the more formalized International Helsinki Federation for Human Rights, which recruited prominent Western Europeans to help Helsinki groups in the East fight on against Soviet governments. Both organizations wrote reports based on country visits, and both NGOs lobbied Western governments to take action when faced with rights-violating regimes.

The similarities end there. Fundamentally, what differentiates Amnesty from HRW is the fact that while Amnesty distinguishes itself as a membership-based movement spanning 150 countries,[9] HRW emphasizes its professional, legal focus on paid, on-the-ground researchers with international outposts in international capitals and major cities.[10] Though both HRW and Amnesty have central offices that serve as focal points, the ability of staff at the international level to make policy decisions is often curtailed by Amnesty's membership demands, while HRW can move much more quickly with executive decisions.

The effect of membership

Membership organizations must take into account the values and interests of their members. Like the model of democratic governments,

---

[9] www.amnesty.org/en/who-we-are (accessed August 2, 2009).
[10] www.hrw.org/en/node/75138 (accessed August 2, 2009).

leaders are held accountable in that they can lose their seats. Because membership organizations are accountable both to members and the board, this creates credibility because they have to establish common interests with many individuals. Membership maintenance is also costly.

For Amnesty, the membership has always been a point of healthy tension. There is a recognition that the membership, composed of individuals mostly organized into national sections, is both the lifeblood and the burden of the organization. However, the dominant view of the leadership prior to the 1990s was a need to centralize the advocacy of the organization precisely because of the involvement of the membership, who themselves were not human rights experts.[11] This explains why Amnesty has always had a central director, whether Benenson himself or the IS and International Executive Committee (IEC),[12] that decides the agenda. At the same time, staff at the headquarters worked very hard to ensure that national sections could have discretion in campaigns to take into account local variation.[13]

On the one hand, the membership of Amnesty is the first entity mentioned by its Statute, and the membership funds the organization and makes the ultimate decisions on changes to the mandate. Members provide the headquarters in London the volunteer labor that drives the Amnesty machine. Amnesty members routinely petition their own governments and stage picketing events and rallies. The core function of Amnesty members, however, has traditionally been writing letters on behalf of prisoners. The prisoner adoptions are coordinated at the international level by researchers or other high-level officials and carried out by individual members organized in adoption groups. Volunteers also facilitate research – Amnesty frequently recruits country-level experts for work in coordination groups, which helped with some of the research functions in London.

On the other hand, membership demands can change the direction of the organization quite dramatically, or make it much more difficult to push policies through. Annual and later biennial meetings attended

---

[11] Author interview with former Amnesty International senior staff, June 22, 2009.

[12] Author interview with former Amnesty International board member, July 13, 2009.

[13] Author interview with former Amnesty International staff, February 27, 2009.

by the membership (called International Council Meetings, or ICMs) serve as the official policy-making body of the NGO.[14] While ICMs capture the diversity among the national sections, the diversity has, at many points in the history of Amnesty, prevented policy changes from happening for over a decade. For example, the issue of gay rights first emerged at the end of the 1970s.[15] However, it was not until 1991 that the ICM finally approved a statute change to include the adoption of homosexuals as prisoners of conscience.[16] The discursive nature of decision-making contributed to the democratic nature of the NGO, with all participants following the same rules of engagement until decisions were made. Discussions were the glue that kept the international, and often disagreeing, membership together.[17]

The other governing body of Amnesty is the IEC. The IEC's official job is to oversee and ensure the execution of tasks as mandated in the ICMs; it is the board at the international level. The IEC is also seen as the representative of the membership when ICMs are not in session.[18] De facto, it, and even more so the IS, make many important day-to-day and quarterly decisions. While the IS's formal job is administration, in practice the concentration of resources at the international level ensured that the London office had quite a bit of influence directing the NGO overall; consequently, the predominant characterization of Amnesty as "centralized."[19]

While there is a fundamental tension between the demands of the membership and the needs of a central body to coordinate the disparate parts of an organization in Amnesty, HRW faces far fewer constraints on its decision-making precisely because it is not a membership organization. Early on, decisions went through Aryeh Neier,

---

[14] www.amnesty.org/en/who-we-are/accountability/statute (accessed August 2, 2009).
[15] Author interview, July 13, 2009.
[16] Although homosexuals were adopted prior to this date, they were not considered a prisoner of conscience if their arrest or persecution did not come from an existing Amnesty concern, mainly freedom of speech and expression. The change to the statute allowed homosexuals who were arrested purely for being homosexual to be counted as prisoners of conscience as well.
[17] Author interview with former Amnesty senior staff, April 24, 2009.
[18] Author interview, July 13, 2009.
[19] Author interview with former Amnesty staff, June 16, 2009; author interview, June 22, 2009; author interview with former Amnesty International staff, June 26, 2009.

who served as the first head of Americas Watch and vice chair of
the Helsinki Watch board and, after 1988, the executive director of
HRW. Neier's personality, stature, and vision shaped much of the
early expansion of Americas Watch in particular. Neier, described as
"fearless" by a former colleague,[20] would attack the Reagan administration's human rights policies in Central America, unabashed that
his organization had been created the same year Reagan was inaugu-
rated (Neier 2003). Because all of the Watch committees were sister
organizations that were independent insofar as name and regional
director went, decisions were made very independently. The accounts
of early experiences routinely reflect a period of great autonomy for
the directors of the various Watch committees, who could more or less
decide on the projects they wanted to do because Neier encouraged
creativity on the part of his lieutenants.[21] A great deal of decision-
making power, both on the part of extensions of Watch committee
work, as well as strategy and planning, was left to the directors of the
Watch committees, with Neier weighing in on anything that might
seem problematic.[22]

Neier left in 1993 in the middle of a period of intense growth. As
Laber writes, "Human Rights Watch went through a stormy period
in the early 1990s, when we seemed unable to cope with our own
momentum" (Laber 2002: 375). When current Executive Director
Kenneth Roth stepped into Neier's shoes, he consented to some of
the organizational suggestions made by a consulting firm that had
been tapped by the board. Although HRW had been in existence
since 1988, the Watch committees were left relatively autonomous
under Neier.[23] Under the leadership of Roth and guided by Program
Director Cynthia Brown, HRW went through a dramatic organizational change in 1994. Structures designed to unify the messages
and overall strategic and legal advocacy of HRW were implemented,
and Brown created several offices to achieve that goal of organizational coherence. Two key offices, the General Counsel and Program
Director, ensured accuracy in the application of international law in
reports written by researchers and the fit of the work with existing

[20] Author interview with former HRW senior staff, July 30, 2009.
[21] Author interview with former HRW senior staff, July 27, 2009; author
interview, July 30, 2009.
[22] Author interview with former HRW senior staff, July 14, 2009.
[23] Author interview with former HRW senior staff, February 27, 2009.

publications, respectively. Other key offices that spanned across the Watch committees, rechristened "Regions" in the new organizational scheme, helped keep the overall coherence of the organization in communications, advocacy, and development, or fundraising. The associate director's position, which Roth had occupied prior to Neier's departure, established a permanent place in helping the executive director maintain board relations. These new positions helped create a locus of consistent and shared decision-making, rather than the more ad hoc and personalized style in HRW's formative years.

Since 1999, HRW has started a new form of outreach in different metropolitan centers around the world through the creation of city committees. New York and Los Angeles were the first of these committees, designed for three primary purposes: fundraising, advocacy, and outreach. While these city committees do not operate outside of HRW's overall strategy, they do help link the NGO to various policymakers at the local and domestic levels. This strategy has moved beyond the United States, as HRW hopes to expand its extra-US funding into the developing world in the hopes of expanding its influence in developing centers of power.[24]

In summary, HRW and Amnesty have faced different types of struggles to find the right structure throughout their histories precisely because of the role of membership. HRW researchers and the regional directors experienced a long period of independence during Neier's years, and the structural changes that began in 1994 were resisted by some.[25] The two NGOs faced different demands because of their audiences. HRW needed to get the attention of diplomats and state officials. Amnesty, on the other hand, responded to demands from its membership, forcing it to centralize research functions because it relied upon the membership for decentralized action.[26]

Membership is an avenue by which to assess the credibility of NGOs because the presence/lack of membership signals the efforts of the organization to forge common interests with a larger public audience, and can also indicate commitment to an NGO's ideals. The adoption of economic, social, and cultural rights as "Amnesty rights,"

---

[24] See "Soros to Donate $100 million to Human Rights Group," *New York Times*, September 6, 2010.

[25] Author interview, July 30, 2009; see also Laber 2002: 375–78.

[26] Author interview with former Amnesty senior staff, June 8, 2009.

which took more than ten years for Amnesty to do, was finally pro-
pelled forward by desires to increase membership in the developing
world. HRW can change research direction rather quickly, leading the
way in establishing women's rights, landmines, and the International
Criminal Court as human rights issues.

Sources of funding

One of the points that NGO analysts inevitably refer to is the source
of funding. Funding signals to whom an NGO is beholden, affect-
ing the way an NGO operates in terms of prioritizing certain issues
or techniques. Having government donors indicates a co-optation
of agenda, and perhaps even open collaboration. Funding from governments, in other words, compromises critical things that human
rights NGOs want as part of their image: independence and impartiality. Both Amnesty and HRW have avoided government funding.
For Amnesty founder Benenson, taking government funding would
compromise the ability to work among the various factions of the
Cold War. By taking money only from individuals, he hoped that having such disparate funders would legitimize Amnesty's actions along
more universalistic lines, to go along with the Threes scheme for
adoption groups. Among the major human rights NGOs, Amnesty
alone tends to shirk funding from foundations, and intergovernmental organizations as well. The traditional funding scheme of relying
upon individual contributions led to a series of financial woes in the
1970s and again in the 1980s. Put differently, Amnesty has chosen to
have a large number of diffuse principals, consistent with its membership-driven orientation. This led to the innovation of direct mail, first
proposed by Ginetta Sagan from the US section of Amnesty. The success of the direct mail campaign would have enormous consequences
for the internal debates about the centrality of the IS vis-à-vis national
sections, but it also revitalized the US section and gave Amnesty more
generally a huge boost by reinforcing the sustainability of the financial model based on individual donors.

HRW has toed a similar line on government funding, but it has
long taken money from large foundations. The Ford Foundation was
one of the key early donors to Helsinki Watch, and in fact remained
its sole donor in the early days (Laber 2002: 104). The International
Helsinki Federation for Human Rights drew funding from Ford and

several other foundations. A $3.5 million grant from the MacArthur Foundation jump-started the last two Watch committees, Africa and the Middle East, at the end of the 1980s. Ford Foundation representatives have also held positions on the board, and were instrumental in pushing the idea of an overall "mega-Watch" that eventually became HRW.[27] HRW accepts individual donations as well.

From an evaluative perspective, the credibility of both HRW and Amnesty is not necessarily enhanced by their reluctance to accept government funding. It may contribute to the idea that human rights work comes from many parts of the world, but the funding for both of these NGOs by and large comes from individuals and foundations located in the West and global North. Moreover, government funding may not necessarily make NGO claims false. Similar to the fact that biased conflict mediators are not necessarily less credible, knowing that an NGO takes government funding is simply another part of an NGO's make-up, and may help us interpret the reports it distributes. Although the tendency is to assume that governments might unduly sway the reporting of human rights NGOs toward ideological agendas, there is no reason to believe that taking money from large donors like Ford Foundation does not have a similar effect. The focus therefore, when examining funding, should not be the sources of funding, writ large, but rather the number of funders, or principals, that hold the NGO accountable, as Gourevitch and Lake argue in the opening chapter. Diffuse principals *individually* exert less control over what an NGO does, but having a wide variety of donors contributes to the credibility of the NGO in terms of not being beholden to a narrow or biased agenda.

Central agenda-setting

Having fewer agenda-setters leads to more coherent advocacy policies, which I argue makes human rights NGOs more credible. Having a clear advocacy message conveys internal agreement, especially when the organization gets large and spreads across different geographic regions. But it also conveys consensus on often contentious issues that have to travel across cultural borders. Are women's rights human rights? Should economic, social, and cultural rights be counted as human rights too?

[27] Author interview, July 14, 2009.

Amnesty decided early on that the research, report writing, and case distribution functions should be centralized in the IS. Although in recent years such core tasks have devolved to a certain degree to national sections, for much of the 1960s to 1980s, the IS controlled the agenda for what counted as human rights within the NGO. The IS was the primary fact-finder for all prisoner cases, and ultimately it set the agenda for who Amnesty would take on as a case, creating rules for who counted as an Amnesty case. Coincidentally, this time period has been defined as one when human rights became an agenda item in the public mindset (Cmiel 1999).

The Research Department within the IS at Amnesty made choices on close calls for prisoner adoption cases, and most of the time, the countries they chose to report on were selected without much external approval. The power of the Research Department in this era has been documented elsewhere (Hopgood 2006). Thus, for example, the IS was often at the center of making the criteria for deciding which prisoners should be adopted, following the general rules set out by the ICMs and IEC. Cases were rarely clear-cut, and in fact, a Borderline Committee of three eminent representatives from various national sections was established in 1968 to deal with problematic cases such as Nelson Mandela or Angela Davis. But by the 1980s, it was clear that the Research Department had simply stopped sending such cases to the Borderline Committee, rendering the external review irrelevant.[28]

Choosing cases now (and then) serves a very important agenda-setting function in Amnesty. The IS also set up the rules for how to distribute case materials to the various national sections, coordinating activity between different national sections and the IS on the actual advocacy work. In between ICMs and IEC meetings, the IS had a very wide berth in terms of finding new cases, researching them, and distributing the relevant information to the various national sections and local adoption groups. In 1984, the Membership and Campaigns Department was created out of two existing bodies to balance out the power of research within Amnesty. It tried to emphasize the need to grow membership in non-Western countries, and why the IS needed

---

[28] The 1989 ICM officially dissolved the Borderline Committee and created the Mandate Review Committee to take over its duties, which by then were trivial.

to respond to the needs of current national sections.[29] However, the IS still held considerable sway with its research reports, and was able to control the agenda despite sometimes vehement protests from national sections. For instance, in the late 1970s, Amnesty issued a report on torture in both Syria and Israel. Without calling either side's actions more pernicious, and merely by dint of mentioning Israel's actions, the IS received an irate response from members of the US section. That type of reaction confirmed the "argument for the center to retain policy control, because if the center did not contain policy control, you would find particular national sections demanding that we treat particular countries or subjects in a particular way, and that was felt not to be in the best interests of the movement, nor to be intellectually honest."[30]

While the IS centralizes many of the functions of the NGO, changing the advocacy strategies and issues within Amnesty often requires several ICMs to iron out consensus among members. The aforementioned addition of homosexuals as prisoners of conscience was one such debate. ICMs originally convened yearly, and provided a forum in which some of the most powerful and outspoken national sections – the British, Dutch, Germans, and Swedish – proposed Amnesty policies regarding various countries. This practice of national sections creating resolutions on single countries was gradually phased out and filtered through the IEC in the 1970s. Generally speaking, despite the fact that tensions between the IS and national sections would come to a head at the end of the 1980s into the early 1990s, the membership still recognized the importance of protecting the research function from too much interference, as it did serve a core reason for Amnesty's prominence as an international NGO.[31]

Similarly, HRW's message arises from its research. The directors of the Watch committees, now the directors of Programs, have always served a very important agenda-setting function. As documented earlier, Neier's management style in the early days encouraged creativity in finding human rights in less traditional places, such as chronicling police brutality. Directors were encouraged to think about things creatively, and could choose topics and countries, distributing resources

[29] Author interview, June 8, 2009.
[30] Author interview, June 16, 2009.
[31] Author interview, June 8, 2009.

as needed. Depending on the country, but more often the region, the same countries Americas Watch tarnished as bad guys could be allies in getting states targeted by Asia Watch to change their behavior. Alongside directors' agenda-setting power is the deference to expertise: researchers are given leeway to pursue relevant and timely research topics, as senior leadership often leave specific subjects of human rights reporting to individual analysts.

New human rights research programs could be started with Neier's blessing. Cynthia Brown was able to assemble the women's rights research program in a few months in 1990 after informal discussions with various staff about the need to respond to criticisms made by women's groups about the reluctance of "human rights" to take on women. Despite some resistance to adopting women's rights as part of the scope of HRW's work, Brown created a blueprint for the oldest such thematic program in the organization.[32]

The power of the directors in vetoing changes was also part of their discretion. Rakiya Omaar, who was the first director of Africa Watch, believed that rights in Africa had to proceed piecemeal in order to be successful, and the new women's rights program simply should have no place in her region. Until her departure from the post in 1992, she successfully opposed the inclusion of women's rights into the Africa Watch agenda. Omaar's refusal to include such rights, which she supported with strong reasoning, demonstrates the power of directors.[33]

Some of the power of discretion was inevitably eroded when more layers of bureaucracy were created in 1994. Although directors still had a lot of sway in their reports, they had to document pre- and post-mission the purpose and findings of research trips. Reports had to be checked for quality and consistency, which slowed down the rapid rate at which they were released.[34] As a former senior staffer recalled, reports that took a week to turn around and release to the public could take months under the new system. HRW lost its "maverick" quality as the "lean, mean alternative to Amnesty" under the 1994 changes.[35]

Providing information about human rights abuses is at the core of how an international human rights NGO operates. As the number

[32] Author interview, July 30, 2009.
[33] Author interview, July 14, 2009.
[34] Author interview, July 30, 2009.
[35] Author interview, July 27, 2009.

of agenda-setters on the issues an NGO takes on grows, the institutionalized checks on accuracy may erode, while at the same time increasing the speed of information dissemination. Fewer agenda-setters raise the credibility of an NGO's allegations, while increasing agenda-setters also increases the likelihood of errors and inconsistent NGO messaging. Amnesty's more developed national sections moved to take some of the research power away from the center early in the 1990s. The US section has had an independent research function for eight years. The devolution of research tasks from the IS has made coordination much more difficult in recent years.[36] For HRW, the establishment of rules under which all of the Watch committees operate has created coherence across regional and thematic programs, at the expense of speed and timeliness. In both NGOs, clearly those that control the information control the organization. Agenda-setting rests with those who are closest to the research, and the two NGOs seem to be moving in opposite directions. More agenda-setters have entered for Amnesty, while HRW has tried to harness the independence of the regional difference under one banner. Centralized agenda-setting leads to more credibility, whereas decentralizing such agenda-setting can lead to decreased credibility.

Structure as a determinant of credibility

Why do we find some international human rights NGOs more credible than others? What makes some so convincing that we would be willing to believe their allegations, and is there a limit to the believability of their claims?

First, human rights NGOs must satisfy some basic knowledge condition. Accuracy of initial reports and a demonstrated track record of accuracy help to reinforce that knowledge claim. But implicit in the evaluation of the accuracy of a claim is an assessment of how an NGO's political position fits in with that of the evaluator. If the evaluator is the target of human rights abuse claims, perhaps that individual or state will be less likely to admit the credibility of Amnesty's or HRW's accusations, and discredit the accuracy of their claims. If the evaluator is the enemy of the subject of an HRW report, that individual or state will be more likely to find the NGO's monitoring credible.

[36] Author interview with Amnesty USA senior staff, April 6, 2009.

When George H. W. Bush used an Amnesty report to justify his invasion of Iraq in 1991, the accuracy of allegations the that Kuwaiti emir
made of the mistreatment of civilians was heavily discounted by other
sources, but he and others who supported US policy used Amnesty's
credibility to justify military action (Harlow 2006; Willcox 2005:
160–62).[37] Credibility is in the eye of the beholder.

Credibility must rest on other factors as well, beyond accuracy. That
the Iraq report did not sink Amnesty as a credible source for human
rights monitoring attests to credibility beyond accuracy. Despite the
fact the NGO's enemies have made quite a bit of noise about it and
other Amnesty blunders, it remains a credible organization. Similarly,
the allegations of HRW's anti-Semitism have not sunk the credibility
of its reporting in other areas.[38]

I have explored various facets of organizational structure that contribute to a notion of credibility. First, membership organizations are
more credible because they have to satisfy the whims of more than just
a few. Membership helps to establish common interests with a par-
ticipatory audience, but the maintenance of this continued network
of support can drain the resources of the organization. The continued
appeal of Amnesty and its ability to generate financial contributions
speaks to its credibility as a monitor of human rights. HRW's comparative lack of membership does count against it in this instance.
Nonetheless, HRW, unlike Amnesty, does plant its own people in-
country for its reports, rather than relying upon local reporting. Such
actions are costly and can be risky as well. This contributes to the
accuracy of its reports in terms of verification of purported events,
even if report contributors are not members of HRW per se.

Second, the importance of information for both NGOs has led to a
historical focus on the producers of research, who set the agenda. Both

---

[37] Ironically, it was this press release that also got Amnesty in trouble for
distributing misinformation about Iraqi soldiers' role in killing civilians –
the allegations in the report later proved to be overstated at best, and
false otherwise. Nonetheless, the information about babies thrown out of
incubators was used by Bush, among others, to support the invasion of Iraq
(for an openly biased account, see cosmos.ucc.ie/cs1064/jabowen/IPSC/
articles/article0004573.html (accessed July 28, 2009).

[38] See www.ngo-monitor.org/article/human_rights_watch_hrw_ (accessed
January 24, 2011). In 2009, a story broke about a senior HRW analyst's
extensive Nazi memorabilia collection, further fueling criticism of HRW's
judgments of the Israel–Palestine conflict.

NGOs satisfy the condition that the fewer agenda-setters, the more credible the actor. Neither NGO has faced serious public problems of multiple agenda-setters representing the same NGO and contradicting one another. While HRW has moved to solidify the mechanisms that guarantee a consistent message across divisions, Amnesty has moved in the opposite direction by delegating research functions to national sections. Centralized agenda-setting makes it easier for third-party verification of information to occur, as both the research and the advocacy positions of the NGO are defined and uniform across different sections.

Third, neither NGO accepts government funding as a hard and fast rule. This helps contribute to their credibility, building ties with non-government audiences and lending itself to scrutiny from principals that are independent from the targets of NGO advocacy. Amnesty's staff are accountable to their funders, the membership, and the ICMs help to regularly evaluate the performance of the international NGO as a whole. The structure of Amnesty creates many, often conflicting, principals to which the staff respond. HRW's constituency is much smaller. Because they do not claim to be a membership organization, and because they receive a fair amount of foundation funding, they are accountable to fewer donors.

Structural criteria are subject to the evaluation of various audiences, but they concretize the reasons for why some NGOs might seem more accurate or credible to certain actors. More democratic, membership-based practices might be less credible than having experts decide on the agenda of an NGO and vice versa. Perhaps individual donors are seen as fickle and uninformed, compared to specialists in foundation offices. Nonetheless, if NGOs want to claim to be impartial advocates of human rights, the structural characteristics of membership-driven, undisputed agenda-setter(s), and more funding sources distinguishes some NGOs as more credible as monitors of international human rights.

PART II

Humanitarian NGOs

Dilemmas of information and
accountability: foreign aid donors
and local development NGOs

CAREW BOULDING

Introduction

On a busy street in Sopocachi, a fashionable neighborhood of Bolivia's
capital city La Paz a few blocks from the embassy district, there is a
large well-maintained building housing the main offices of a prominent health care NGO called PROCOSI. Like many thriving NGOs in
developing countries, PROCOSI has been very successful at obtaining grants from international donors like the United States (through
USAID) and the European Union, as well as grants from the government of Bolivia and international NGOs like CARE and Save the
Children. With this funding, PROCOSI runs health care programs all
across Bolivia. The office is staffed by well-educated, relatively well-
off Bolivians and shares many features with offices of the major aid
agencies in La Paz: it is comfortable and professional, glossy posters
and brochures detailing successful projects and pictures of those in
need adorn the walls, and professionally dressed staff members work
at computers.

NGOs like PROCOSI have become increasingly important middlemen for the delivery of aid in developing countries. Since the 1980s,
most foreign aid donor organizations (both governmental and private, multilateral and bilateral) rely on grassroots NGOs in developing countries to help carry out their projects. Using local NGOs
as service providers is seen as beneficial to donors for several reasons. First, since grassroots NGOs are based in the communities they
serve, they are thought to have access to local knowledge about what
types of projects are most needed, and have the know-how to effectively carry them out. Second, supporting local NGOs is seen as good
for civil society and good for democracy because these organizations promote community involvement and democratic participation.

More fundamentally, grassroots NGOs are seen as virtuous. Like other nonprofits, they are seen as mission-driven organizations with goals that are a natural fit for foreign aid donors, including things like sustainable development, empowering women, educating children, or improving access to health care. And, because of their non-governmental, not-for-profit, and issue-centered nature, they are seen as having common interests with donors, making them more trustworthy and less prone to corruption than governments or businesses involved in similar services.

Despite this attractive package, foreign aid donors face a particular dilemma in selecting grassroots NGOs to fund: it is difficult to accurately measure the degree of "common interest" that an NGO shares with a donor when the NGOs are actively seeking funding and may rely on that funding for survival. Many of the qualities that make an NGO "good" are quite hard to measure (good intentions, honesty, and access to local knowledge, for example). These attributes would be hard to measure and evaluate in the best of circumstances, but foreign aid programs are frequently responding to critical humanitarian needs. There is a strong ethical imperative to use resources directly to provide food to the hungry, medicine to the sick, or clean water to the poor instead of diverting it to costly monitoring and evaluation procedures. Further complicating matters, NGOs, by virtue of being nonprofit, mission-driven ethical organizations, were supposed to be the *solution* to these types of dilemmas with unscrupulous governments or for-profit contractors, which has made it difficult for donors and NGOs to recognize the accountability problems that remain.

There is considerable variation in the size, capacity, expertise, honesty, and effectiveness of local development NGOs. How can donors distinguish good NGOs from bad? The contrast between the extremely good (a well-intentioned and effective organization) and the extremely bad (a fraudulent, ineffective organization) might seem obvious, but the majority of NGOs somewhere in the middle represent more of a dilemma for donors. How do donors distinguish between organizations that are somewhere in between? These dilemmas of credibility also matter to the NGOs themselves. How do virtuous organizations establish their own credibility and reputation in the absence of clear indicators of quality or reliable verification?

In this chapter, I discuss a number of issues that complicate the dynamic between foreign aid donors and grassroots NGOs in developing countries, drawing primarily on examples from Bolivia. I argue that it is quite difficult for donors to accurately assess the true quality of local development NGOs. Since reliable indicators of quality are hard to come by, donors rely on a number of less than perfect signals to select NGO partners, biasing evaluation toward the more tangible aspects of NGO activity and performance. Relying on these signals, in turn, creates incentives for NGOs to invest in improving their appearance on the sometimes-superficial indicators that donors observe (things like websites, professional offices, glossy reports, and so on) – in some cases at a cost to their true performance. These pressures result in a number of less than ideal outcomes, including a tendency to favor older, larger, and more established organizations over younger, smaller organizations, regardless of quality. Although these tensions in no way suggest that NGOs are not doing a tremendous amount of good work in the developing world, they do point to the pressures that NGOs are under, and offer some explanations for why development aid to NGOs has not been the "magic bullet" early advocates hoped for.

The chapter proceeds as follows: in the next section I give an overview of the role that NGOs play in the foreign aid process, and the multiple audiences they must respond to. Then, I address the question of why credibility is particularly difficult for NGOs to establish in this arena, followed by a discussion of the implications for donors faced with selecting NGOs in a difficult information environment. The next section looks at the issue from the perspective of the NGOs, discussing the tradeoffs between seeking credibility with international donors and credibility with local communities, followed by conclusions.

NGOs involved in development assistance: an overview of the actors

Non-governmental organizations play many roles in the foreign aid process, both as donors and recipients of aid. As donors, NGOs from wealthy countries administer development and relief operations in poorer countries. This type of aid is often called Private Voluntary Aid (PVA). Private aid is the purview of large, established international NGOs such as CARE, Save the Children, Oxfam, World Vision, Catholic Relief Services, International Rescue Committee, and others. These organizations, although private, act much like other large donors in that they frequently contract with local NGOs to help carry out services. Although there are certainly interesting questions related to accountability of NGOs as donors, this chapter focuses on NGOs in their other main role in the foreign aid process: as recipients of aid.

For the purposes of this chapter, I focus on local development NGOs. These organizations can be defined as nonprofit, development-oriented organizations based in developing countries. Or, as the World Bank defines them in Operational Directive 14.70, "private organizations that pursue activities to relieve suffering, promote the interests of the poor, protect the environment, provide basic social services, or undertake community development." Local development NGOs range in scale from very small community-based organizations in a single community, to large and professional national networks. Development assistance from all sources now includes partnerships with NGOs in developing countries. Since the 1980s multilateral donors like the World Bank, bilateral donors like USAID, and international NGOs alike target funding toward local development NGOs as a way to support local communities and deliver development assistance services at the local level.

In the language of principal–agent relationships, NGOs that receive foreign aid funding can be thought of as the agents of the foreign aid donors, who act as the principals (see Chapter 1, this volume). The donor gives the NGO financial resources in order to carry out some specific tasks (such as improving agricultural services, opening a health clinic, offering classes, etc.). In this sense, local development NGOs can be thought of as not-for-profit contractors, similar to nonprofits in the developed world that in some cases contract with governments to provide public services.[1] I should note that identifying local development NGOs as the agents of foreign donors is somewhat controversial. NGO advocates would argue that NGOs are primarily responsible to their community and to their core mission (improving health care or reducing poverty, for example) and that they use the foreign funds to achieve those ends. However, for the purposes of

[1] For a discussion of the economics of not-for-profit provision of public services outside of the context of foreign aid, see Francois (2003).

closely examining accountability between donors and NGOs, it is a useful framework.[2]

Even if we think of NGOs as agents and foreign donors as principals, the most important additional audience is clearly the community in question. The relationship between an NGO and its community depends on the type of NGO and the type of work they are doing. Some NGOs are mainly interested in delivery services, but others are more involved in community development and advocacy. In both of these cases NGOs can be members of or advocates for the target community at the same time that they help a donor carry out a project in that community. They are middlemen, giving access and information to donors and delivering services and resources to their community.

There can, however, also be a strong tension between the need to respond to the directives of the donor, and the need to respond to the wishes of the community in question. An NGO can be caught between needing to show local credibility to donors as proof of their access to local knowledge at the same time they may be facing criticism from community members that they are trying to please international donors at the expense of listening to local citizens. This tradeoff is a familiar story in the developing world. As Carrie Meyer writes, "Southern NGOs that are too successful in attracting donor funds are subject to criticism. They may be labeled disparagingly as BINGOS (big NGOs) and DONGOS (donor organized NGOs)" (Meyer 1995). Meyer presents a formal model of these tradeoffs, showing that an NGO manager faced with a potentially compromising foreign grant can rationally accept the grant, even knowing it might damage the NGO's local reputation if the grant is large enough.

Other NGOs make up another critical audience for NGOs involved in foreign aid. Other NGOs may actually compete for funding from the same donor sources, or they may act as advocates for a particular segment of the community, or as policy watchdogs on development issues. Early work on NGOs points to the NGO community as a great

---

[2] Eric Werker and Faisal Ahmed point out that thinking of NGOs in terms of not-for-profit contracting is a good framework for understanding local development NGOs. Work on not-for-profit contracting in the developed world predicts that NGOs should have an advantage in providing goods and services where information on quality is difficult to verify and where the temptations to shirk on quality are very high for for-profit providers, which is very much the case for development work (2008).

strength, and characterizes the cooperative relationships between NGOs as part of their comparative advantage in doing development work. However, the fact that competitive bidding processes for foreign grants pit NGOs against one another complicates this dynamic. As Alexander Cooley and James Ron (2002) point out, this competition can undercut the previously cooperative relationships between NGOs that made them attractive in the first place.

In sum, NGOs are serving multiple audiences and must respond to pressures from several sources: their community, their members (in the case of more membership-based organizations), the local government, and other NGOs who may be competitors or collaborators. These audiences are outside of their more formal contractual relationship with foreign donors (principals) who contract with NGOs (agents) to provide goods or services. The next section explores the tensions and tradeoffs generated by these multiple audiences, and the problems of credibility that they create.

Why is credibility a problem?

Why is credibility a particular problem for local development NGOs involved in foreign aid? Certainly many different types of organizations operate in environments with multiple audiences or multiple principals. A few characteristics of the NGO–foreign aid dynamic make credibility a difficult issue. First, obtaining high-quality information on the goods and services provided by NGOs is very difficult both because the tangible factors can be hard to evaluate (is the NGO spending the money prudently? Is the project effective?), and because many of the qualities that are important are in fact intangible (honesty, motivation, etc.). Additionally, there are very few sources of external verification to evaluate an NGO's performance. These informational difficulties are compounded by a reluctance on the part of many donors to admit that more formal accountability might be necessary. In this section, I detail these particular challenges of establishing credibility for NGOs.

First, it is helpful to be specific about what credibility means. In this context, the primary concern over credibility is the donors' ability to believe NGOs' claims that they are capable, honest organizations in a good position locally to carry out development projects (and the NGOs' concern to make those claims credible). In contrast to NGOs that are devoted to monitoring the behavior of others, the question for these NGOs is one of self-reporting. As the previous section makes clear, local development NGOs must respond to several different audiences. Credibility to each of the audiences is important in different ways, and involves important tradeoffs I will discuss later, but first I will consider the relationship between NGOs and donors.

Gourevitch and Lake argue that, in general, NGOs are more likely to be credible when four conditions are met. Specifically, NGOs are more credible when:

(1) there are common interests between the audience and the NGO;
(2) the NGO makes costly efforts to signal commitment to their cause;
(3) there are penalties for misrepresentation; and
(4) there is some external verification of NGO claims.

Local development NGOs represent a type of NGO that falls short on most of these conditions. In many cases, local NGOs do share common interests with donors, and this continues to be an important source of successful NGO–donor partnerships. However, on the three other counts local development NGOs fare much worse. Unlike in wealthier countries, there are frequently few alternative professional careers for highly-educated skilled workers, making the choice of working in an NGO a good one regardless of ideology. So employment in an NGO is far from a costly signal. Similarly, there are few serious penalties for misrepresentation, and in some cases poorly-functioning NGOs may be rewarded with grants aimed at improving their capacity or organization. And finally, with a few exceptions, there are few actors to act as reliable external verifiers.

There has also been a reluctance to let go of the idea of NGOs as the "magic bullet" of development aid for several reasons. First, foreign aid is characterized by an ethical imperative to act quickly and efficiently to deal with pressing human problems. Because of this ethical imperative to provide as many services, or as much relief as possible, it has been difficult to make the case that monitoring and evaluation are as critical as the core mission – getting food to hungry children, providing medical care to critically ill patients, providing a village with clean water, etc. Because of this sense of urgency, and a general sense of faith that NGOs are good organizations doing good work, there has been some reluctance to seriously investigate the dilemmas of accountability – and the tradeoffs – that may be involved in funding NGOs. Second, NGOs were supposed to be the *solution* to this problem with governments. Giving money to NGOs was supposed to ease the frustrating problems of giving to corrupt governments by offering a less corrupt alternative.

The best-case scenario (and the reason the aid world fell in love with NGOs) is an organization that is already effectively promoting the goals of the donor (high level of "common interest" in the language of Gourevitch and Lake). Imagine a grassroots NGO that provides education and microfinance services to women. Committed staff members, who have chosen this less lucrative profession with the sincere intention of promoting social change, run the organization. They have a successful model of engaging women's groups, offering seminars, developing business plans and repayment rates, and structuring small loans to maximize the benefits to the women. A donor in this scenario can simply give more money to expand the successful programs the NGO has already developed, and the issues of measurement, evaluation, and accountability are resolved through similarity of interest. And, in addition to all these good things, funding these NGOs should have positive political externalities: increased social capital and trust, increased political participation, and a growing acceptance of democratic norms and procedures, for example.

The worst-case scenario is an NGO that is dishonest and only seeking aid dollars for private gain, with no intention of carrying out the projects proposed, or no actual capacity to do so. While most donors would like to think that these extremes should be easy to recognize, the muddy middle is more of a dilemma – why is it difficult to distinguish easily between these two types?

First, direct information on the quality of NGOs is difficult to obtain. Qualities like good intentions, honesty, etc. are hard to observe, and measuring NGO activity and performance – especially local grassroots NGO activity and performance – is a difficult task. Why? NGOs are involved in a wide range of issue areas and activities, making simple comparisons across categories difficult. Unlike profit-motivated businesses that can be evaluated by their bottom line regardless of the goods or services they provide, there is no comparable "bottom line" to compare NGOs in different sectors. Werker and Ahmed (2008: 78) explain this dilemma very clearly:

Nongovernmental organizations deliver goods and services to a population that provides little feedback on the range or quality of product delivered. Compared to usual market or political settings, beneficiaries have a weakened ability to use market forces to penalize and reward NGOs. Citizens can vote out an incumbent from office and consumers can choose not to purchase a product from a for-profit provider, but villagers may be hostage to the particular development scheme that happens to be funded by the designated local NGO.

To further complicate matters, the goals of the organizations can be quite different as well, making the choice of the most appropriate metric for evaluation challenging. For example, should a health-care NGO be evaluated in terms of health services provided or in terms of changes in actual health outcomes among those they serve? And how should that organization be compared with one that focuses on education, or women's empowerment, or agricultural services? (For examples of the range of NGO activities in one developing country, see Table 5.1 a list of NGOs by sector in Bolivia).

Second, and perhaps more important, measurement of NGO performance is difficult because the quality of an NGO may actually be determined to some degree by unobservable characteristics like honesty, resistance to corruption, and access to local knowledge. Directly measuring those characteristics in a consistent manner is a formidable challenge. One solution might be to dismiss these intangible characteristics as less important than more easily measured factors like the debt to spending ratio, the number of employees, etc., but this tactic misses one of the main reasons NGOs are attractive in the first place. In fact, for some donors, these less tangible benefits or outcomes of NGO activity – things like building local organizational capacity, strengthening civil society, or empowering women or minority groups – are, in fact, the point. For example, although better health outcomes may be one desired outcome of funding an NGO, the more immediate goals are to create jobs, strengthen civil society and community involvement surrounding health issues, etc. That these tangible and intangible qualities often go together in a successful NGO is one reason that serious attention to monitoring and evaluation has come relatively late in the interactions between donors and grassroots NGOs.

This informational problem is often referenced in critiques of the foreign aid process and the relationship between donors and local organizations. For example, William Easterly, in his sweeping critique of development aid, calls for a total reorientation of aid giving away from offering a "plan" to fix problems, and toward a mode of "searching" for solutions based on local knowledge (Easterly 2006). However, he readily acknowledges that this task is no easy one, and that offering aid often changes the incentives for local organizations in negative ways. Critiques of aid targeting civil society organizations also point to the problem of identifying which organizations are part of the organic local civil society scene, and which are responding solely to the incentive of donor promises of funding (Howell and Pearce 2002; Pearce 2000).

Finally, in the case of local development NGOs, there are few organizations that serve as reliable external verifiers of NGO quality or behavior. However, there are several potential verifiers that warrant mention. First, the developing country government can play an important role in registering and monitoring NGOs. In many countries there are formal legal requirements for NGOs to register as nonprofit organizations and submit to some types of audits. Obviously, the enforcement of these kinds of rules varies widely in the developing world. Governments can also play an important role in their relationships to donors in setting the priorities for foreign aid programs. In many cases, NGOs receiving aid are providing goods and services typically associated with government public goods provision (for example, water and sewage systems, electrical grids, primary education, basic health care, etc.). Developing country governments have an interest in how these public goods are being created, and may play a role in monitoring how effective they are – especially when the government can take some credit for delivering the goods and services in question. This role is an important one, but it is also limited. In most cases, if the government had a strong capacity for monitoring the work of the NGOs, it would be providing more of the essential public goods in the first place.

Responding to the lack of reliable external verifiers of NGO activities, not-for-profit consulting firms that offer certification aimed at ranking the quality of NGOs have entered the scene. One example, ForeignAID Ratings LLC, offered fee-based certifications to local development NGOs, evaluating the organizations in terms of social impact, accountability, institutional development, non-violence, and financial efficiency and health of an organization. They reviewed the organization's spending and revenue, audited the programs they run, and interviewed people in the community the NGO serves. Their business goal was to provide reliable ratings of grassroots NGOs to facilitate the process of choosing NGO partners, collecting fees from both potential donors and NGOs. For donors, a list of "foreign aid certified" NGOs was available for purchase. From the other side, an NGO seeking to attract foreign aid could apply for "Foreign Aid Certification," which involves paying a fee for third-party certification and ratings, which the NGO can then use to attract donors. Additionally, access to a database of potential donors was available for purchase, as were a variety of consulting services designed to make NGOs more attractive to donors. This organization was fairly successful and had several high-profile clients, including USAID and the Bolivian NGO PROCOSI mentioned in the introduction. However, this type of for-profit certification scheme is still very new and has yet to make a big difference in the dynamics of NGO contracting. And by 2011, the organization ForeignAID Ratings was no longer in business.

Implications for donors

These dilemmas of obtaining accurate information have important implications for foreign aid donors seeking NGO partners in developing countries. Because information on the true quality of NGOs is costly and hard to obtain, donors rely on imperfect signals in order to select NGO partners. These signals include things like size, age, visibility, professionalization of the NGO, as well as ties the NGO may have to other donors. By relying on these imperfect measures of quality, donors actually help create and maintain an environment in which NGOs have strong incentives to invest in visible signals of quality even when it comes at a cost to their core mission. Once NGOs have been selected and contracts given, there is a real tradeoff between resources spent on expensive monitoring and evaluation programs for NGO partners and resources spent on core project activities.

Imagine a project manager at a development agency in charge of implementing a large-scale health program. Working with local NGOs may be an official mandate from the agency, or it may be a practical necessity, but how does the manager select partners? Most aid agencies have competitive bidding procedures, but often there are informal channels for information about NGOs (and to encourage

NGOs to apply) as well.[3] Based on interviews with staff at aid agencies and NGOs in Bolivia, I have identified several shortcuts that help time- and resource-pressed aid agency staff make decisions about NGOs.[4] Most of the people I interviewed saw few problems with this system, although some recognized that the pressure to disburse funds quickly sometimes comes at a cost to quality.

As in other professional arenas, personal relationships are very important, even when competitive bidding procedures are in place. Informal networking and reputation can still be a major factor in how grants are allocated. These informal processes work in several ways. First, personal relationships with NGO staff or employees, or with third parties who can recommend the NGO, are important shortcuts for managers seeking NGOs with which to work. Second, donors pay close attention to existing relationships between NGOs and other donors. NGOs that have been very successful at attracting big grants from one donor may find that other donors are more interested in them. In some cases, this is a very good proxy for capacity – there may only be a few top NGOs working in a certain area. But it can also lead to snowballing, where each aid agency assumes the previous agency did careful vetting whether they did or not. Other signals are more obvious (and in some ways more superficial). NGOs that are large, well established (at least several years old), and professionalized (nice websites, attractive offices, etc.) are more likely to attract foreign aid funding.

When do these shortcuts provide "good" information and when are they unreliable? Many of these shortcuts are quite reasonable from the perspective of a donor with money to spend and limited time. And, in many cases, these shortcuts may lead to the selection of high-quality NGOs that are experienced with the foreign aid process, and who are well equipped to receive foreign funding. However, many of

---

[3] It should also be noted that aid agencies themselves are subjected to less-than-ideal incentive structures as agencies that are delegated the task of distributing funds from a principal (usually a donor country government). In fact, aid agencies themselves face a dilemma of credibility, and often turn to producing glossy reports, focusing on short-term gains, and over-emphasizing less important but more tangible aspects of their projects in an effort to prove their own effectiveness (Easterly 2002).

[4] Author interviews during the summer of 2004 (funded by the Center for Iberian and Latin American Studies at UCSD) and January 2007 (funded by the University of California Institute for Global Conflict and Cooperation).

these shortcuts seem to favor easy information over important information, and they do little to advance the conditions of credibility laid out by Gourevitch and Lake (common interests, costly efforts, penalties for misrepresentation, or outside verification).

Relying on these shortcuts as heuristics for NGO quality has implications for the development of the NGO scene in a developing country. First, it privileges larger, well-established NGOs at the expense of newer and smaller NGOs, even if the small, young NGO has more of the qualities that a donor is looking for. For example, staff of a large NGO with an office in the capital are more likely to know people in common with aid workers, which can help secure personal recommendations. A small, regional, health-care NGO, on the other hand, might be very well intentioned and possess the kind of local connections that would make for a successful program, but may not have connections in the capital or have received media attention. The NGOs who first sought international funding in the 1980s and 1990s when it became available have an advantage over organizations that formed later. Although new NGOs do certainly continue to get funding, the older, more established NGOs have a longer track record and are more likely to already have existing ties with the government, other donors, and other NGOs. Since existing contracts with other donors send a signal that the NGO is capable and trustworthy, early achievers maintain a privileged position. If the early donors selected their NGO partners well, this bias may not be a problem, but it is far from a perfect selection mechanism.

Once NGOs have been selected and enter into a contractual relationship with a donor, the question of monitoring and evaluation remains. Monitoring and evaluation of the performance of grassroots NGOs receiving foreign aid funding has gained increasing attention, and since the 1990s nearly all donors make mention of accountability and have some formal reporting requirements for NGOs receiving funding. There is also a growing body of technical literature on the organization of NGOs, building capacity, and monitoring and evaluation (for example, Adams 2001; Buckmaster 1999; Charlish *et al.* 2003; Fowler 2002; Hilhorst 2002; Kendall and Knapp 1999; Riddell 1999). Although this seems like a step in the right direction for increasing the flow of information between NGOs and donors, there continues to be a bias toward indicators that are easily obtained and compared across sectors. Thus evaluative schemes tend to over-emphasize the quantitative characteristics that are most easily measured and verified (things like percentage of the budget spent on programs versus administration, number of employees, etc.) which capture only a small part of what donors are really interested in. Additionally, the focus on reporting statistics on these indicators can be a heavy burden for smaller NGOs.

This tendency towards evaluation based on easy indicators holds true in developed countries as well as developing ones. As an example a look at a US-based organization that ranks charities in the United States is useful. Charity Navigator, which bills itself as "America's premier independent charity evaluator" (www. charitynavigator.org), ranks major US charity organizations according to their organization "efficiency" and "capacity." Efficiency is measured by looking at the organization's spending and fundraising figures and calculating:

(1) the percent of total functional expenses spent on programs and services;
(2) the percentage of total functional expenses spent on management/general;
(3) the percentage of total functional expenses spent on fundraising; and
(4) the ratio of money spent on fundraising to money raised.

Capacity is measured through growth figures – both primary revenue growth and growth of program expenses – and the "working capital ratio," a figure which indicates how long the organization could continue meeting its obligations with no further income. Basically, organizations that are spending more this year than last get better marks than organizations that remain the same. And ones with some savings in the bank are better than those with very little saved (although too much saving can also earn poor marks). Although Charity Navigator ranks US-based charities in an effort to provide information to potential philanthropists, their ranking system is similar to many other efforts to measure the performance of NGOs. These indicators, while convenient for generating comparative rankings, do very little to capture the more intangible qualities that may actually determine an NGO's effectiveness. All of which is to say that the informational difficulties between NGOs and donors are severe, and not easily resolved.

Implications for NGOs

The dilemma of credibility for NGOs creates a number of tradeoffs between the signals NGOs must send to be perceived as high-quality organizations by donors, and the actions that might actually make them high-quality organizations. For example, time and money spent in developing attractive websites does little to improve the capacity of an NGO to deliver services in rural areas where few people have access to the Internet. But having a professional website may attract donors, which would help increase the services the NGO could offer to the rural poor. Additionally, the actions that make an NGO more accountable to international donors may come at a cost to their credibility with local audiences. As NGOs devote resources to demonstrating accountability to foreign donors, they may be undermining their credibility to their local community as they are increasingly seen as agents of international donors. For example, activists among the rural poor may resent resources diverted from core programs to maintaining a website, or they may trust an NGO less once it becomes clear the NGO is acting as an agent of the United States or another big donor.

These dilemmas can be characterized in terms of two major tradeoffs for local development NGOs. First, there is a tradeoff in terms of resources: the more resources devoted toward demonstrating credibility to donors means fewer resources devoted to building ties in the community. In some cases, such as devoting a small portion of the budget to developing a professional website, this tradeoff is minimal. In other cases, such as investing heavily in expensive offices and four-wheel-drive vehicles, seeking expensive certifications, or generating program evaluations to demonstrate capacity to donors, the tradeoff might be more costly. Second, there is an ideological tradeoff in which local donors give up autonomy and some part of their ideological credibility to their community in exchange for financial resources from international donors. In Bolivia, for example, local agricultural NGOs were sometimes reluctant to partner with USAID out of fear of being seen as an agent of the US government involved in coca eradication programs. NGOs working on indigenous land issues in Bolivia have faced a similarly difficult tradeoff. Indigenous communities were already skeptical of accepting NGO advocacy on their behalf, but in some cases were very hostile to the idea of working with an NGO funded by foreign donors, even though foreign donors offered critical funds. In Ecuador, a major environmental NGO, Fundación Natura, lost its more radical members when it accepted USAID funding in the 1980s (Meyer 1995).

This tradeoff between what makes NGOs attractive to donors and what makes them good at representing local interests has been observed in many different contexts in the developing world, often with negative consequences. For example, a comprehensive study of foreign-funded NGOs in Russia following the transition to democracy showed clear evidence of such tradeoffs. Although Western assistance increased the organizational capacity of NGOs "by providing tangible equipment and training for NGOs," the resources came at a steep cost to the independence and effectiveness of the NGOs (Henderson 2002: 140). As Sarah Henderson explains,

Rather than fostering horizontal networks, small grassroots initiatives, and ultimately, civic development, foreign aid contributes to the emergence of a vertical, institutionalized, and isolated (although well-funded) civic community. The result is "principled clientelism": despite funders' self-proclaimed moral intentions, the outcome is the development of unequal, vertical relationships between domestic groups and Western donor agencies. (2002: 140)

Henderson makes the case that foreign-funded NGOs in Russia are more likely to emphasize short-term results over long-term effectiveness, more likely to tailor their agenda to reflect Western interests, and more likely to waste money on duplicate programs because donors were willing to fund them. Overall, her conclusions are quite damning. Rather than offering helpful resources, Henderson sees Western aid to Russian NGOs as creating a system of incentives that "encourages donors as well as grant recipients to behave in ways that hinder rather than facilitate civic development" (2002: 141).

Clifford Bob (2005) makes similar observations about the contortions that local activist groups must go through in order to capture the attention – and the resources – of international donors. He argues that worthy causes and social injustices the world over go unnoticed because they lack marketing cachet – not because they are less worthy than the few causes that catapult to the top of the limited attention span of people living in wealthy countries. NGOs are both heroes and villains in this dynamic. In some cases, international NGOs are the key to gaining national and international attention for important causes (Keck and Sikkink 1998). In other cases, however, the resources and assistance that donors offer create perverse incentives for local organizations trying to gain attention for their cause. In particular, local activists are under a lot of pressure to market their message in a way that is palatable to the Western donor imagination: "under pressure to sell their causes to the rest of the world, local leaders may end up undermining their original goals or alienating the domestic constituencies they ostensibly represent" (Bob 2002b: 37).

Alnoor Ebrahim (2003) points out that NGOs adopt many different strategies in order to establish their accountability but that there is a tradeoff between the efforts to become more accountable to donors (through things like generating reports, disclosures, performance assessments, etc.) and efforts to become more accountable to community members (through things like increasing participation, self-regulation, and social audits). In particular, Ebrahim finds that pressures on NGOs from the donor community have emphasized "upward" and "external" accountability to the donors at a cost to "downward" and "internal" accountability to members of the community. Ebrahim worries that the implication of this tradeoff may be devastating to NGOs in the long run, arguing that the "current emphasis among NGOs and donors on the upward and external dimensions of accountability is problematic in that it encourages the formation of relationships with highly imbalanced accountabilities. In such cases, patrons can abuse their powers of punishment by threatening NGOs with a loss of funds, by imposing conditionalities, or by tarnishing NGO reputations" (826). Ebrahim also points out that the pressure for NGOs to be more accountable to donors also tends to reward NGOs for "short-term responses with quick and tangible impacts, while neglecting longer-term strategic responses that address more complex issues of social and political change" (826).

Identifying these tradeoffs offers no easy solution. Even if the tradeoffs are clear, and an NGO knows that they will lose credibility with local members by accepting a contract or a foreign grant, there can be strong rational incentives to accept the funding. The case of the environmental NGO Fundación Natura in Ecuador illustrates this point: even though the NGO initially lost members, and several more radical NGOs were formed by disillusioned former members, in the long run the funding from USAID allowed Natura to grow considerably.

Meyer (1995) demonstrates these tradeoffs using a game theoretic model of an NGO manager faced with the choice of accepting a foreign grant that will compromise the reputation of the NGO to local members. Even in the case of an ideologically committed manager, and clear tradeoffs between the ideology of the NGO and the donor, it can be in the best interest of the manager to accept the funding. Because the new resources can be used to build new membership, and pursue the goals of the NGO, the initial loss of membership or credibility can be tolerated.

To return to the example that opened this chapter, consider the successful, early-achieving health-care NGO PROCOSI in Bolivia. PROCOSI is a good match for what donors are looking for in an NGO. First, it has a long history of completed projects and a stable organization. Second, as a network of thirty-four member organizations, PROCOSI appears to have the organizational and technical capacity to carry out large-scale health projects. In terms of the shortcuts discussed above, it has multiple official partners, including large international NGOs and foreign donors. Third, PROCOSI has demonstrated a willingness to undergo monitoring and evaluation, both by obtaining certification through Foreign Aid Ratings, and undergoing extensive evaluation programs sponsored by USAID to build capacity and improve effectiveness. PROCOSI also utilizes the International Standards Organization (ISO) guidelines.

In fact, these efforts can be thought of as movement toward establishing credibility with donors: PROCOSI is sending costly signals in the form of paying for verification and producing the necessary reports; it is also seeking out third-party verification in the form of Foreign Aid Ratings and other program evaluations. A look at PROCOSI's public website confirms that the NGO recognizes these shortcuts as important information cues about the quality and capacity of its organization. The main page of the website (www.procosi.org.bo) features several items that clearly signal to donors that PROCOSI is a large, established, professional NGO. First, the logos of USAID and the European Union are prominently displayed on the main page, as well as links to other major sources of funding. Having previously been selected as a partner for USAID or the European Union is a powerful signal that PROCOSI is a big player in health care in Bolivia. Second, as additional signals of size and capacity, the main page displays a list of all nine departments in Bolivia where PROCOSI offers services, showing that it is an organization with national reach. There is also an image with the logos of dozens of other NGOs that are part of the PROCOSI network.

On one hand, this is simply clever marketing. But what does PROCOSI gain by firmly placing itself in the camp of the international development community? What does it lose? The organization gains funding and credibility, which facilitates its work. It also gains a privileged position in the community – PROCOSI consults with the government and is seen as the leader in the field. However, in pursuing these signals, PROCOSI may lose some degree of independence and flexibility. More seriously, it is possible that the organization loses some credibility in rural communities that are suspicious of outsiders. In trying to appeal to donors, a large, professional NGO like PROCOSI becomes more like the donors – more like an international aid agency – and less like the recipients they are targeting. This transition may make the donors more comfortable, but might undermine their credibility to their own constituents to some extent.

It is important to note that these tensions are dynamic, not static. PROCOSI has adjusted its strategy to meet growing concerns over accountability from donors. And, as an early successful grant recipient, PROCOSI is well positioned to do so – communication from the many donors is regular and established, and PROCOSI has the resources to adjust its strategy. Other smaller organizations may be much less able to provide these reassurances to donors. This reinforces the inequality that Bob (2005) observes between organizations and movements that are able to gain the attention of international donors, and those that are not. Again, this observation is not a condemnation of organizations like PROCOSI, which is playing the game quite well, but it does make clear that the tradeoffs involved are not costless.

Conclusions

As this discussion has shown, the dilemmas of information and credibility for local development NGOs involved in foreign aid are formidable, and they create difficult pressures for both donors and NGOs. High-quality information about NGOs is difficult to obtain, making direct observation of NGO impact or performance challenging for donors (and for scholars). The difficulty in obtaining accurate information has resulted in a bias toward measuring the more tangible

Table 5.1. *NGOs in Bolivia by sector and sub-sector, 2005*

Sector	Sub-sector	Number of NGOs	Number of projects
Agriculture	Farming	136	327
	Agro-industry	32	49
	Forestry	59	103
	Livestock	76	138
	Fisheries	11	15
Legal assistance	Legal advice	6	12
Communication	Roads	10	11
	Alternative technologies	18	24
	Press	3	6
	Radio	14	17
	Television	6	8
Education and culture	Culture	36	64
	Adult education	52	92
	Special education	31	60
	Occasional education (workshops)	34	46
	Formal/regular education	56	112
Energy	Electricity	13	15
	Solar power	8	13
Institutional Strengthening	Municipalities	61	109
	NGOs	23	67
	Other organizations	80	226
	Prefectures	3	3
Environment	Biodiversity conservation	27	59
	Natural resource management	35	62
	Environmental improvement	55	76
	Zoning (territorial demarcation)	12	18
Mining	Cooperatives	9	19
	Other	7	11
Small industry/ handicrafts	Handicrafts	45	65
	Small business	42	74
	Small industry	17	27

Table 5.1 (*cont.*)

Sector	Sub-sector	Number of NGOs	Number of projects
	Textiles	32	51
Health	Dental health	15	18
	Maternal health/birth	9	12
	Prenatal health	14	18
	Child health and development	20	33
	Cancer detection and prevention for women	2	2
	Drug addiction and mental health	7	9
	Sexually transmitted diseases and HIV/AIDS	13	17
	Acute illnesses (cholera)	13	17
	Acute respiratory illnesses	4	4
	Essential medications	12	18
	Traditional medicine	11	13
	Other illnesses (tuberculosis, chagas, malaria)	36	78
	Family planning	12	66
	Immunizations	8	9
	Services for the disabled	6	8
	Health education	50	90
	Indigenous health care	9	14
	Oral health	4	7
	Sanitation	5	7
Basic sanitation	Drinking water	47	77
	Waste disposal	8	9
	Human waste disposal	29	43
Housing	Self-construction	11	15
	Construction	10	11
	Repairs	10	22
	Urban planning	3	6

Source: VIPFE 2006.

aspects of NGO activity and performance, even when those are not the most important or the most interesting metrics.

Additionally, because of the high cost of the necessary information, and the large range of potential outcomes of interest, donors rely on shortcuts to distinguish one type from another. This has several implications. First, NGOs that already receive funding, that are already large, professionalized, and effective, are more likely to receive foreign aid funding than organizations that are small, new, and unfunded. There may be a real path dependence in NGO funding, which might be excluding innovative new actors. However, it is also possible that this is a fairly reliable selection process – if the choices of the NGO partners made by the early donors are sound. If so, then there is certainly bias in the selection of NGOs but not necessarily to the detriment of good organizations being chosen for funding. This scenario – of an NGO scene dominated by a few well-established titans – is not the vision of local knowledge and fledging grassroots organizations than many envision, but it may work fairly well.

Finally, there is a tendency in the donor community and scholarly work on these issues to conflate two things that are very different: the good intentions of NGOs and the effectiveness of NGOs at providing goods or services in the aid process. Although good intentions may well be an indicator of good quality on other dimensions, this may also be a troublesome oversimplification. A promising research agenda to extend this inquiry would be to explore how well the shortcuts and measurements used for evaluating NGOs actually correlate with their quality on the less-tangible scales.

It is easy to think of the dilemma of credibility as primarily a problem for donors. Who should you trust? How can you choose the best organization to support? But it is important to recognize that the inherent problems of credibility in this relationship create incentives for both donors and recipients to change their behavior in ways that, over time, bias the distribution of aid toward NGOs that are best able to meet the standards of professionalization – regardless of whether they are actually the best-qualified organizations working in an area.

6 | In defense of virtue: credibility, legitimacy dilemmas, and the case of Islamic Relief

LAURA THAUT, JANICE GROSS STEIN, AND
MICHAEL BARNETT

Humanitarian organizations, like most virtuous organizations, help us live an ethical life. It is often impossible practically, or prohibitively expensive, to do the right thing on our own. Many of us are deeply concerned about human suffering in places like Darfur, but cannot directly help these distant strangers. Instead the most that we can do is support humanitarian agencies that have the desire and the capacity to act in ways that are consistent with our values. By supporting humanitarian organizations we turn them into our ethical agents. We contribute to humanitarian organizations because we believe both in what they stand for and that they can and will do what they promise.

What happens to virtuous organizations when beliefs about their values and their effectiveness are shaken or can no longer be sustained by faith, when their legitimacy and their credibility are questioned? For much of their history humanitarian organizations were credible in large part because they were legitimate, a legitimacy based largely on their social purpose. Acting in the name of humanity and according to universal principles, they were helping the world's most vulnerable populations. Yet over the last several decades the "virtue" of humanitarian organizations has been challenged; whether their actions are truly consistent with the values of the international community – a question of legitimacy – and whether they can credibly carry out their stated goals – an issue of credibility – came into question.

In response to the growing legitimacy crisis, the humanitarian sector has moved in several directions to try to restore its legitimacy and recover its credibility. In some cases the sector was forced to comply with new reporting requirements by funding agencies, which can be understood easily as a consequence of what happens when donors decide, following Ronald Reagan's famous line regarding the

Soviet Union, to "trust but verify" what their agents do. In other cases, though, individual agencies and the entire sector undertook different kinds of reforms designed to recover their legitimacy and enhance their shaken credibility. Why they did so, how they did so, and whether and how such responses made a difference raises several issues that we explore in this chapter.

We argue that the perceived loss of legitimacy caused humanitarian agencies to engage in reforms. Legitimacy is related to but is not synonymous with credibility. As defined by Gourevitch and Lake in this volume, credibility exists whenever "statements are believable or accepted as truthful by one or more audiences." Credibility is value neutral; it has no intrinsic normative content. Mother Teresa can be credible, but so too can thugs, bullies, and zombies. Legitimacy, on the other hand, has a clear normative content. Mother Teresa had something more than credibility – she had legitimacy. Thugs, bullies, and zombies might have credibility, to the extent that we believe their threats, but that hardly means that they have legitimacy. Credibility and legitimacy differ in another important way, a difference that appears particularly important when considering non-governmental organizations (NGOs) – how we understand the basis of their interests. As Gourevitch and Lake note, many contemporary understandings of credibility, especially those that derive from a rationalist or game-theoretic tradition, assume that statements are most credible when they are consistent with the actor's interests. The core issue is: what are their interests? If we assume that their interests are narrow, that is, consumed by organizational concerns such as survival, a larger budget, and a bigger share of the turf, then the more credible they are then the less legitimacy they will have. Yet most humanitarian organizations can only operate if their credibility is tied to normative content and they do not appear to be operating according to narrowly-defined self-interest. This creates a much tighter relationship between legitimacy and credibility for these kinds of organizations. Shorn of their legitimacy, humanitarian organizations cannot be credible. And even when they are legitimate, an inability to deliver what they promise – seemingly only an issue of credibility – will over time compromise their legitimacy.

It is not surprising, then, that humanitarian agencies want to be viewed not just as credible but also as legitimate. Legitimacy has two elements: substantive legitimacy, which concerns whether the social purpose of the organization is consistent with the values of the community; and procedural legitimacy, whether it is operating in ways that are consistent with modern standards of practice. Substantive legitimacy overlaps with but is not identical to virtue. When we speak of an actor as virtuous, we imply that their actions reveal something about their character. Although ethicists debate these character traits and the impact of context, virtue is usually attributed to a person or an organization that seeks justice and the development of the full potential of fellow human beings. Being seen as virtuous helps further an organization's substantive legitimacy. Virtue, just like substantive legitimacy, cannot be normatively neutral but rather depends on a prior moral commitment.

Procedural legitimacy speaks to the question of whether the actor is abiding by accepted standards of practice. These standards cannot be determined ahistorically but rather are context dependent. There are many ways in which procedures might enhance or diminish the legitimacy of the organization, but for our purposes, we are most interested in those "modern" processes that give confidence to outside audiences that: practices are not driven by self-interest (thus enhancing legitimacy); and processes are consistent with stated purposes (thereby increasing credibility).

By distinguishing between legitimacy and credibility, we draw attention to the normative, institutional, social, and cultural contexts that shape the perceived virtue of NGOs. First, this distinction illuminates how legitimacy, like credibility, is audience dependent. What counts as "legitimate" depends on community standards. Different communities are likely to have different assessments of, and use different metrics to evaluate, the substantive and procedural legitimacy of the same organization. One community's legitimate organization will be another community's illegitimate organization, and one community's metrics for proper procedures will trigger another community's alarm at improper procedures. Second, different organizations see themselves as agents of different kinds of principals, and the same organization may see itself as the agent for different principals at the same time. Humanitarian agencies are connected to different communities and in this way are agents of more than one group of principals. When donors "hire" aid agencies to deliver services, for example, when the United States contracts an organization like World Vision International, does it become an agent of the government? World Vision International has a broad membership and collects largely unrestricted funds from a broad base of donors. To what extent do those who give to World Vision view themselves as principals and relief workers in Haiti as their agents? And more to the point, do aid organizations see themselves as the agents of donors? Staff of World Vision insist that they are the agents of their beneficiaries, who do not hire them in any contractual sense but rather avail themselves of World Vision's services. UNHCR staff claim that they represent states, international refugee law, and the refugees that they serve. Third, the distinction between substantive and procedural legitimacy focuses attention on the possibility of legitimacy dilemmas. By this we mean that the attempt by an organization to address a loss of legitimacy and recover its virtue with one audience that undermines its legitimacy and virtue with another. Humanitarian agencies that attempt to maintain their legitimacy with donor governments by engaging in various kinds of action that might make it appear to be the "instrument" of states can undermine their perceived virtue to the extent that, virtue depends on being connected to the values of the international community and not the interests of states. These legitimacy dilemmas also undermine the credibility of these organizations. As we argued, credibility is not independent of legitimacy for humanitarian organizations.

This chapter begins by exploring the legitimacy dilemmas of international humanitarian agencies generally and then examines the case of Islamic Relief in the context of these dilemmas. The first section begins by discussing the concept of legitimacy in general and in the specific circumstance of humanitarian action; introduces the concept of "moral suspect" in the context of virtuous agencies that are suspect to identifiable communities; identifies how environmental changes, largely emanating from the West, began to raise questions regarding their legitimacy; and explores the response by individual agencies and the sector to these challenges. These developments, we then argue, potentially increase the aid agency's legitimacy with its donors at the potential cost of legitimacy with its recipients – a prominent theme of the post-Cold War period as aid agencies became increasingly associated with the political agendas of their largest donors. These legitimacy deficits create serious challenges to the credibility and legitimacy of these organizations, challenges that go beyond their effectiveness.

The second section applies these arguments to the case of Islamic Relief (IR), a British-based relief and development agency. We are particularly interested in three features. Like other relief and development agencies, Islamic Relief had to address charges that challenged its claims to virtue, and interestingly, part of its response was to put significant resources into self-monitoring. It did so in part because it was an Islamic agency based in the West – that is, as a moral suspect, its claims to virtue were scrutinized by non-Islamic, Western audiences, especially after 9/11. These developments, in turn, led Islamic Relief to undertake responses that were intended to shore up its substantive and procedural legitimacy, and its credibility. Not all areas were scrupulously monitored – specifically, financial transparency – related to procedural legitimacy – received considerably more attention than program evaluation that is more closely tied to credibility. Although Islamic Relief is no different from other agencies in terms of its self-monitoring priorities, its urgent focus on procedural legitimacy owed considerably to its desire to address the growing Western suspicion of everything Islamic. These responses allowed it to generate greater symbolic capital which translated directly into financial and political capital. Yet these same responses, which were designed to increase its legitimacy with a Western audience, had potentially negative consequences for its substantive legitimacy with some Islamic audiences. We conclude by discussing the ambiguity of virtue and of monitoring and their consequences for legitimacy and credibility.

Virtue under attack

The ethic of humanitarian action, as James Orbinski noted in 1999 when he accepted the Nobel Peace Prize for Médecins Sans Frontières, is constructed as an "ethic framed in a morality" that is not reducible to "rules of right conduct and technical performance" (Orbinski 1999). Indeed, there may seem to be little reason to question the virtue of humanitarian agencies whose aim is to save lives, restore dignity, remove conditions of risk that plague vulnerable populations, and create solidarity. If there remain any doubts regarding their virtue, the humanitarian principles of impartiality, neutrality, and independence should erase them. By pledging to help anyone who needs it, to remain above the fray of local conflicts, and to remain untainted by the political interests of others, humanitarian agencies demonstrate that their ambitions are apolitical and beyond reproach (Terry 2003).

Yet over the last several years the legitimacy of humanitarian organizations has been attacked on two fronts. Some of these charges go to their substantive legitimacy, that is, whether they are acting in a way that is consistent with the values and aspirations of the community. There are several lines of critique. One is that aid organizations are less virtuous than they seem – humanitarian organizations are organizations, all organizations are fundamentally concerned with their organizational survival, and humanitarian organizations are more attentive to their survival and growth than they are to their beneficiaries. In this sense, they are self-interested, with no more automatic entitlement to legitimacy – and credibility – than more overtly self-interested actors (Polman 2010).

Second, some humanitarian organizations want to do more than save lives, they also want to produce social change. But what counts as desirable social change is in the eye of the beholder. And as aid agencies have increasingly moved from saving lives to saving societies, from trying to address symptoms to attacking the causes of suffering, they venture increasingly into politics (Barnett 2008). Along these lines, some see Western humanitarian agencies as promoters of Western values, acting not in accordance with universalism but rather particularism. A related argument accuses faith-based agencies of attempting to promote religious values, a charge leveled at both Christian and Islamic agencies. Perhaps the most damning critique comes from Western states that are the principal funders and supporters of aid organizations – that humanitarian agencies are not acting like the agents they are supposed to be. After the end of the Cold War, states became increasingly interested in using humanitarianism to further their foreign policy interests. Humanitarian and development assistance could be useful in containing the dangers of failed states and in furthering the security, political, and economic interests of donors by ensuring that failed states became democratic, legitimate, rights-embracing, peace-loving states. Donor states could even avoid more dangerous entanglements by using humanitarianism as a "fig leaf" (Barnett and Weiss 2008).

These challenges to the substantive legitimacy of aid agencies highlight several important issues. Legitimacy, like virtue, is context and community dependent. One person's virtuous organization is another person's moral suspect. Environmental changes can play havoc with the substantive legitimacy of aid agencies. All aid agencies, because they cross boundaries – territorial, political, social, cultural, and moral – run the risk of becoming moral outcasts. Lastly, while most aid agencies claim a cosmopolitan identity because they are acting in the name of humanity, the identity of most agencies is modified in significant ways by their national, religious, or sectarian association.

Critics also question the procedural legitimacy and the credibility of humanitarian agencies; that is, whether they follow appropriate procedures and whether they do what they say they are going to do. Virtue is not enough because aid agencies must demonstrate that they are capable of delivering what they promise. Some accuse humanitarian agencies of doing more harm than good not only because the circumstances are challenging but also because they are organizationally challenged (Terry 2003). Over the last two decades humanitarian agencies have been charged with lacking professionalism, failing to operate according to modern systems of management, and neglecting to provide basic evidence regarding their effectiveness. The allegation that agencies do not adequately measure and monitor the outcomes and the impact of what they do is a direct attack on their credibility (Singer 2010: ch. 5). In short, these virtuous organizations might want to do the right thing but their lack of professionalism (the amateurism associated with their voluntary status), technical incapacity (staff lack training in their chosen vocations and there is little attempt to develop best practices), and lack of bureaucratic acumen (often improvised activities that do not take advantage of possible economies of scale and standardization) leave aid agencies doing the wrong thing time and again.

Different audiences are likely to care more about one dimension of legitimacy than another and therefore come to different conclusions about credibility. Official donors have emphasized procedural legitimacy, accepting that aid agencies that are impartial, neutral, and independent are likely to be virtuous, but that they may fail to meet standards of modern systems of procedural legitimacy, especially with respect to the tracking of financial flows. Individual or small donors, on the other hand, are more likely to consider substantive legitimacy issues in choosing whether to support an aid agency. We are not asserting that households do not care about whether aid agencies are effective, accountable, or spend most of their money on staff, because they do, a reason why organizations like Charity Navigator have become popular. Instead, households likely make a first cut in terms of the identity of the organization and then try to identify that organization within the population that is judged most efficient and effective. No firm judgments can be made about beneficiaries because the evidence about their judgments is thin. What we do know suggests that some recipients do a fair bit of profiling even as they care about some of the factors that go to the heart of procedural legitimacy and effectiveness.

Although we have distinguished between procedural and substantive legitimacy, and the relationship of both to credibility, they are entangled. Principals at times tried to use procedural issues to force aid agencies to act consistently with their interests, and there were ethical agents who wanted to develop their procedural legitimacy to shore up their substantive legitimacy. And at times the attempt by a humanitarian organization to shore up the legitimacy deficit with one audience created a legitimacy – and consequently, a credibility – deficit with another. This enmeshment can be seen in several different areas. One is the growing insistence by states that aid agencies develop new reporting mechanisms to demonstrate that they are using their money wisely and effectively, a development that was a consequence of the growing interest and investment of resources by states in humanitarian action. This demand relates directly to credibility. Between 1990 and 2000, aid levels rose from $2.1 billion to $5.9 billion, a nearly threefold increase. Moreover, as a percentage of official development assistance, humanitarian aid rose from an average of 5.83 percent between 1989 and 1993 to 10.5 percent in 2000.[1] A few donors were responsible for much of this increase, and they now comprise an oligopoly. The United States was the lead donor by a factor of three; in 1999, for instance, its outlays exceeded the total assistance of twelve large Western donors. Between 1995 and 1997 it provided 20 percent of total assistance, and then in the following three years its contribution rose to 30 percent. The second largest donor is the European Community Humanitarian Organization (ECHO), followed by the United Kingdom, several European countries, Canada, and Japan. Many states expected something in return for this increase in giving; at the very least, they wanted evidence that their money was being well spent and achieving the outcomes they expected. States began introducing mechanisms that were intended to control the way their "implementing partners" spent the money.

Yet this strong emphasis on procedural legitimacy and on effectiveness, designed in part to shape substantive legitimacy as defined

---

[1] Macrae 2002, 15. For a good overview, see Randel and German 2002.

by the donors, challenged the substantive legitimacy as defined by others, including the humanitarian agencies themselves. One way that aid agencies demonstrate their legitimacy is by adhering to the principles of impartiality, neutrality, and independence. However, the more states insisted on controlling the spending of their agents, the more humanitarian agencies protested that being treated as an agent was compromising their legitimacy. This objection was partly self-serving, but not entirely. Humanitarian agencies bristled at these procedural mechanisms and insistence on outcome measures and assessments of impact not only because their autonomy and independence is critical to their identity, but also because they feared that they would no longer be seen as agents of humanity, operating with moral authority. Monitoring is not necessarily value neutral, and the procedural mechanisms that were designed to improve the credibility of aid agencies, that is, to control their spending, increase their procedural legitimacy, and demonstrate their effectiveness might well undermine their substantive legitimacy.

The push to accountability can also create friction and conflict between procedural and substantive legitimacy where enhancing the one can undermine the other (Slim 2002; Smilie and Minear 2004: 215–24). Aid agencies had their own reasons for adopting new mechanisms of accountability. Many wanted to better understand the results of what they were doing (Stein 2008). But one critical factor was the push by donors to apply the principles of "new public management" that originated with the neoliberal orthodoxy of the 1980s to humanitarian organizations. Neoliberals wanted to reduce the state's role in the delivery of public services and, instead, rely on commercial and voluntary organizations that they saw as more efficient and effective. Because government agencies justified the shift from the public to the private and voluntary sectors on the grounds that these sectors were more efficient, they introduced monitoring mechanisms to reduce the possibility of either slack or shirking (Macrae 2002: 18–21).

Until the 1990s humanitarian organizations largely escaped the consequences of the ideology of new public management. Because humanitarian assistance was a minor part of the foreign aid budget, states did not view humanitarianism as central to their foreign policy goals and trusted that humanitarian agencies were efficient and effective, then, they had little reason to absorb the monitoring costs.

However, once humanitarian funding increased and humanitarianism became more central to security goals, states began to question the effectiveness of humanitarian organizations (de Waal 1997: 78–9). States introduced new reporting requirements, developed new kinds of contracts, and demanded greater evidence of results. In short, whereas once aid agencies could use the money in ways that were consistent with their principles, now powerful donors were insisting on the adoption of modern monitoring mechanisms to ensure that humanitarian organizations became increasingly rational organizations operating in ways that were consistent with the interests of donors and producing the results they promised.

How did humanitarian agencies respond to these attacks on their substantive and procedural legitimacy and to the challenges to their credibility? Much depends on the source of their legitimacy deficit, the kind of agency they are, and the audience they are trying to accommodate. Table 6.1 identifies a menu of strategies that humanitarian organizations used to enhance procedural and substantive legitimacy as well as credibility, but, as we argue, using one kind of strategy may sharpen a different kind of deficit.

Strategies to enhance procedural legitimacy and credibility are costly. Monitoring compliance with codes, meeting reporting requirements, providing time and resources for evaluation all consume financial and human resources. We would expect that agencies would use the strategies that are likely to be least costly and bring the greatest benefits. To be credible, however, agencies must invest sufficient financial and human resources to meet reporting requirements and to develop some measure of outcomes. These are all "costly signals." One important indicator of an agency's commitment to comply with monitoring requirements is the investment it makes in financial and human resources.

In part to ease these dilemmas, in part to lessen the intervention of donors, and in part to deal with the explosion of agencies working on the ground, the humanitarian sector developed voluntary codes of conduct during the 1990s. More aid organizations than ever before were marching to their own beat, wreaking havoc in the field and sullying the reputation of the "good" agencies. Perhaps the most influential code was developed by the International Red Cross and Red Crescent Movement. The Movement espouses seven fundamental principles:

Table 6.1. *Strategies to enhance legitimacy*

	Official donors	Private donors	Beneficiaries
Procedural legitimacy	• Adopt codes of conduct • Sign on to monitoring bodies • Implement organizational reforms (professionalization, rationalization, bureaucratization) that promote compliance with internal and external monitoring mechanisms • Promote transparency by making information available	• Increase transparency in how funds are allocated and used (enhanced reporting)	• Reform aid delivery or development assistance to enhance perceived effectiveness
Substantive legitimacy	• Emphasize commitment to humanitarian principles of impartiality, neutrality, independence • Promote partnerships with well-respected aid agencies	• Emphasize cultural principles and motivation • Emphasize work with beneficiaries of shared cultural identity	• Build stronger ties in communities • Emphasize shared values and principles, including cultural identity • Distance agency from suspect Western or other identity

humanity, impartiality, neutrality, independence, voluntary service, unity, and universality.[2] The Code is used by monitoring bodies or institutions such as the UK Disaster Emergencies Committee (DEC), and it became integrated into the work of the Sphere Project, NGOs

[2] International Committee of the Red Cross (ICRC), International Red Cross and Red Crescent Movement, www.icrc.org/Web/eng/siteengO.nsf/htmlall/movement?OpenDocument (accessed August 8, 2009).

in Disaster Relief, and the People in Aid. Procedural accountability is central to the principles enshrined in these codes. For example, the People in Aid Code, to which DEC members are signatories, outlines guidelines for proper staff management, human resources policies, and a set of indicators that establish benchmarks for evaluating compliance with these guidelines. The People in Aid Code notes in its discussion of its human resources strategy that the agencies must develop and monitor "operational plans and budgets" in order to "reflect fully our responsibilities for staff management, support, and development and well-being."[3] The demonstration of appropriate procedures is not simply for internal consumption but rather, as the report by People in Aid demonstrates, central to their activities.

The Code is more than merely making staff better at their jobs or happier in their roles. It is fundamentally about organizational efficiency and effectiveness. Sometimes external factors prompted action: host governments, partners, and the wider community all need the reassurance that the agencies with which they work will demonstrate professionalism in all their activities. Donors require that their funds be committed to agencies that can demonstrate effective human resource management. For example, the Disasters Emergency Committee (DEC), which raises substantial funds from the British public in times of crisis internationally, states that members need to have "a demonstrable commitment to achieving People In Aid standards and a willingness to be evaluated against them."[4]

The adoption of the principles, strategies, and indicators embedded in these kinds of codes are intended to signal to donors and host countries (and beneficiaries) that an agency is virtuous because it is a procedurally legitimate humanitarian actor. Indeed, aid agencies often prominently display the various codes on their websites, a code that is more likely to be noticed by potential funders than by potential beneficiaries.[5]

---

[3] People in Aid, Human Resource Strategy Indicators, www.peopleinaid.org/code/online.aspx (accessed August 8, 2009).
[4] Human Resource Strategy: Why is this important? www.peopleinaid.org/code/online.aspx (accessed August 8, 2009).
[5] As Barnett (2008: 254) notes "Because organizations are rewarded for conforming to rules and legitimating principles, and punished if they do not, they will tend to model themselves after those organizational forms that have legitimacy."

Although we have emphasized the view from donors and Western governments, the view from the beneficiaries also matters. Building relationships with and assuring the support of the host governments and the communities in which humanitarian agencies operate is integral to the success of relief and development projects. That a humanitarian agency may be party to recognized codes of conduct and be well respected in the international community may be of little significance to the beneficiaries. Instead, beneficiaries are more apt to evaluate the credibility of a humanitarian agency by the effectiveness of its work on the ground, and by its substantive legitimacy, including the religious identity of the agency and the history of partnership in the community or host country.

Islamic Relief

Islamic Relief's reception area resembles those of many other agencies – comfortable but hardly sumptuous, a waiting area that contains annual reports and publicity materials, and photographs and posters of their work around the world. Yet, on the day that we visited in January 2010, it had a distinctive artifact: on the wall, nearly the first thing a visitor sees when entering the building, was a framed copy of a list of the most transparent aid agencies according to the quarterly *Charity Finance*. Islamic Relief saves lives, but it chose to emphasize its transparency. Certainly many other aid agencies over the last decade have worked hard to professionalize, but Islamic Relief's decision to put its resources into transparency, and the significance of this accomplishment, can only be understood by recognizing the role of its Islamic identity. It sent a very costly signal. In doing so we do not dismiss the kinds of cost–benefit calculations that led Islamic Relief to choose this direction. As one executive confessed, financial transparency is a lot cheaper than program accountability, the litmus test of credibility. Yet these calculations have to be placed in context. The view from headquarters was that its donors trusted the organization, but worried that if they gave to Islamic Relief they might get into trouble with Western authorities who were increasing their monitoring of Islamic charities as part of the war on terrorism. To protect its donor base – and to signal that Muslims are more than terrorists, Islamic Relief had to increase its transparency and professionalize in a manner that would alleviate any suspicion on the part of Western authorities. This section explains why Islamic Relief placed transparency, and especially financial transparency, at the center of its attempt to communicate its virtue and increase its procedural legitimacy.

Established in 1984 in response to the humanitarian crises in Ethiopia and the Sudan, Islamic Relief is a religious agency headquartered in Birmingham, England, with an annual budget in 2007 of approximately $75.9 million,[6] operations in twenty-four countries and liaison offices in twelve countries (de Cordier 2009). Like many other humanitarian agencies, Islamic Relief's mission evolved in the 1990s to include a long-term development focus, and it further expanded in response to the tsunami of 2004 and the earthquake in Pakistan in 2005.[7] Yet Islamic Relief is unlike many other Western-based aid agencies because of its Islamic identity. It is the creation of Dr. Hany al-Bana, an Egyptian who attended medical school in Birmingham in the mid 1980s. While he was visiting Sudan in December 1983 for a medical conference, he learned about the plight of the refugees and was struck not only by the tremendous need but also by the absence of Muslim agencies. Wanting to do something to alleviate the suffering and provide an opportunity for Muslims living abroad to contribute to the effort, he began soliciting donations from friends and strangers. He was successful beyond his expectations. Muslims responded

---

[6] UK Charity Commission, "About Charities: IR Worldwide," www.charity-commission.gov.uk/ShowCharity/RegisterOfCharities/CharityWithPartB. aspx?RegisteredCharityNumber=328158&SubsidiaryNumber=0 (accessed March 4, 2009).

[7] Regarding the origin of Islamic Relief, see Islamic Relief Worldwide, 2008; "Islamic Relief Beliefs, Values and Code of Conduct." Available at www. islamic-refief.com/In Depth/downloads/IRs%20Beliefs,%Values%20and%20 Code%20of%20Conduct.pdf (accessed February 15, 2009); Islamic Relief 2006. Annual Report and Financial Statements. Islamic Relief, www. islamic-relief.com/Whoweare/FinancialReportsMain.aspx?depID=2 (accessed January 14, 2009); and Kirmani and Khan 2008. Bellion-Jourdan (2000: 15) notes that "in the mid-1980s, several relief organizations were created to come to the aid of Afghans," as the "Egyptian Union of Doctors created a humanitarian branch, the Lajnat al-Ighatha al-Insaniya (Human Relief Agency); in 1986, the Organization for Social Reform in Kuwait created the Lajnat ad-DaŌwa al-Islamiya (Islamic Mission Agency) to collect funds for Afghanistan; and in 1987, Yusuf Islam ... founded Muslim Aid. These organizations and others such as IIRO, the IR Agency (international network of the Sudanese organization IARA), and Human Concern International regrouped themselves in Peshawar as the Islamic Coordination Council, in which also Kuwaiti and Saudi Red Cross associations take part."

with the opportunity to give to an Islamic relief agency, and a growing number wanted to contribute their time as well as money; most dramatically, he tapped into a strong interest among student associations, and these students began to volunteer for the organization and get the message out.[8] First-generation Pakistani students attending the local university in Birmingham were especially prominent; they volunteered in impressive numbers. Islamic Relief was on its way.

Although it is the *Islamic* in Islamic Relief that is central to our account, we want to note that this organization contains many of the fault lines that exist within Islam in a globalizing world. It is an Islamic agency based in the West. It was founded by an Egyptian national, and nearly all of its trustees are from the Arab world; yet much of its staff is from the non-Arab world, including a very visible group of British-born descendants of Pakistani immigrants. There are generational divides, with an older group committed to more traditional notions of charity and a younger group that is more committed to social change. Although most staff are Muslim, there are religious differences; some are devout, some are converts from the West, and others are more cultural than religious Muslims. There are gender differences. There are class differences, with some staff from elite families in the Arab world and others from working-class families in Britain. One long-time staff tried to tidy up these cleavages by observing that Islamic Relief has three divisions: a "Muslim Brotherhood" (not the organization but rather a cluster of pious), a more corporate-oriented group, and an "old school" development cadre. But these differences matter more to the staff than they do to a Western audience that assumes that "Islamic" says it all.

Giving while Islamic

Unlike other Western aid agencies that are presumed virtuous until proven otherwise, Islamic Relief was not given that latitude, not before 9/11 and especially not afterwards. As a "moral suspect," there was no golden age. Staff can easily recall episodes prior to 9/11 when Islamic Relief's virtue was challenged and describe being in a constant state of tension and worry. Many staff say that they were motivated

---

[8] Barnett interview with Dr. Hany al-Banna, Minneapolis, MN, April 23, 2008.

to work for an Islamic agency precisely because they wanted to prove to the West that Muslims are more than terrorists. Islamic Relief's legitimacy deficit is compounded by its relatively young age. Unlike veteran aid agencies such as Oxfam, which can rely on name recognition to overcome doubts, new agencies such as Islamic Relief need to prove their merit, and Islamic Relief tried to do so at a time when the entire sector was being pressured to professionalize, modernize, and rationalize.[9] Being young and Muslim in the West isn't easy, not for individuals and not for aid agencies.

Developments after 9/11 intensified the climate of fear and raised the risks. One senior manager at Islamic Relief reflected that "After 2001, yes, you are suspected everywhere ... even agencies that you dealt with in the past suspect you."[10] As another staff member reflected, Islamic Relief became "more subject to scrutiny – generously so."[11] At stake was the organization's financial survival.[12] Western authorities were increasingly fearful that Islamic charities were, knowingly or unknowingly, helping finance terrorism. In response, they began working to separate the "good," from the "bad." But, in a climate in which Islamic charities were almost guilty until proven innocent, donors worried about getting into trouble with Western governments and finding themselves on watch lists; in response, they became more more fearful of, and less giving to, and consequently, donors became a lot more fearful of giving to Islamic agencies such as Islamic Relief. Additionally, various Western NGOs that might otherwise partner with Islamic Relief became more reticent.[13] In short, while the donors continued to trust Islamic Relief, they worried that their donations might run afoul of Western authorities who did not necessarily trust the agency.

---

[9] Islamic agencies generally emerged as actors in the humanitarian field in the 1980s in places like Cairo, Tehran, Algiers, Beirut, and Gaza, but it would be another decade before they developed significant international relief programs. For data on the increase in the number of Islamic aid agencies in Africa from 1980 to 2000, see Salih 2002: 56.

[10] Interview by Thaut, Birmingham, UK, July 16, 2008.

[11] Interview by Barnett and Stein, Birmingham, January 14, 2010.

[12] As Shawn Flanigan (2006) notes, there is a fear that "[n]onprofit organizations based in the United States and Western Europe may divert the funds of unknowing donors toward terrorist organizations, or may provide a legitimate disguise for donors consciously seeking to support resistance movements abroad."

[13] Islamic Relief received approximately £3 million in annual donor support from the Middle East prior to 2001; it now collects less than half that total.

This was no small matter. Muslims, many of whom live in the West, comprise the bulk of its donor base, and they donate to Islamic Relief for reasons largely related to their religious identity. For many it is a way to perform their religious duty of *zakat* by giving to an Islamic agency that operates in Muslim societies. Others give when Muslim populations experience a natural disaster. And still others give to show solidarity with their co-religionists in places like Palestine, Afghanistan, and Iraq.[14] In addition to private donations, which made up nearly 90 percent of their support, Islamic Relief enjoyed official assistance from Gulf Arab states. In order to survive, Islamic Relief had to reassure Western authorities about its capacity to manage and control its financial flows. It had to address its procedural legitimacy.

Nothing to hide

Islamic Relief worked hard to become as transparent as possible and to convince Western authorities that it had nothing to hide. An event in the mid 1990s foreshadowed the post-2001 developments and put Islamic Relief on a state of alert. In Paris, Algerian-associated groups committed several acts of terrorism, and the French newspaper *Le Figaro* charged that various Islamic relief agencies, including Islamic Relief, were supporting terrorist organizations. Islamic Relief fought the charges in court, and won. It learned several lessons, including the need for more oversight of its local partners and the central importance of the capacity to produce exonerating evidence. It began subjecting potential partners to a "partner appraisal character." As recalled by an architect of the process, Islamic Relief wanted to monitor and evaluate the "capacity and character" of its local associates. It also began keeping better financial records and stood ready to provide them at a moment's notice. This experience forewarned Islamic Relief of the kinds of accusations it would have to address, and forewarned is forearmed.

After 9/11 and in response to new government regulations and oversight activities, Islamic Relief moved to increase its transparency and reassure Western authorities that it was a high-quality, efficient, bona fide relief agency with transparent financial flows.

---

[14] Interview by author, written notes, Islamic Relief Worldwide, Birmingham, UK, July 30, 2008; Khan *et al.* 2009. See also de Cordier 2009; Khan 2012.

It introduced a "Quality Management System" that established benchmarks by which, first, its field offices could assess their work, and, second, headquarters could evaluate local offices in the areas of governance, program management, and office management. It provided more and better information about the agency and its projects to beneficiaries and stakeholders. It encouraged partner agencies, institutional donors, and beneficiaries to involve themselves throughout the life cycle of a project, which would improve quality, increase accountability, and provide greater assurance to funders. Yet Islamic Relief concentrated its energies on financial transparency. It expanded its annual reports. It put all its financial records online. It entered its annual reports into competitions for awards for transparency. It sought external audits of its local operations from PricewaterhouseCoopers, chosen purposely because of its name recognition and thus its ability to help firm up Islamic Relief's procedural legitimacy and therefore its credibility. It worked closely with the Office of Foreign Assets Control in the US Department of Treasury.[15] In these and other ways Islamic Relief attempted to convince authorities that it had nothing to hide.

Card-carrying humanitarians

At a conference in Cairo in June 2008 that the three of us attended, one of Islamic Relief's senior staff was trying to convey what it is like to be an Islamic agency in a post-9/11 climate. With considerable drama, he pulled out his billfold and withdrew his business card and then passed it around the room for all to see. He then asked the group to identify what, if anything, distinguished his card from the typical card from a Western aid agency. Barely waiting for an answer, he pointed out that his card identifies many of the sector-wide associations to which Islamic Relief belongs, and that by embossing their names on the Islamic Relief card the agency was reassuring its funders. Following a well-worn survival strategy of many minorities, Islamic Relief began to seek "credibility by association," as one staff member put it, and ultimately to become a leader in the profession.

---

[15] www.ustreas.gov/offices/enforcement/ofac.

Critical to Islamic Relief's strategy to increase its legitimacy and credibility was its deliberate association with existing and emerging professional associations. It identified with existing codes of conduct and the guidelines for humanitarian action. It emphasized its commitment to the humanitarian principles of impartiality, neutrality, and independence. It publicized its commitment to the emerging professional associations, including Sphere, which established benchmarks for minimum standards for relief. It joined the UK-based Disaster Emergency Committee (DEC), an umbrella organization whose very select British-based members are renowned for their leadership and commitment to accountability.[16] This strategy improved its credibility with Western authorities and its access to populations in non-Muslim countries. According to a program officer, Islamic Relief wanted to work in China but, at first, the government and local communities were suspicious of Islamic Relief's presence because of its faith-based identity. Islamic Relief was finally able to gain access by emphasizing the professionalism of its programs and its commitment to the codes of conduct and fundamental humanitarian principles. Once it began its work, moreover, it adopted a model of partnership with local organizations in order to provide further evidence of its impartiality.

Because Islamic Relief is an Islamic agency, it constantly runs the risk of guilt by association; that is, if one Muslim agency is found guilty of funding improper activities, all Islamic agencies suffer by association. Consequently, Islamic Relief worked with other Islamic agencies and governments to ensure their compliance with Western standards of transparency. Islamic Relief also began working with other Islamic charities and donors to increase their transparency and encouraged them to adopt the regulations that would be credible to a Western audience. One long-time Islamic Relief executive repeated Dr. Hany's motto: "We need to ARM charities." ARM stood for assist in building capacity, regulate charities, and monitor *zakat*. Islamic Relief created the Muslim Charities Forum and encouraged Arab states, particularly its large donors from the Gulf, to accept regulations to increase their transparency in giving.

---

[16] Disaster Emergency Committee (DEC) 2008, "Public Accountability and Governance," www.dec.org.uk/item/295 (accessed February 18, 2009).

Islamic Relief also wanted to be seen as a leader in the professionalization and institutionalization of the sector. As one senior staff
member observed:

We should not have to struggle to meet minimum standards; instead, we
should help to develop those standards. We owe that to the people we work
with and for. In addition, we need that to survive in a world that often
looks at Muslim charities with suspicion. To get to that leadership position,
we need to perform better than we do now. Performing better has to do
with structure, process, job satisfaction, cordial relations, a positive work
environment, technical expertise, and priority-setting.[17]

Improving its operations would not only increase its effectiveness
but would also raise its standing in the aid sector, which would help
Islamic Relief survive. By associating itself with many professional
associations and standard-setting bodies, it demonstrated its commitment to excellence and simultaneously reduced the "Islamic" and
elevated the "aid" in "Islamic aid agency." Islamic Relief also sought
to be a leader in furthering greater understanding and cooperation
between Western and Muslim aid agencies. Dr. Hany founded the
Humanitarian Forum, an organization designed to increase greater
collaboration and understanding between Western and Southern aid
agencies. It became a charter member of the Montreux Initiative, a
Swiss-sponsored project whose mandate includes the development of
mechanisms for creating greater cooperation between Western and
Islamic agencies.[18]

The benefits and costs of legitimacy in the West

Islamic Relief's steady effort to increase its legitimacy and credibility
with Western audiences had two important consequences. One is that
the strategy, by and large, worked, and there is no better evidence
than the comfort of most Western governments with Islamic Relief.
Western governments wanted to eliminate the "bad" Islamic agencies,
but they also wanted to promote the "good" ones. Many Western
governments want to engage the Muslim world in order to win their
"hearts and minds" and view humanitarian action instrumentally as

---

[17] Interview by Barnett and Stein, Birmingham, January 14, 2010.
[18] www.eda.admin.ch/eda/en/home/topics/peasec/peac/confre/conrel.html.

part of this broader strategy. To overcome the suspicion of Muslim populations, Western governments need to work with intermediaries, but not just any intermediaries – they must be credible. This strategy is nicely captured by a working group report commissioned by USAID. It concluded that the US government should increase its cooperation with and assistance to legitimate Muslim charities because of the centrality of humanitarian principles in Islam, the potential for Islamic charities to draw on significant resources from religiously motivated donors, and the expectation that Islamic aid agencies may be better received within the Muslim world than other, Western secular or faith-based agencies. The terms of the bargain are clear: an exchange of resources for greater transparency. "Strengthening the governance and transparency of Muslim charities," the experts conclude, "should be an integral part of this assistance" (Alterman *et al.* 2005).

Islamic Relief began to capitalize on its advantage of access to Muslim populations in comparison to non-Islamic agencies.[19] One staff member observed that:

In comparison to MSF's [Médecins Sans Frontières'] work with beneficiaries, Islamic Relief is better able to work in Muslim communities because [Islamic Relief] makes people more comfortable; they will trust Islamic Relief, and will come to them not as though Islamic Relief is foreign, but as if Islamic Relief is from the local community. Islamic Relief is identified in Palestine as a Palestinian charity, and in Yemen, as a Yemeni charity. Islamic Relief is not associated with a Western, white identity.[20]

Reflecting on how its liminal characteristic gives it a niche position in the aid world, Dr. Hany El-Banna noted that "Islamic Relief is in a unique position as an aid agency founded in the West but based on Islamic humanitarian principles," which "gives [Islamic Relief] an important role as a bridge between cultures, communities, and civilizations" (Islamic Relief 2006). Many staff credited its rising

---

[19] Laura Hammond notes that the "fusing of charitable work with spiritual duty is a central tenet of Islam, and those following this approach may be accorded more trust by Muslim communities because it is more familiar than the self-declared secular approach to humanitarianism that many international aid agencies espouse" (Hammond 2008: 188). See also Benthall 1999, 2003, 2007; de Cordier 2009.

[20] Interview by Thaut, written notes, Islamic Relief Worldwide, Birmingham, UK, July 16, 2008.

popularity, evidenced by its growing number of partnerships, with its "Western" and "professional" standing with access to Muslim populations.[21] Indeed, at a moment when the choice of Islamic partners narrowed substantially because of Western regulations and constraints, Islamic Relief became an ideal collaborator.[22] Just as Islamic Relief attempted to increase its legitimacy by associating with branded aid agencies in the West, many of these Western aid agencies attempted to increase their acceptability to local populations by associating with Islamic Relief. One Islamic Relief employee tells the following story. Islamic Relief was working with a well-known Western aid agency in a *madrassa* (religious school); the Western relief agency was helping to broaden the curriculum and Islamic Relief was helping with sanitation and water.[23] At one point the Western aid agency ran into difficulty selling its curricular reforms, and it turned to Islamic Relief for assistance. Rather than emphasizing the reform's connection to universal values, which the Western aid agency had done, Islamic Relief reframed the project within an Islamic perspective. Explaining why Islamic Relief was able to accomplish what the Western aid agency could not, he emphasized that because Islamic Relief is an *Islamic* agency and offered a Quranic perspective, it was not seen as a "Western imperialist."[24] It was not just the recitation of Islamic

---

[21] As Laura Hammond (2008: 187) argues, because "Western-based aid agencies are working in countries with large Muslim populations," it behooves them to partner with the "local and international Islamic organizations" that are welcome in Muslim communities.

[22] Interview by Thaut, Birmingham, UK, August 5, 2008.

[23] Islamic Relief's partners and institutional donors have included the UK government's Department for International Development (DfID), World Food Program (WFP), European Commission (EC), European Commission Humanitarian Organization (ECHO), the Catholic Overseas Development Agency, and Christian Aid, among others.

[24] Interview by Thaut, Birmingham, UK, July 28, 2008. Other staff members note that, depending on the community, Islamic Relief may or may not work with local religious leaders. As one staff member emphasized, "It doesn't matter if it is a religious leader, business leader, or some other person who fills a leadership role in the community, you have to work with these leaders to gain acceptance and trust." Another employee notes that although IR's work with religious leaders varies depending on the project, in emergency situations it is good to work with religious leaders because they are respected and can be very powerful in the communities. "It can backfire if you don't," an employee cautioned.

principles, it was the recitation of Islamic principles by an Islamic agency that made the message credible to local beneficiaries.

There is some evidence that Islamic Relief's increased legitimacy and credibility with Western governments came at some expense of its legitimacy within the Muslim world. As one staff member said, "We have a delicate balancing act."[25] Becoming more transparent, more willing to work with Western governments, and collaborating and vouching for Western aid agencies that are viewed suspiciously by local populations all take a toll on Islamic Relief's legitimacy with both its donors and its beneficiaries.

Islamic Relief gets most of its donations from private sources, which are overwhelmingly Muslim (Khan 2012). Many Muslims want to perform their religious duty through international relief activities and Islamic Relief is well known for its transparency and professionalism. It enjoys a significant level of trust relative to other Muslim aid agencies, and Muslim donors have less reason to fear that their names will end up on a government watch list. Donors also like the fact that Islamic Relief presents a "good image" of Muslim organizations. Yet, in order to increase its legitimacy and credibility with Western governments, Islamic Relief deemphasized its Islamic identity. Islamic Relief faces a legitimacy – and credibility – trap. As an Islamic agency operating in the West it is a moral suspect in Western eyes, and as a Western-based agency operating in the Islamic world, it is a moral suspect in the eyes of the local population – and the more it is identified with the West and Western values the less legitimate and credible it becomes to local, Muslim populations. A Western "seal of approval" has its price and, in the worst of all possible worlds, both Western and Islamic societies may see Islamic Relief as something akin to a "double agent."

A high-ranking staff member told a revealing story. A staff member, who presented Islamic Relief's work to a large gathering of potential donors at a conference in Saudi Arabia, emphasized that Islamic Relief does not discriminate on the basis of religion and spoke of its support for an orphanage in Bosnia that cares for both Christian and Muslim children. One member of the audience rose and condemned Islamic Relief for helping people who had been killing Muslims. At the end of the conference a major donor wrote a check for the aid agencies at

---

[25] Interview by Barnett and Stein, January 14, 2010.

the conference, but insisted that Islamic Relief did not deserve any of the money because of its "impartiality." Virtue in the eyes of Western donors may not be virtue in the eyes of all Muslim donors.

In order to balance these pressures, Islamic Relief carefully calibrates what it does. It highlights its Islamic identity when speaking to Muslim audiences. Islamic Relief will wait until it feels completely accepted by the local population before partnering with a Western agency.[26] It also seeks the approval of religious authorities, especially when it is working on new and sensitive issues.[27] As it moves more deeply into development, it tries to identify how and in what ways its work on the ground is connected to the Quran. It works closely with the European Council of Senior Scholars and Yussuf Qaradani, a widely respected Islamic scholar working in the United States. In 2007, the Department for International Development (DfID) in the United Kingdom awarded Islamic Relief a grant of £130,000 to begin an international consultation on Islam and HIV/AIDS, a taboo subject in the Muslim world. The funding from an international donor was essential if Islamic Relief wanted to work on this kind of large policy issue; individual donors will contribute to specific projects such as health care and education, but generally will not support large-scale policy-relevant work. Nor was it likely that individual Muslim donors would contribute to a project as sensitive as HIV/AIDS. Yet institutional funding from Britain required Islamic Relief to formulate policy positions and initiate dialogues on a very difficult issue (Khan and van Eekelen 2008).

To develop an HIV/AIDS program, Islamic Relief had to communicate with the Muslim world as a Muslim aid agency. In November 2007, Islamic Relief initiated a five-day international conference on

---

[26] Interview by Thaut, Islamic Relief Worldwide, Birmingham, UK, 28 July 2008; Barnett and Stein, January 14, 2010.

[27] The importance of its commitment to professionalism and accountability is noted in the following example told by a staff member: when the religious identity of Islamic Relief caused one of the largest donors to fear that beneficiaries in Darfur would view Islamic Relief as associated with the Sudanese government, the donor ultimately changed its mind when it observed the work that Islamic Relief carried out with the United Nations Office for the Coordination of Humanitarian Affairs (OCHA). In such cases, Islamic Relief reduced the negative perceptions of the agency by demonstrating its commitment to the Code of Conduct and the Sphere guidelines.

Islam and HIV/AIDS and began to develop an action plan. Islamic Relief needs to be legitimated by Islamic scholars and leaders in the Muslim world to open the door to broader projects (Alterman *et al.* 2005: 13; Khan and van Eekelen 2008). "When you have the acceptance of the local religious leaders, you can have access to communities … respected Muslim scholars are influential," confirmed an Islamic Relief regional program coordinator.[28]

Conclusion

Virtue is in the eye of the beholder. Because it is, there is always ambiguity as to who counts as a virtuous actor and whether and when virtue translates into legitimacy and credibility. We argue that there are no automatic processes of translation and that context shapes the construction of both legitimacy and credibility. Dependent on community practices and politics, an organization that makes a claim to virtue may well have to make a considerable effort to defend its claim. Asserting its virtue may not be enough. Particularly on issues of procedural legitimacy and credibility – its capacity and intention to deliver what it promises – even a virtuous actor may have to send costly signals. This is particularly the case when organizations speak to multiple audiences, with different identities, needs, and interests. All virtuous organizations cross boundaries, and while they may claim that their virtues are timeless and universal, they are nevertheless bound by time and place. What is significant, moreover, is that the claim of a humanitarian agency to be virtuous is dependent on substantive and procedural legitimacy, and on effectiveness. Two decades ago claims to virtue would not have been dependent on particular systems of accountability, transparency, codes of conduct, and outcome measures, but today the virtue of many humanitarian organizations, especially those that operate in the West, does. What constitutes credibility and procedural legitimacy has its time and place.

This is the story of Islamic Relief. It is deeply concerned about its legitimacy and, consequently, about its credibility with Western governments. Largely as a result of the special time and place in which it was created and developed, Islamic Relief gave particular attention to

---

[28] Interview by Thaut, Islamic Relief Worldwide, Birmingham, UK, July 28, 2008.

one dimension – its procedural legitimacy, especially the transparency of its financial flows. It invested less effort and resources into program evaluation than some of its counterparts because its overwhelming challenge was to demonstrate its credentials in an environment that was suspicious of what Islamic charities did with the funds that they raised. In a deliberate and strategic response, consistent with the predictions of Gourevitch and Lake, Islamic Relief sent very costly signals to enhance its credibility in the West.

That was not all that Islamic Relief did. Islamic Relief tried to demonstrate its common interests by promoting autonomous governance structures, professionalizing, stressing its technical proficiency, and associating with established NGOs. Islamic Relief did all this and more to reinforce its credibility. It also attempted to shore up its legitimacy by emphasizing how its values are universal and beyond reproach.

Islamic Relief, like many aid agencies, has invested heavily in improving its procedures. One of the striking features of the monitoring mechanisms that exist in the humanitarian sector is that the information they produce seems to be less important than that these systems exist. We are at least partly in the realm of symbolic politics. Constructing symbols requires effort and resources, and aid agencies have spent considerable energy trying to develop systems of management, transparency, and accountability to demonstrate that they have no secrets. At times these systems do help agencies to learn about what works and to improve how they do what they do, generally the defining attribute of credibility. Yet part of the value of these exercises seems to be to convince watching audiences that their willingness to engage in these performative practices is prima facie evidence that they are virtuous. Importantly, their virtue is established mainly through financial practices – not program outcomes.

In part because the virtue is in the symbolic practices, Islamic Relief has strong incentives to monitor its own performance and provide transparent results, more so than secular humanitarian agencies. Nevertheless, it is difficult to judge how credible its monitoring and transparency are. It is, after all, self-monitoring. But it certainly is putting significant economic, human, and political resources into making transparent its financial transactions. The problem is not unique to Islamic Relief but generic to the humanitarian sector, a carryover from the time when humanitarians proclaimed their virtue and were widely believed. Virtue is no longer enough. In the case of Islamic Relief, precisely because its commitment to monitoring, transparency, and evaluation is deeply self-interested, it cannot demonstrate that its self-monitoring is credible. That, too, is a generic problem in the humanitarian sector. There are no monitors to monitor the self-monitors.

Making this investment of resources to enhance procedural legitimacy may help reduce the legitimacy crisis of Islamic Relief with one audience, but at some cost with another. The legitimacy dilemma, as is true of all dilemmas, is not easy to solve. Efforts to increase procedural legitimacy in the eyes of Western official donors by associating more strongly with Western partner agencies may have a negative impact on substantive legitimacy with the local community. How can agencies navigate this dilemma? There are no obvious answers. Arguably Western governments and institutional donors are interested in procedural legitimacy and accountability, whereas Muslim donors, beneficiaries, leaders, or governments tend to privilege the substantive legitimacy conferred by Islamic religious identity and principles. Accentuating one might come at the expense of the other, given the current political climate. In the contest over whose perception matters, or whose opinion counts, most of the largest international aid agencies have demonstrated time and again that they care more about what their funders in the West think, about whether they are credible to the large institutional donors. This does not mean that they ignore their recipients; they don't and they clearly do care about those they help. Nevertheless, there is no way to avoid these legitimacy and credibility dilemmas. How humanitarian agencies resolve these dilemmas depends very much on who has the political, financial, and symbolic capital.

It is arguable that Islamic Relief and other aid agencies would be better served by an independent, arm's-length monitoring system in which it had no choice but to participate. Were such a system in place, Islamic Relief could avoid many of the difficult tradeoffs between dimensions of credibility, procedural legitimacy, and substantive legitimacy that we have examined in this chapter. It could explain to its Muslim donors and beneficiaries that it had no choice but to submit itself to monitoring. It could escape some, but not all, of the most difficult legitimacy traps that it currently faces. Islamic Relief faces conflicts between dimensions of its substantive legitimacy, conflicts that go far beyond monitoring and speak directly to who it is. When it refuses to discriminate on the basis of religion or ethnicity in the assistance it provides, that is who Islamic Relief is. That commitment to non-discrimination is part of its identity, a part which conflicts with other dimensions of its identity and legitimacy. There is no simple answer to these kinds of conflicts. These legitimacy dilemmas may be the fate of humanitarian organizations that try to bridge cultures, religions, and worlds and serve others even while they serve their own. These agencies run the risk of being seen as moral suspects in all the communities they seek to serve.

7 Monitoring repayment in online peer-to-peer lending

CRAIG MCINTOSH

Introduction

Credit markets present a particularly well-defined credibility problem because outcomes are transparent (repayment), and both borrower and lender must sustain a reputation in order to permit the leveraging of capital. Institutions such as credit bureaus and credit ratings agencies exist in order to provide measures of the quality of borrowers and of banks. In the new NGO-driven microfinance lending sector, this well-defined problem becomes more complex because investors seek a double bottom line, pursuing social as well as financial gains. This introduces a fundamentally different form of credibility problem, one related more broadly to the humanitarian NGO problem of assuring donors of the social efficacy of their interventions. Nonprofit microfinance institutions (MFIs) solicit direct donations or investments from private individuals, typically using social benefits to the borrowers as motivation. Recent evaluation studies that have failed to find a transformative impact of microfinance have raised questions about these claims (Banerjee *et al.* 2009; Karlan and Zinman 2009), and complicated the question of whether we should think of microfinance as a financial service or a humanitarian activity.

Peer-to-peer (P2P) microfinance is a new modality that has emerged in recent years, allowing private parties to provide lending capital directly through the Internet to borrowers in developing countries (Bruett 2007; Flannery 2007). The institution is created by linking local NGOs (developing-country MFIs) with an international NGO monitor/fundraiser (the P2P institution). The best-established microfinance P2P lender in the United States is Kiva.org. To use it, individuals go online to view details on the loan terms and business

The author is grateful to Bryan Diaz and Summer Starr for their excellent research assistance on this project.

investment of an individual entrepreneur in the developing world, as well as a picture and some personal information of the entrepreneur, and the repayment performance and financial details of the MFI sourcing the actual loan on the ground. Loans made through Kiva are zero interest both for the lender and for Kiva itself, while the loan to the entrepreneur is made at the MFI's typical rates. The entrepreneur then repays the MFI and the MFI repays the P2P institution, and the original lender can then either reloan the principal or donate it to Kiva's operations. The five-year-old organization has lent $100 million to 200,000 borrowers with repayment rates of more than 98 percent.

Kiva serves as a particularly interesting case in the context of this volume because it is both a monitor of other NGOs and a quasi-humanitarian NGO with a need to maintain its credibility with a donor base. It represents a clear example of a network of NGOs creating a set of private, voluntary standards that permit a completely new form of quasi-humanitarian activity. This complex, high-tech network enables lending between private individuals across developed and developing countries in the absence of any domestic or international regulator who could enforce the credit contract. The mechanism is, therefore, entirely dependent on the credibility of Kiva itself. Kiva's system for establishing the financial credibility of its NGO microfinance collaborators is simple and successful, but some aspects of the humanitarian credibility of Kiva have been under attack. David Roodman of the Center for Global Development used data posted on Kiva's own website to criticize their operations, showing that more than 95 percent of the loans presented on Kiva have, in fact, already been disbursed to the clients by the time they are put online. This chapter documents a specific case in which an allegation of misrepresentation was made against the organization, and the concrete ways in which it responded in order to maintain its credibility. As we shall show, Kiva's primary response – similar to that of Islamic Relief when its credibility was similarly challenged (see Chapter 6, this volume) – was to increase its already high level of transparency.

Yet, two additional issues are raised here in terms of the credibility of P2P microfinance. First, by comparing the default rates of the loans posted on Kiva to the overall rates in the MFIs that issue the loans we demonstrate that the MFIs are paying off loans through Kiva even when the underlying loan is in default. The very robust MFI scoring system that Kiva has devised makes this an entirely rational response, but this suggests that the loan is really made to the MFI and not to the ultimate borrower. Next, we argue that the types of clients who are posted on Kiva are very likely to have received loans in the absence of the P2P channel. This in no way negates the role of P2P venues in increasing access to finance for MFIs, but does again imply that the apparent personal link between the donor and a specific client is mostly illusory. These three issues (pre-financing of loans, MFIs paying off defaulted loans, and redirection of credit) raise complex questions as to the nature of the claims being made by this NGO intermediary and the ways in which the credibility of such institutions should be evaluated.

These issues are germane because P2P microfinance appeals precisely by offering a very personalized form of NGO activity: the targets of Kiva's activities are the individual recipients of the micro-loans, and the ultimate principal is the public. The specific attraction of such a vehicle to potential donors is precisely the decentralized, human-to-human nature of the link (as compared to investing in a social enterprise fund, giving money to an MFI, or giving political support to higher aid spending, for example).[1] This personalized link, however, passes through the hands of two layers of NGO intermediary. We can think of the operations of Kiva in terms of being two sequential principal–agent games: Kiva delegating the monitoring of borrowers to local MFIs, and the lender delegating monitoring of the MFIs to Kiva. Both of these PA problems must be solved simultaneously in order for the P2P channel to be fully incentive-compatible. To the extent that P2P microfinance is a financial service, this two-layered contract functions spectacularly well. At the same time, the very success of the Kiva scoring mechanism in generating high MFI repayment creates a tension with the premise that one peer is extending credit to another.

This in turn raises complex questions about institutional reputation and the exact nature of the claim being made by Kiva: are they saying that people *like* the ones on the website will have credit extended to

[1] Claims made by this NGO are likely to be credible because of a common interest between the NGO and its audience (again quite personalized in the husband-and-wife Flannery team, founders of Kiva), and because of a very clear set of penalties established by Kiva.

them if you use the P2P channel, or are they making the claim that the *individual* shown on the website will be extended a loan *if and only if it* is funded through Kiva? Despite the highly formalized system of private standards used by Kiva to score its partner MFIs, the credibility of claims such as these will have to be established with the general public in a manner quite typical of the broader set of NGO institutions considered in this book.

On the one hand, this chapter documents a surprising success story. Faced by a delegation problem (lender/donors in one country need to monitor the attributes and behavior of borrowers in another) and the absence of a legal mechanism (because credit bureaus don't exist in the borrower's country), an interlinking set of NGOs spring up to meet the need. The umbrella NGO seeks to be transparent and therefore makes data on its activities freely available, and when a watchdog uses that data to criticize the credibility of the NGO the institution responds immediately, altering the nature of the claims made. At a deeper level, however, it is a cautionary tale about the way that the self-interested incentives of institutional players drive the actual functioning of NGO monitoring institutions. The Kiva monitoring system works admirably as a financial contract, but the lifeblood of the organization appears to be in the personal, individual nature of the link it creates between lender and borrower. This chapter probes the extent to which a quasi-humanitarian organization such as Kiva can be credible to its audience if its financial claims are robust but the human connection underlying its appeal is largely illusory. If its practices were fully disclosed, it might threaten the perception of common interests between Kiva and its donors, make it more difficult to build bonds around common values, and further undermine its credibility (see Chapter 1, this volume). It is not clear that the Kiva audience is affected by these criticisms, but it is clear those who run Kiva are concerned enough to have altered their presentation and framing of their activities.

Criticism of the timing of Kiva's loans, and the response

David Roodman of the Center for Global Development wrote a short blog which ended up being very widely circulated, illustrating that the large majority of Kiva clients actually had their loans disbursed to them *before* the loans were officially funded by Kiva investors.[2] This criticism triggered a response from Kiva and an alteration in the claims made on their website, which is in itself a fascinating window into the strengths and weaknesses of NGO monitoring. In his original critique, Roodman makes the following statement:

Kiva is the path-breaking, fast-growing person-to-person microlending site. It works this way: Kiva posts pictures and stories of people needing loans. You give your money to Kiva. Kiva sends it to a microlender. The lender makes the loan to a person you choose. He or she ordinarily repays. You get your money back with no interest. It's like eBay for microcredit.

You knew that, right? Well guess what: you're wrong, and so is Kiva's diagram. Less than 5 percent of Kiva loans are disbursed *after* they are listed and funded on Kiva's site. Just today, for example, Kiva listed a loan for Phong Mut in Cambodia and at this writing only $25 of the needed $800 has been raised. But you needn't worry about whether Phong Mut will get the loan because it was disbursed last month. And if she defaults, you might not hear about it: the intermediating microlender MAXIMA might cover for her in order to keep its Kiva-listed repayment rate high.

In short, the person-to-person donor-to-borrower connections created by Kiva are partly fictional. I suspect that most Kiva users do not realize this. Yet Kiva prides itself on transparency.[3]

Roodman does not provide any detailed statistics on the nature of the pre-lending problem, but he posts an extract of data from the Kiva website that can be used to form a visual representation of the problem. The Kiva data posted by Roodman provides information on 8,204 individual loans from eighty-seven MFIs that were posted on the website between August 22 and October 1, 2009. In the following frequency plots, zero represents the day on which a loan is posted to the Kiva website. While it is the case that fewer than 5 percent of the loans are disbursed after having been posted on Kiva, it is also the case that fewer than 5 percent of the loans are disbursed more than a month prior to being posted. Hence while the pre-funding phenomenon is pervasive, it is temporally very limited. In the bottom panel

---

[2] David Roodman, "Kiva Is Not Quite What It Seems," October 2, 2009, available at http://blogs.cgdev.org/open_book/2009/10/kiva-is-not-quite-what-it-seems.php.

[3] *Ibid.*

we see that more than 50 percent of the loans posted are funded in the first day and 95 percent are funded within two weeks.

Roodman illustrates the importance of (and potential abuses of) personalization using the "save a child" campaigns sponsored by numerous international NGOs over several decades. He describes an investigative exposé run by the *Chicago Tribune* in 1998 that documented patchy or no benefits accruing to sponsored children, and at the more extreme end of the spectrum, forged holiday letters sent from sponsored children who had died several years previously. In trying to understand whether this personalized link is important, Roodman says:

Undoubtedly some hard-sell charlatanry was at work. But the problem was deeper than that: a tension between creating the psychological experience of connection that raised money and the realities of fighting poverty. Often the fairest and most effective way to help poor children is by building assets for the whole community such as schools, clinics, and wells. Often charities contract with locals to build these things. Often things go wrong because of corruption, bad luck, or arrogance among outsiders thinking they know what will work. In the best cases, charities learn from failure. All these factors break the connection between giving and benefit, sponsor and child. But admitting that would have threatened the funding base.[4]

This blog received widespread discussion on online forums such as the Development Finance listserve run by the Ohio State University. The furor was sufficient to provoke a response from Matt Flannery, the CEO of Kiva.

Most of Kiva's users have very casual knowledge of microfinance. In fact a large percentage of them had never heard of microfinance before Kiva and had never donated or lent to an international cause. This presents a major challenge in terms of simultaneously educating them and empowering them to make an impact in our field.

Our approach to this challenge has been to provide a very easy way to engage users, and provide a wealth of information to them as they become more curious. The oversimplified nature of our homepage reflects this broad strategy. Certainly the Kiva homepage does not describe the nuances of microfinance or Kiva's approach. In fact, it largely ignores the details.

---

[4] *Ibid.*

Days between listing on Kiva and disbursement to client

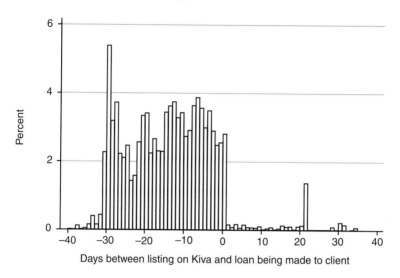

Days to be funded on Kiva

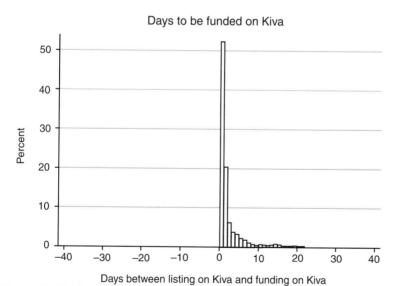

Figure 7.1 Timing of lending, posting, and online funding through Kiva

However, it is our intention to provide every last detail of the mechanics of Kiva to those curious users. My hope is that, for those that care to delve deeper, users can learn all they need to know – and more – by looking at our website alone.[5]

Flannery explains the pre-financing of loans on Kiva as a phenomenon that emerged over the course of time. Early MFIs did indeed wait for funding from Kiva to disburse, but as time passed they worked with larger and more liquid MFIs, and these partners saw that the loans were funded so quickly once posted on Kiva that there was no point in waiting for them to be posted before making the loans (the figures presented above confirm this).

Perhaps Flannery's most interesting rejoinder in terms of thinking through the long-term viability of NGOs as monitoring organizations is the following:

Further, I want to assert that Kiva doesn't fear that complete honesty would undermine growth! In my humble experience, I've learned that honesty creates stronger bonds between the organization and its constituencies. Time after time, this lesson has been reinforced, and it is a lesson which affects many operational decisions within the organization to this day.[6]

Here, however, his reponse may be disingenuous: while it is certainly the case that the long-term viability of Kiva as an intermediary depends on a reputation for veracity, it is also the case that a large part of the rapid growth of Kiva relative to the more unpersonalized vehicles through which private parties in rich countries can fund microfinance is precisely the appearance of a direct human link. Hence, it is far from clear whether Kiva will grow more quickly in the coming years through being straightforward about the real link with the MFIs or through continuing to market an appearance of individualization that is not strictly correct.

Kiva did, however, undertake a redesign of their website that attempts to clarify the details of the chain that connects "peer to peer" through their service. It is interesting to compare the old flow chart with the new one.

[5] Matt Flannery, "Matt Flannery, Kiva CEO and Co-Founder, Replies," October 12, 2009, available at http://blogs.cgdev.org/open_book/2009/10/matt-flannery-kiva-ceo-and-co-founder-replies.php.
[6] *Ibid.*

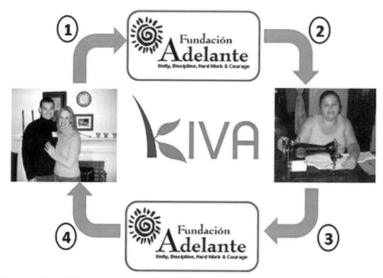

Figure 7.2a Old Kiva website flow charts

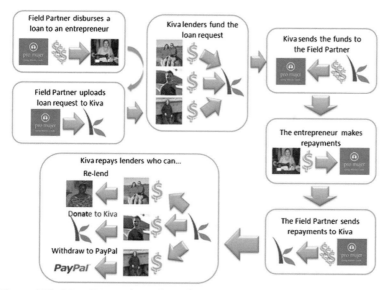

Figure 7.2b New Kiva website flow chart

Several substantive changes appear here. First, the new graphic reverses the relative timing of disbursement and posting of the loan. Second, the new graphic makes much clearer the central role played by the MFI in collecting and relaying payments. Hence the response to Roodman's criticism seems to have come primarily in amplifying the apparent role of the MFIs and in dropping any explicit claims that the funding of the loan on Kiva preceeds disbursement.

Two primary questions arise in thinking through the timing issue. The first is, should we care? Flannery points out that the MFIs themselves exist in a competitive, customer-focused market and hence have no interest in making borrowers wait for credit when their competitors will not. Flannery does not make the additional, relatively obvious point that requiring MFI field staff to make two visits to disburse will impose substantial additional costs on the lender, thereby decreasing the benefits of using Kiva financing and decreasing the sustainability of the organization if they do use Kiva. Hence the issue of having loans pre-financed by a time period rarely exceeding a month may appear relatively unimportant (and indeed efficient) in the grand scheme of things.

Having introduced the current debate over the credibility of Kiva's claims, we now formalize the reputation problem in credit markets in order to argue that the "target" of Kiva's operations are not in a simple way the personalities viewed on the website at the time that lending decisions are made. We begin by tying the monitoring problem explicitly to the institution of credit bureaus, and describe in some detail the way that Kiva's internal monitoring system works. With this structure established, we explore the specific types of clients likely to be newly lent to as a result of the expansion of P2P microfinance versus those shown on the website, and show that a disconnect exists. We then consider the strategic incentives created by the monitoring systems in terms of default, and show that this implies that the true "target" of the use of Kiva is not the pictured borrowers but the NGOs from whom they receive credit.

Formalizing the critique of Kiva: the role of credit market information

Microfinance lenders typically use joint liability (Besley and Coate 1995; Ghatak and Guinnane 1999), dynamic incentives (Morduch 1999), and social capital as collateral in order to attempt to compel repayment on uncollateralized loans. NGO MFIs lend to loss-making market segments that would be unserved in a purely profit-driven market, and these financial losses are justified by the social impact of the activity. The sources of funding for microfinance (whether private donations, support from development agencies, or concessional loans from development banks) typically have at least partially humanitarian objectives.[7] To achieve its "double bottom line," then, a microfinance lender must perform both as a financial institution and as a development institution.[8]

The signal formal institution for screening and monitoring in lending markets is a credit bureau (Jappelli and Pagano 1993; Padilla and Pagano 1997, 2000). Bureaus expand uncollateralized lending because they strengthen the ability to punish through the scoring mechanism rather than through seizure of assets. In terms of their organizational structure, such information sharing systems may be public (credit registries) or private (credit bureaus) (Luoto *et al.* 2007). Public registries may contain broader information on utility payments, legal actions, or liens, but private bureaus offer sophisticated services tailored exactly to the needs of private-sector lenders. Most middle-income countries have for years featured some degree of credit reporting on individuals who participate in the formal banking system, but until recently this represented a small and stable share of the population. With the explosion of microfinance and other "bottom of the pyramid" lending, however, formal repayment information is now being collected for a large new entrepreneurial class. The creation of credit bureaus to cover these markets, and particularly the integration of such bureaus with well-established, pre-existing commercial bank bureaus, therefore promises to be an avenue toward building the "missing middle" of the credit ladder (de Janvry *et al.* 2010; McIntosh and Wydick 2005).

In developed-country contexts, the presence of dense credit histories and real-time credit reporting systems allow "reputation" to be captured very succinctly in a credit score, most commonly the FICO

---

[7] An estimated US $5 billion has flowed from the developed world to microfinance lenders over the past decade.

[8] Despite the unarguable success of MFIs as financial institutions, the past year has seen the release of several careful studies indicating that the socioeconomic impact of microfinance is likely to be modest (Banerjee *et al.* 2009; Karlan and Zinman 2009).

score.[9] In the dense US credit reporting environment, P2P lending markets such as Prosper.com are enabled by good credit information in two ways. First, the bureau reduces adverse selection by preventing those with bad prior reputations from getting access to P2P loans. Second, once a loan is given, the presence of credit reporting incentivizes high repayment by linking credit availability from all lenders to the repayment on the P2P loan, and thereby combats moral hazard. The tremendous punitive capacity of scores such as the FICO score in the United States allow countries with strong information systems to dispense entirely with the intermediation of banks: P2P lending venues such as Proper.com are able to offer limited liability lending to complete strangers by private individuals.

For a borrower located in a developing country, however, few avenues may exist through which to signal quality to prospective lenders. Particularly when these prospective lenders are in a different country and have poor information-gathering capacity, the set of feasible contracts may feature such severe asymmetric information as to preclude any transfers at all. If anything, the importance of screening and monitoring are greater in pro-poor credit products such as microfinance lending than in mortgage lending, where the collateral on the loan should make the loan self-policing. Microfinance loans are "limited liability" loans because the lender is only able to force the borrower to surrender assets worth a fraction of the loan in the case of default, and so borrowers are not fully financially liable for the loans they take (Besley and Coate 1995; Ghatak 1999; Stiglitz 1990). In this environment lenders need to maintain other kinds of incentives (such as group lending or the denial of future credit) in order to compel repayment (Wydick 1999). Over the course of the past decade microfinance markets have evolved overlapping formal and informal institutions that serve to screen and monitor (de Janvry *et al.* 2010; Navajas *et al.* 2003).

Microfinance P2P websites can be distinguished strategically by the fact that they do not link to any independent source of information on the reputation of the borrower. They may or may not attempt to create some internal reputation for the borrower, but fundamentally the screening and monitoring required to conduct uncollateralized

---

[9] The US credit reporting system is dominated by three firms: TransUnion, Experian, and Equifax.

lending are left to the microfinance lender alone. P2P lending appears to be inherently limited liability in the sense that the infrastructure required to collect and liquidate collateral is complex and difficult to delegate, and therefore cannot be conducted online between strangers in a cost-effective manner. This combination of features focuses the strategic incentives in microfinance P2P lending on the local microfinance lender, the only party that can credibly collect from locals as well as credibly contract in a dynamic sense with outside entities.

To overcome their informational disadvantage, P2P credit markets that connect rich-world lenders to poor-world borrowers must look for creative ways to score institutions and to enforce contracts with them once money has changed hands. What has emerged with rich-to-poor P2P sites such as Kiva.org is a multi-tiered system of credit scoring. At the most basic level, these new systems are working. From its startup in 2005, Kiva.org has reached 200,000 borrowers and lent almost $100 million. Despite this breakneck growth, Kiva has an overall default rate of less than 2 percent and a delinquency rate of less than two-tenths of a percent among the lenders currently using the system (relative to typical microfinance default rates of 2–5 percent).[10] The premier US-based P2P lending outlet is Prosper.com, which has disbursed almost $200 million, and reports a ninety-day delinquency rate of around 2 percent on all credit classes of loans.[11]

Kiva offers loans only through in-country MFIs, and Kiva scores the MFI on the institution's repayment record to Kiva borrowers, thereby generating strong incentives for the MFI to control default even though the individual carries little or no reputational capital in the system. Kiva does not currently score the individuals requesting loans. Rather, Kiva scores its field partners with a five-star rating system. This is an amalgamation of reputation scores from third parties such as MIX (The Microfinance Information Exchange),[12] financial information such as current portfolio size and risk, audits conducted by Kiva through local auditing agencies and journal entries about borrowers written by Kiva Fellows. Kiva mostly uses their rating system to distinguish newer partners who do not have an established track record and may not be found on international microfinance indices

---

[10] www.kivadata.org/summary.html.
[11] www.prosper.com/invest/performance.aspx.
[12] www.mixmarket.org.

(like MIX) from their more established counterparts.[13] The most common form of punishment is the closing of the account.

Only one case has been documented where a Kiva rating was lowered rather than closing the account. This was due to a portfolio-wide delinquency in payments. MIFEX, a savings and loan cooperative (credit union) located in Guayaquil, Ecuador, specializes in agricultural loans and has collection periods that do not align well with Kiva's system. Kiva disclosed that "MIFEX has recently come up against liquidity challenges that have affected their repayment performance on Kiva."[14] This was the cause for the demotion from three stars to one star. More commonly, Kiva has had to punish their field partners by closing their account for more serious violations, most commonly incorrect use of funds or insolvency.[15] Five cases have been reported where Kiva has had to take such action. Four were for misuse of funds and one was for insolvency. These violations were uncovered during routine field partner audits.

Individual microfinance borrowers in developing countries have long-term relationships with the MFI and repay under joint liability contracts that tie future credit access both for the individual and the group to the individual's current repayment, thereby generating strong incentives to repay even though these loans are typically uncollateralized. The MFI, in turn, forms a long-term relationship with the P2P site, and the future access of the entire MFI to zero-interest Kiva credit is tied to the repayment performance of each loan made to the MFI. Hence loans are repaid in this four-step chain despite the fact that no party has a credible relationship with an organization more than one link above them in the chain. That is to say, an MFI borrower would not repay Kiva without the MFI in between them, and the MFI would not repay the private "lender" of funds without Kiva in between them.

We can represent the flow of information and monitoring in the following way (see Figure 7.3).

---

[13] www.mixmarket.org.

[14] MIFEX Partner Page: www.kiva.org/about/aboutPartner?id=7.

[15] Cases of misuse: Seed: www.kiva.org/about/aboutPartner?id=32.WITEP: www.kiva.org/about/aboutPartner?id=11.AE&I: www.kiva.org/about/aboutPartner?id=53.RAFODE: www.kiva.org/about/aboutPartner?id=33.WEEC: www.kiva.org/about/aboutPartner?id=6.

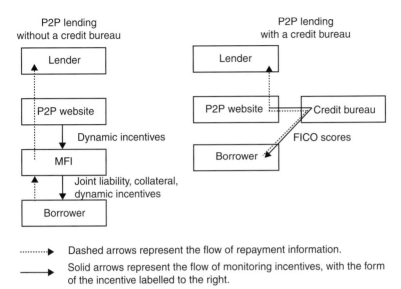

Figure 7.3 Flow chart of money and information in P2P lending

Information on individual repayment does not need to reach the lender in a microfinance P2P system (and to our knowledge no such P2P lenders report on the repayment performance of the individual borrower). Without a bureau, only the MFI has the capacity to monitor and enforce repayment on the borrower, and so borrower-level repayment information is irrelevant to the P2P website's ability to maintain the contract. What is necessary is that the MFI's reputation is at stake with the P2P website, and hence the mechanism credibly delegates the responsibility for monitoring onto the only agent able to carry it out. This system is thus fundamentally one of a relationship between institutions, and the bottom-level link of MFI to borrower exists independent of the other links created by the mechanism. The presence of a credit bureau, on the other hand, confers upon the P2P website the ability to directly monitor and punish the behavior of the borrower, and so the P2P mechanism is engaged in a fully individualized contract with the recipient of the loan.

Seen from this perspective, only where a bureau exists can we really refer to such lending as "P2P." Where we require a local lender as intermediary to issue and monitor the loan then such lending might better be called "P2MFI" because the actual repayment of the individual who gets the loan becomes irrelevant and only the MFI's overall record of repayment to the website intermediary determines future access to capital. The critical repercussion of this monitoring regime is that it delinks the apparent "target" of the use of Kiva (the person whose picture is shown on the website) from the actual target, namely the MFI itself. We now investigate in more depth two ways in which this delinkage takes place.

Client selection and who gets listed on Kiva

The fact that a borrower gets a loan funded through Kiva does not imply that the borrower would not have gotten a loan in the absence of the P2P NGO. In this sense P2P microfinance does not necessarily *cause* credit to be extended to all the borrowers funded by their activities. It is entirely possible that there is a new client to whom the MFI would never have made a loan before and who they find knowing that they will be able to get them funded on Kiva. Indeed, the very rapid funding of loans indicates precisely that the MFI would be rational to pre-fund the loan even if it wouldn't have made the loan without access to Kiva. Hence Kiva can be causal to the creation of a new loan even with pre-financing. Conversely, even if the loan is disbursed after posting on Kiva, it appears quite likely on inspection that many, if not most, of the clients listed on Kiva would have received funding from the MFI even if the MFI did not use Kiva. Therefore pre-funding and the extent to which Kiva funding *causes* a specific loan to be made are logically distinct concepts.

In order to present a very simple framework in which to consider this question of who would have been funded in the absence of Kiva, we present a stylized model of microfinance lending. Kiva neither pays interest to individuals using its website, nor does it charge interest to the MFIs. Hence it represents a free source of lending capital, except for the (not insubstantial) fixed costs per loan imposed by providing the photographs and narratives required for posting. For an MFI to choose to use Kiva, the P2P portal must represent a new and lower-cost source of capital. Our model considers how this fall in the costs of capital alters selection in a credit market.

We assume that MFIs are interest rate price-takers in local lending markets, and that every potential client wants to borrow one unit of capital. The profitability of a given individual for the MFI is therefore simply a function of the repayment probability and the cost of capital. The lender uses a scoring model to convert a set of borrower-level observable attributes X_i into the predicted probability of repayment, given by $p_i(X_i)$. While it is most straightforward to think of this score as a formalized quantity such as a FICO score in a market that features centralized bureaus and scoring services, it may represent a more informal reputation in markets based more heavily on personal relationships and reputational capital.[16]

An MFI has access to capital at a cost c, and it then lends it at a rate r, and so the problem of the lender is to maximize the sum of profits across all potential borrowers, or

$$Max\sum_i \left[p_i(X_i)(1+r) - (1+c) \right].$$

The MFI lender will give loans to all borrowers with positive expected profits, and the lowest-profit individual given a loan is the person on whom the lender expects exactly to break even. We can solve for the identity of this "break-even borrower,"

$$\underline{p}(X_i) = \frac{1+c}{1+r}.$$

Beginning from this market equilibrium, we can now model the effects of access capital from a P2P institution. The MFI will only use the P2P capital if it is cheaper than the other sources of liquidity available, and so for all participating MFIs we assume that the P2P institution lowers the cost of capital from c^0 to c^1. Examining changes in the break-even borrower, we see that $\frac{d\underline{p}}{dc} = \frac{1}{1+r} > 0$. This says that as the cost of capital falls, the MFI will be willing to lend to an individual with lower expected returns, and so $\underline{p}^0 > \underline{p}^1$. While the MFI may *use* P2P capital to lend to people that it would have lent to before, and while the *profit* from lending to those people may

---

[16] Note that we can considerably broaden the scope of the argument by thinking of $p(X_i)$ as being a social weighting function in microfinance markets, where gender-based or pro-poor targeting will cause clients other than the most profitable to be thought of as desirable in the lender's objective function.

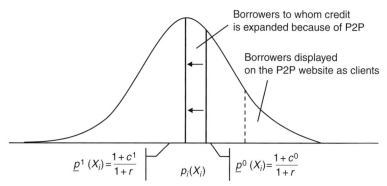

Figure 7.4 Impacts of P2P credit on MFI market access

increase as a result of having lower-cost capital, the causal effect of this new liquidity source is to expand access to a group of individuals less reliable as clients than those that were being served before.

We can think of the MFI as a lower-tier lender and the loan targeting process of the P2P site as a higher-tier lender. The simplest assumption to make is that the selection criteria of these two different layers of lenders are the same, meaning that a client who is attractive to one is also attractive to the other. In this case, it is the values with the highest value of $p(X_i)$ that will be most attractive to list on the P2P site. This creates a disconnect between the individual identities of those represented on the P2P site and those causally brought in to the market by the use of P2P credit. Figure 7.4 draws the density function of $p(X_i)$ to illustrate the tension.

The introduction of less expensive P2P financing pushes the break-even borrower down from $\underline{p}^0$ to $\underline{p}^1$, and hence brings a new set of borrowers into the MF marketplace. For each loan given, the MFI is asked to provide a specific borrower to the P2P institution, and particularly if these borrowers are individually scored then the MFI begins from the right-hand tail of its repayment distribution in selecting which borrowers to display on the website. Because the number of clients must match, the density between $\underline{p}^0$ and $\underline{p}^1$ will equal the density to the right of the dashed vertical line, which represents the least reliable borrower that will appear on the website.

Hence, there is likely to be a disconnect between the types of people shown on P2P microfinance websites and the types of people who actually receive credit as a result of the existence of such P2P institutions. There is no direct causal claim of the type "we will not fund this person if their Kiva loan is not fully funded," and so as long as the picture recipient does in fact get a loan, then the contract stipulated on the website has been nominally fulfilled. An MFI that was, for example, expanding into new remote areas with marginal credit but posting only those nearby borrowers on whom it was easy to gather the information required by Kiva might never show on the website a borrower who would not have received credit in the absence of Kiva.

Default in a P2P microfinance system

A large literature describes the "joint liability" contracts used by microfinance lenders. Such contracts are designed to coerce repayment in the absence of collateral by making future lending to any individual member of a group conditional upon successful repayment of the group loan. The idea is that borrowers are then forced to cross-insure, and also have incentives to monitor each other's actions and do what they can to induce their fellow members to repay. In this way the group carries a reputation which drives incentives to select and insure. Again, an analogy exists for the actions of an MFI lender once an organization like Kiva begins to score repayment.

The incentive to cross-insure takes on an unusual dimension with P2P loans, because normal loans to an MFI are made to the institution, which can then deal with default on any specific sub-loan as it wishes. The other sources of lending liquidity available to the MFI are not linked to the underlying repayment performance of individual borrowers. A development bank making a loan to an MFI will care only about the repayment of the MFI to the bank, and not whether the sub-loans made by the MFI were repaid. Only P2P-linked credit attempts to make this link, and this introduces a very clear set of strategic incentives for the MFI, effectively pushing it to the extreme of perfectly insuring all repayment on sub-loans. Since the cost to the MFI of paying off a loan to Kiva on which there was actually default are very low (the average individual loan size is $650) and the benefits from retaining a good relationship with Kiva are large (the average partner MFI has acquired over $850,000 in lending capital from Kiva), the MFI simply pays off the loans when the borrower defaults.

Take a lender with a stable default rate who has set aside an adequate loan loss reserve. In any period default is predicted correctly on average and the reserve exactly covers default without changing the cost of capital. Default by the portion of the MFI's portfolio arising from P2P funding, however, carries an externality effect on the whole portfolio, because the rating of the MFI will fall, constricting access to P2P credit for the whole institution. If the punitive effect of default on a single group is larger than the cost of repaying that loan, the MFI will face a strictly lower cost of capital if it uses its loan loss reserve to repay all group loans made through the P2P with the loan loss reserve than if it allows these groups to be registered as defaulters. This says that there is a threshold punitive value of the MFI's reputation to the P2P beyond which the MFI will choose to provide P2P lenders with 100 percent repayment, regardless of the real performance of those loans. This suggests that no link at all exists between the underlying reliability of the clients and their apparent repayment performance to Kiva.

Kiva also features an option called "default protection," under which the MFI can explicitly choose to indicate that they will pay off the loan in case of default by the underlying borrower. There are no micro-data available at present for the use of the option at the loan level, but a visual inspection shows that even many MFIs not explicitly offering default protection nonetheless have exactly zero default through Kiva. Hence, whether this coverage is explicit or implicit, the scoring incentives are sufficiently strong to make all MFIs that use Kiva on an ongoing basis pay them off when they default.

One way of establishing this dissonance in default rates empirically is to compare the default rates reported by partner MFIs to Kiva with the overall institutional default rates of these same organizations as reported to the MixMarket, a microfinance website. Using the sample of loans from August to October 2009, the historical default rate on all Kiva loans is exactly zero for MFIs representing 99.89 percent of the loans made through Kiva, and 0.0103 for the sole institution that records any history of default in this time window. How do these default rates through Kiva compare to default in the MFIs as a whole? To answer this question, we can link the MFI-level information provided by Kiva with data from the MixMarket, the most comprehensive repository of performance statistics for microfinance lenders. We are able to match 105 of the 133 MFIs provided by Kiva to the

MixMarket, and we can compare repayment performance through the P2P channel to overall repayment in the MFI as a whole.

Table 7.1 uses the broader Kiva data reflecting the whole history of the institution, and provides average outcomes across MFIs, broken down by the partner risk rating of the MFI as rated by Kiva. The table provides clear evidence of the threshold effect suggested above; there is a clear break in performance in Kiva for those MFIs with two or fewer stars, where the average default rate is 12.3 percent, and those with three or more, where default is 0.01 percent. Interestingly, this does *not* correspond at all to the default rates found in those organizations overall, where the loan write-off rates are 1.29 percent and 1.55 percent, respectively. That is, institutional default is *higher* in the group of lenders who maintain virtually zero default to Kiva. Clearly, the Kiva contract of scoring MFIs is dividing them into two groups, one of which chooses to pay off loans to Kiva all the time no matter what, and the other of which ends up with higher default to Kiva than it does overall. The fact that the detailed lending data on the MFIs still given access to the website as of the August–October 2009 period shows only a single active MFI with any history of default indicates just how strongly Kiva is using dynamic incentives to select only for those lenders willing to protect Kiva's users against any default risk whatsoever.

Taking the analogy to the level of the lending institution, we see MFIs as "groups of groups," and the fact that P2P lending scores the institutions on loans made to its underlying clients induces exactly the same incentive to collectivize risk and cross-insure loans. The core difference is that, unlike in the informal and sometimes contentious environment of a microfinance group, the MFI provides a "firm" to centralize this decision. We would therefore expect that the ultimate success of MFIs at preventing any default from their underlying group loans to Kiva will be much higher than the success of the microfinance groups at inducing repayment among their individual members. Seen from this perspective, it is the tremendous *success* of P2P microfinance in placing repayment incentives on the parties below them in the funding chain that makes the link between the apparent and actual recipient of credit so tenuous.

Table 7.1. *Repayment performance through Kiva versus overall, MFI level*

		Kiva's "partner risk rating"					
		CLOSED	1 (worst)	2	3	4	5 (best)
Data from Kiva.org	Number of MFIs	22	8	4	27	44	28
	Default rate in Kiva (percent)	9.47	14.47	12.99	0.01	0	0
	Months using Kiva	38	34	26	15	21	27
Data from Mixmarket	Loans through Kiva	184,028	539,281	374,294	344,154	914,467	1,905,673
	MFI writeoff rate (percent)	1.64	1.29	0.96	2.4	1.42	0.82
	MFI total number of borrowers	15,637	8,264	8,175	9,589	21,986	37,805
	MFI total lending portfolio	1,347,512	2,456,956	1,342,635	3,028,124	8,643,090	18,817,747

Conclusion

P2P microfinance has been enabled by the rise of a creative new set of multilevel monitoring contracts. The general public delegates monitoring to Kiva, which in turn delegates monitoring of the final loans to the MFIs that make them. The system works because Kiva has developed a highly effective, credit-bureau-like system for scoring MFIs and thereby has created a well-defined internal form of reputation. In this financial sense we have a reputation based on clearly monitorable and observable outcomes, and the mechanism is a success. The reputation that Kiva bears as a humanitarian organization, however, is more typical of an international NGO: there are no clear metrics for their performance in terms of social impact on the intended beneficiaries. Kiva's multi-layered system has imposed strong incentives on international intermediaries, has generated vanishingly small default rates, and yet has opened Kiva up to criticism for failing to honor the spirit of the contract offered by their website. Despite its success, Kiva's credibility is at issue.

Peer-to-peer microfinance websites are complex monitoring institutions that must serve a variety of purposes to be effective. It is unclear, prima facie, whether these NGOs should be viewed as financial institutions or humanitarian institutions. One way of synthesizing the issues presented here is that the private standards they have developed to prevent problems on the financial side are so effective that they induce distortions on the humanitarian side. Specifically, the offer of interest-free funding to MFIs on the ground is highly attractive, but in order to receive this funding they must remain in excellent standing with Kiva in terms of repayment. The financial incentives of local MFIs cause them to do three things. First, they pre-disburse loans prior to posting them on Kiva so that they do not have to visit clients twice in order to make loans. Then, in order to get the Kiva loans filled quickly they desire to post both needy and reliable clients on the website, precisely the type of client to whom they would have lent anyway. Finally, the MFIs have very strong incentives to repay the loan for the client even in the event that the loan goes into default. The resulting contract looks a great deal more like a risk-free loan to the MFI, a claim presumably of substantially more limited emotional appeal. Hence systems such as Kiva.org are inherently not P2P, but rather P2MFI; the actual target is the intermediary MFI and not the other peer.

These new multi-party institutions are a great success story in interlinked NGO monitoring of transparent, externally verifiable outcomes such as repayment. The broader reputation of P2P microfinance lenders as organizations providing social benefits and a meaningful and credible service to the general public, however, is likely to be the key to their future growth. Ultimately, the question of credibility in the humanitarian dimension of P2P microfinance relates to the precise nature of the service being offered by these NGOs. Does the public see P2P sites as a generalized avenue to support microfinance, analogous to donating/lending money directly to an MFI, or do they value the direct human link created most effectively by P2P lenders? The rapid growth of Kiva and its competitors (combined with a rumored decline in contributions to the websites of major MFIs in recent years) suggests that it is the latter. In other words, the personalization offered by Kiva is a more effective substitute for direct MFI fundraising. More subtly, if indeed people value the direct personal link, do they see the individuals pictured on the website as emblematic of a type of beneficiary, or do they in fact value the idea that their money has gone directly to fund a person who would not otherwise have received a loan? Developing countries may not possess the institutional depth to support genuine *peer* to *peer* lending, in which case the public would need to be satisfied with the less glamorous claim of P2P microfinance as P2MFI.

The argument here is not that Kiva makes any incorrect claims. Everything on its website (given the recent revisions prompted by Roodman) is correct: the stated individuals do in fact receive those loans on those terms, and the MFI repays loans to Kiva with exactly the frequency given. The emotional power of Kiva's framing does likely draw in more funds, thus expanding the number of people who get grants. The argument is rather that those individuals in all likelihood would have received loans in the absence of Kiva. Seen in the principal–agent framework, these new P2P lenders serve as a powerful example of NGOs emerging to solve contracting and credibility problems that are not easily spanned by legal codes (in this case, both because the borrower countries do not have strong credit reporting institutions and because the lender and borrower are in different countries). The strategic indirectness of the linkage, however, raises an underlying set of issues about the actual causal effects of institutions seeking to link peer with peer, and the claims that can credibly be made by P2P lenders. These institutions are emblematic of both the promise and the pitfalls of delegating complex networks of NGO intermediaries to serve as monitors. Overall, though, we see Kiva struggling with how to sustain its credibility while still presenting an emotional appeal to its donors. Like other NGOs examined in this volume, Kiva increased the transparency of its processes in response to external criticism. The question for the future is whether this will be sufficient in an increasingly crowded marketplace as donors and borrowers become more familiar with the workings of microfinance systems.

Conclusion

8 | *Credibility and compromises*

PETER A. GOUREVITCH AND DAVID A. LAKE

Credible non-governmental organizations (NGOs) may not succeed in bringing about social change. The task may simply be too large, as humanitarian organizations with limited resources and many poor to feed can attest. Others may not share the activists' political agenda, as is perhaps the case in many areas where the demand for ethically grown food or manufactured goods remains small. Credibility is no guarantee of success. NGOs that lack credibility with key audiences, however, are almost certain to fail in their quest to bring about social change. If their claims are not perceived as trustworthy, their statements and efforts will be disregarded. Election monitors from authoritarian countries who certify every election no matter how obviously corrupt have little sway with those who seek to promote democracy (Chapter 2, this volume). Monitors of ethical goods who are sponsored or controlled by manufacturers, such as Kaleen in the case of hand-woven rugs (see Chapter 3, this volume), have difficulty gaining support among consumers. Humanitarian organizations that are too opportunistic – or who become "moral suspects" (Chapter 6, this volume) – will lose the support and confidence of their donors and the targets whose behavior they wish to change. Credibility matters. It may not be sufficient for NGOs seeking to bring about social change, but it is necessary.

Knowing this, NGOs work hard to protect and build their reputations as trustworthy actors. Many NGOs are indeed virtuous. As organizations and individuals they are sincerely committed to their causes. Their virtue, in turn, is the rock upon which their credibility rests. But in a world in which NGOs must be mindful of their organizational interests, and in which skeptical audiences understand this fact, virtue may not be enough. NGOs promote bonds with others around common values – in essence, advertising their virtue and tapping into the desires of others to be virtuous. They adopt autonomous governance structures to minimize conflicts of interest and create a

193

measure of organizational and, especially, fiscal transparency. These strategies were embraced by nearly all the NGOs examined in this book. They also become more professional and integrate themselves into communities of similar professional organizations – demonstrated clearly in the cases of local humanitarian NGOs in Bolivia (Chapter 5, this volume) and Islamic Relief (Chapter 6, this volume), especially once the latter's virtue came under challenge. And when their own efforts at change are hard to observe, as with the case of Rugmark (Chapter 3, this volume), they expend costly effort in more tangible ways, such as building schools, to demonstrate their commitment to their respective causes. NGOs are not passive repositories of credibility created by exogenous circumstances but, rather, seek to shape actively how they are perceived by their audiences.

Much can be learned about credibility when more than one organization occupies a particular field, as occurs in election monitoring (the Carter Center works alongside and in competition with a variety of other Western and other organizations; see Chapter 2, this volume), child labor (Rugmark versus Kaleen, Chapter 3, this volume), human rights (Amnesty International and Human Rights Watch, Chapter 4, this volume), and, of course, in the area of humanitarian relief (see Chapters 5, 6, and 7, this volume). We can also learn from comparisons across organizations and issue areas.

Drawing on such comparisons, it appears that common interests provide a powerful element of credibility for NGOs to their communities of supporters. The more they share values with an audience, the more trusting that audience appears to be. Other audiences, farther removed from these values may, by contrast, be more skeptical.

The need to create and demonstrate common values imposes certain organizational forms on many NGOs. Most basic, the vast majority of NGOs are established as nonprofit corporations. There are a few for-profit monitors today, such as accounting firms offering monitoring services, but they are usually treated more skeptically by those desiring social change. The need to earn a profit exacerbates the conflicts of interest inherent between the organization's need to survive as an organization and the broad social groups it hopes to win over to its cause. Nonprofit status allows an NGO to signal its integrity, to show a willingness to bear a cost (no profits) in service of the virtuous goals it pursues. To affirm this virtue, moreover, NGOs consciously adopt independent boards of directors and diversify sources of financial support, again gaining independence for themselves and attempting to reduce conflicts of interest with various audiences.

The need to demonstrate common interests is more likely than any other condition to create frictions for an NGO in appealing to multiple audiences, which nearly all must do. NGOs may face tensions between their primary donors, who may have a more specific agenda, and their broader base of members or supporters, as the difference between Human Rights Watch and Amnesty International suggests (Chapter 4, this volume). More often, NGOs need to walk a fine line in maintaining the support of their donors and supporters who desire social change and the target countries in which they work (who may also be principals).[1] Access is often important, and it can usually only be provided by the target, who may force the NGO to compromise on its ideals. This is true for all of the cases discussed above, but is particularly acute in election monitoring (Chapter 2, this volume) and the monitoring of ethically-produced goods (Chapter 3, this volume), where access is crucial. Although most humanitarian NGOs seek to navigate this tension by remaining studiously apolitical, the case of Islamic Relief (Chapter 6, this volume) is striking in how efforts to secure the organization's credibility in the West after 9/11 undermined its credibility in the Islamic world – and vice versa. Credibility lies in the eye of the beholder, so the balancing of audiences lies at the core of the strategic problem of credibility.

The credibility of NGOs also hinges in crucial ways on the possibility of external verification. NGOs are often credible because they are themselves subject to monitoring by other parties, including possible legislative hearings, but more often through a free and independent media that knows hypocrisy or scandal "sells" to broader publics.[2] Nooruddin and Sokhey in Chapter 3 point to the possible gullibility of consumers who are swayed by a tag on a product from an NGO

---

[1] See Chapter 1, and the case of Kaleen, Chapter 3.
[2] In Chapter 1 we distinguish between public law, NGO vigilantes who use law to build public support, and private standards set by NGOs. Most private standards and claims made by NGOs on the basis of those standards are not subject to legal review and penalties by courts. The standards often lack precision ("free and fair" elections is ambiguous) and are not obligatory in any event. It would be difficult to hold an NGO to account in a court of law for knowingly violating a private standard that it likely wrote itself. Thus, external verifiers are more likely to be from an independent media intent on revealing hypocrisy.

they may have never heard of before. In their view, this is evidence of a need for greater government regulation. Possibly. This supposed gullibility, however, may also reflect the confidence of consumers that products marked as "fair trade" or "child labor free" must be what they seem, otherwise the manufacturers or stores selling these products would be "called out" for false advertising by a watchful media. Fearful that their reputations would be sullied on the front pages of the news, manufacturers and stores would be reluctant to market products that claim an ethical status they do not deserve. When, for example, a blogger revealed how Kiva actually works, as opposed to the misleading representation on its website, the NGO quickly responded by revamping its description lest its reputation be damaged even further (Chapter 7, this volume).

In turn, audiences can have some confidence that malfeasance and hypocrisy will be revealed. In a crowded field with multiple NGOs, as in election and human rights monitoring or humanitarian aid, sincere or virtuous organizations have an interest in revealing the incompetence, bias, or opportunism of their competitors. Although NGOs often work together in movements and may be reluctant to criticize other organizations for fear of tarnishing them all, they are also rivals that compete for market share in terms of donor contributions. Even in less crowded areas, idealists unhappy with the practices or compromises within organizations may take their stories to the press. Former employees who are themselves highly committed to a cause can be a real danger to any NGO that strays from its mission.

The importance of external verification is suggested by the disproportionate growth of NGOs in countries with independent and vibrant media. Although the comparative absence of NGOs in countries without a free press is undoubtedly correlated with other practices of political repression, it is also likely that an open media that keeps NGOs "honest" is necessary for them to flourish. Most NGOs, as a result, are headquartered in democratic states. In turn, to bolster their credibility, NGOs open themselves to scrutiny by increasing transparency. By facilitating external review, even if few ever actually look, NGOs show that they have nothing to hide. For NGOs, at least, their credibility rests in part on other monitors. As the old proverb (of uncertain origin) suggests, "it's turtles all the way down."

NGOs also enhance their credibility by costly effort. For example, as more political leaders of dubious commitment to honest elections began to invite monitors, the NGOs responded by sending larger missions for longer stays and probing more deeply into electoral practices. As Hyde shows in Chapter 2, as pseudo-democrats engage in more subtle forms of fraud, election monitors maintain their credibility by expanding their efforts and incurring greater costs. On the other hand, Nooruddin and Sokhey (Chapter 3) show that in both the rug and soccer ball industries, and especially the latter, the NGOs have undermined their credibility by employing very limited numbers of inspectors who are, as a result, unlikely to find evidence of child laborers. Not deploying enough inspectors to make finding child laborers reliable occurs, in part, because of the expense of covering so many factories, but it may also reflect the problem of multiple audiences. The NGOs need the cooperation of manufacturers to gain access to factories for inspection, but that same need prevents the sorts of random visits needed to make the process credible. Unwilling to bear the costs of fielding sufficient monitors, and unwilling or unable to alienate the manufacturers whose support they need, the NGOs signal that they are likely to be ineffective and, in turn, that they lack credibility. Indeed, perhaps because inspection efforts themselves are difficult for other audiences to observe, Rugmark has made its biggest impact to the community not by factory or home loom inspections but by building schools in rug-making communities. NGOs also engage in costly effort by professionalizing and integrating into communities of other NGOs, both of which divert resources and effort that might have gone to actually monitoring others or direct aid delivery.

For all NGOs, their credibility also rests on potential penalties for misrepresentation. Many NGOs possess nothing more than their reputations. Accounting firms engaged in monitoring environmental standards may be accused of "green-washing" reports for their clients and survive because of the profitability of other business services they provide. An environmental NGO accused of similar misrepresentation could find itself abandoned by its donors, ignored by others, and soon out of business. Thus, as the human rights NGOs make clear, there is a premium on accuracy in NGO monitoring (Chapter 4, this volume). This may explain why so many NGOs appear to be single purpose organizations without significant other assets or revenue streams. This narrow purview not only avoids conflicts of interest, but leaves them vulnerable in the event they are tempted to "cash in" on their reputations for virtue. As any potential misrepresentation could be fatal, vulnerable organizations must be scrupulous – and that vulnerability, along with the other factors above, gives the rest of us the ability to trust what they say. This source of credibility, however, may be undermined as the NGO community, especially in the area of humanitarian relief, becomes increasingly centralized around a handful of "all-purpose" organizations.

While NGOs have a strong incentive to preserve their "brand," this may not protect them from errors or failures to monitor effectively. Famous commercial brands with vast sums at stake have stumbled: Toyota's several recalls in 2009 and 2010 provide one noteworthy example. The toy manufacturer Mattel took a tremendous reputational hit when it was discovered importing unsafe products made in China. And the factory monitoring movement got its start with a controversy over Nike's labor practices and its failed efforts to resolve the problem internally. There is no reason to believe that NGOs are immune from similar mistakes. Amnesty International almost destroyed itself early in its history when its founder and then leader Peter Berenson appeared to be developing a relationship with British intelligence services (Wong 2008). Nonprofits have responded vigorously to charges of corruption or inappropriately high salaries for top executives. Even the most principled NGOs can err. But overall, the concern for reputation can work to reduce such errors.

Since it is inevitable that NGOs will make errors, how are we to evaluate these? How many errors are too many? When does an NGO fatally undermine its credibility? An important element of evaluation is to consider the relative importance of the sins. All errors are not of equal moral weight. Democracy is the worst form of government except for all others, in a famous turn of phrase. NGOs may be the worst monitors and humanitarian service providers except for all others as well.

The clearest case of error in this volume is the misrepresentation of its microlending model by Kiva, discussed by McIntosh in Chapter 7. Kiva used a highly personalized appeal to raise money for its peer-to-peer (P2P) system. Called to account by a blogger, it became clear that Kiva simplified and perhaps misrepresented the timing of its loans, which had already occurred before a donation was made, and the identity of the borrower, with the donated money actually going to a different person than the one featured on the website.[3] Kiva took the criticism seriously: it reorganized its website to more clearly reflect the flow of money and the role of the MFI, but it still does not make clear the issue of timing. McIntosh suggests that these distortions will in fact be troublesome to donors and undermine credibility.

One could say that in this case "the system" worked. The misrepresentation was revealed. The error, such as it was, was corrected. And yet, it is not clear the error bothered many donors. Kiva continues to grow. Personalization is powerful. We find it in Fair Trade, in CARE, and in many other charities. Connecting to people increases donations. But the mechanism may not be as literal for donors as the critique by McIntosh and others suggest. In this case and perhaps others, the public may not be expecting absolute truth and transparency but a semblance of truth. Donors seek to help the poor, to make a better world by helping them be productive individuals. Skeptical of organizations, many may not expect that their donations are going to the specific people advertised on a website or featured in a commercial. Some misrepresentations, in turn, may be "excusable" and therefore less damaging to an organization's credibility. As long as some poor people are helped, that can be enough for many donors. As *The Economist* noted in a report on monitoring charitable organizations, such NGOs may be aided "by a public that seems unwilling to be freed from its ignorance."[4] It is not just credibility to whom that matters, but it is also credibility for what that may be important.

Credibility can, in sum, be signaled by NGOs. It involves strategic choices by the leadership: how important is credibility to its various audiences, and on what basis do those different publics make their evaluation? Nonetheless, as the theory laid out in Chapter 1 suggests, NGOs can increase their credibility by demonstrating common values, even if this will not suffice for some who want an independent mode of verification from less "interested parties." In these cases, NGOs can enhance their credibility by sending costly signals, opening themselves to external verification, and structuring themselves so that they incur greater penalties for misrepresentation.

---

[3] See David Roodman, "Kiva Is Not Quite What It Seems," October 2, 2009, http://blogs.cgdev.org/open_book/2009/10/Kiva-is-not-quite-what-it-seems.php (accessed April 7, 2010).

[4] "Faith, Hope, and Charities," *The Economist*, November 13, 2010, 69.

Consequences of the need for credibility

All NGOs need credibility and, as above, work to build and maintain their credibility for different audiences with distinct purposes and interests. The need for credibility can, in turn, distort the organization's own goals and practices. Seeking credibility does not necessarily reduce the "effectiveness" of NGOs, a fraught concept for many reasons. Without credibility, many NGOs could not survive or succeed even to the extent they have. Yet, the need for credibility has at least five consequences for how NGOs are structured and how they function that are not recognized sufficiently in the existing literature or, perhaps, by the NGOs themselves.

First, the pressure to be credible leads to an emphasis on procedure at the expense of substance. Because it is difficult to prove the effects of actions, organizations may stress their processes. Islamic Relief shows that it engages in all the proper accounting procedures as a way of claiming that the sources and uses of its funds are beyond suspicion. More generally, charities generally stress the percentage of their budgets going to administration because they are evaluated by Charity Navigator on that criterion, and not on the impact of their giving. Financial transparency is cheaper than program evaluation (as several NGO officials noted to our researchers), and is usually easier to demonstrate. Islamic Relief, again, appears to have devoted more attention to financial transparency than program evaluation once its moral virtue was called into question.

As NGOs are monitored, they are likely to adapt to the criteria used, as happens in any monitoring system. This was famously summarized with the Soviet production model: if nail production is evaluated by weight by the central planner, the plant managers will manufacture one-ton nails. As Boulding argues in Chapter 5, NGOs are likewise pressed to do what their external funders want; perhaps at some costs to the people they seek to serve. They may also "game" the criteria, reclassifying administrative costs as programmatic expenses, hiring grant writers to turn in "professional" applications and reports, and so on. Given that results are nearly always hard to identify, increased monitoring of NGOs will usually privilege process over substance.

Second, greater accountability to their donors causes NGOs to shift their focus "upwards" to their principals at the expense of "downward" responsibility to the members of the local communities with whom they work. External funders tend to favor numerical and tangible information – reports, financial accounting, performance assessments, disclosures and the like. These indicators not only promote a kind of limited transparency, but they serve as costly signals of the NGO's "type." Yet, as Boulding (Chapter 5) also suggests, community members may prefer increasing participation, self-regulation, and social audits (see also Ebrahim 2003). Despite their commitments to local communities, however, NGOs may become more responsive to the needs and concerns of their principals than they are to the groups they are trying to help either as monitors, in the case of child labor for instance, or humanitarian service providers. Thus, the need for credibility may shift power among the various audiences of the NGO. As they are pulled to meet external pressures for information, NGOs are drawn away from the local to the external, be these national or international. This may work well for some processes, such as ethical consumption where the external consumers seek assurances, or for Amnesty International, whose power comes from having a large audience of committed members around the globe. But this same kind of "external" orientation will hurt grassroots groups doing local development work.

The criteria of evaluation affect the dynamics of organizations because they force tradeoffs among constituencies. Doing what the donors want pulls the organization toward the kind of activities and presentations donors like. Several of the cases here show this may cause tension with members: Islamic Relief needs to distance itself from Western actors to reassure its Islamic constituencies, while Western governments fighting terrorism want evidence of engagement with Western donor communities and practices. NGOs in Bolivia complain that catering to the donors takes them away from local communities. The Fair Labor Association has tensions between the need for producer cooperation and criticism from activists that putting producers on the governing board puts the fox in with the chickens.

Third, and related, producing results for principals may draw NGOs into worrying about the immediate, which is often more visible and quantifiable, and away from the long term, which is harder to define and measure. This shifts the emphasis of programs to quick and tangible results and away from more complex, strategic problems of social change. This is most likely to be seen in development projects, which may take years to have an impact.

Fourth, the need for credibility may also lead to the bureaucrat-ization of the organization. To produce numbers and reports, NGOs need staff – people who can gather and analyze data, and translate it into forms easily understood by outsiders. The effect is to create greater bureaucratization, necessary perhaps, but with further con-sequences. It reduces political sensitivity, or acuity, and the ability to respond to changing circumstances on the ground. In keeping with Weberian standards of organization, the NGO becomes less flexible and less responsive to experience.

The type of bureaucracy reflects the logic of the organization's goals and strategy for action. Wong's (Chapter 4) comparison of Amnesty International with Human Rights Watch conveys these differences. Amnesty seeks leverage through the power of mass membership to exert pressure on governments, and so it builds an organization which centralizes the management of informa-tion while decentralizing the activism (for example, letter writing). Conversely, Human Rights Watch seeks to deal with diplomats and state officials, and so does not need the mass membership. Its office is able to make decisions quickly and write comprehensive reports that impress its elite audience. The mechanisms of reputation and thus of credibility are, as a consequence, different between the two organizations. The form of bureaucracy in each conforms to the organization's needs, but also subsequently biases it in particular directions.

Finally, the need for credibility may lead NGOs to engage in offset-ting or compensating actions unrelated to their main missions. NGOs will often undertake virtuous action along one dimension which may obscure what it does in another. As we have already noted, fair trade groups advertise the schools they build. This is certainly a worthy goal, but that is not the core mission of the fair trade system. This is analogous to corporate philanthropy: good will through gifts, which shifts attention away from other criteria.

All of these consequences pull NGOs away from their ability to fulfill their core missions. It would be best if organizations could simply focus on the activities they monitor or deliver the humani-tarian aid they aim to provide. The need for credibility "interferes" with these core activities, but it is also essential if the organizations are to fulfill their missions even in part. It would be inappropri-ate to fault NGOs for paying attention to their credibility, and for expending effort to improve their legitimacy with different audiences. Without credibility they would be even more ineffective in bringing about social change. But at the same time, producing credibility is not without sometimes important and painful consequences for NGOs.

Chains of delegation in NGOs

One important area for further research on the credibility of NGOs is the global "supply chain" problem now confronting many organizations. Global supply chains have, of course, existed for decades in corporations. Toyota, for example, contracts broadly with firms that manufacture components for its automobiles. When you buy a Toyota you are actually buying the output of hundreds of manufacturers about whom you know very little. Consumers may believe that Toyota has strong incentives to monitor and police its suppliers, but we have now seen that this process can be fallible and, as a result, that the company's reputation can suffer severely.

Today, NGOs are also engaged in complex chains of delegation, a kind of vast outsourcing, each with its own "supply chain" of information, verification, dependencies, and power. Kiva is able to extend credit, for instance, because it uses MFIs to verify and enforce loans at the local level. International humanitarian organizations increasingly use local NGOs to implement their programs, as described by Boulding in Chapter 5. Even monitoring organizations increasingly "outsource" their reporting to local observers, who may report on human rights abuses, where and by whom soccer balls are being stitched, and whether elections are corrupt. Indeed, in many cases, these monitoring organizations could not function without local observers. These long chains of delegation complicate and extend the credibility problem. An audience has to trust the primary NGO without knowing how and from whom it acquired information or how it is actually delivering its services. The activist donor has to research not only the NGO but all those upon which that NGO relies. The search costs rise (Ebrahim 2003).

This supply chain problem has led to an additional layer of NGO monitoring. To aid consumers, for instance, Dara O'Rourke has developed a "Good Guide" that measures products on a number of social dimensions – health, safety, and the environment – and provides a composite score available on cell phones when consumers are at stores.[5] It seeks to fill the vacuum of insufficient regulation by telling potential buyers whether the product has antibiotics, hormones, GMOs, or other ethically questionable inputs. In constructing the rating, Good Guide relies heavily on other organizations: Risk Metricks, Asset4, Innovest, KLD, and others that do extensive risk analysis ratings of companies, many of which are the targets of NGO monitoring. Good Guide also partners with other specialized organizations, such as Safemilk, and organizations in various countries that evaluate the composition and safety of products. Importantly, Good Guide relies on the free flow of information on the Internet to construct its ratings. It free rides – as do so many organizations in the monitoring system – on other providers.[6]

Such composite guides, however, magnify the credibility problem by extending the chain of delegation from one NGO to another to another. As chains get longer, the likelihood of error increases, as do the possible distortions discussed in the previous section. And by relying on public information from various sources, as in Good Guide, consumers are still, in the end, dependent on all the NGOs involved providing accurate information for free. How well this supply chain problem is solved deserves significant attention. It also suggests that the credibility problem, no matter how virtuous individual NGOs may be, may not be amenable to a fully private solution, relying exclusively on private bonding mechanisms. Toyota and other firms are having trouble monitoring their supply chains (Gereffi *et al.* 2005); the same is likely to develop as NGOs go down a similar path.

The need for public authority?

Observing NGOs as they go about their business fills us with a mixture of admiration, caution, and advice. The admiration is due to their tremendous commitments to fight for valuable goals in various issues areas, for real achievements in getting information and circulating

---

[5] www.goodguide.com/about/methodology.
[6] In some European countries, government rules require more information on products than in the United States, calling attention to the role of government action, which we examine in the next section.

it to the world, and for providing humanitarian relief in many of the world's most troubled countries. We are all better off because of NGOs and the valuable functions they perform.

The caution arises because there are indeed problems and limits. We have seen a number of issues that arise: conflicting incentives, compromises for organizational imperatives, the need for funds, limits on information gathering, and incomplete information. This leads not to blanket condemnation. The admiration just noted for achievement and dedication limits that. But it does lead to a need for reflection and the questioning of key assumptions.

The most significant item deserving challenge, in our view, is the aggressive separation of the NGOs from government. NGOs differentiate themselves quite sharply along this boundary, praising their own autonomy from government. Governments, in turn, are often the target of their campaigns, as in the case of election monitoring and human rights. And yet, NGOs need governments to do their job. It is incorrect to ask whether NGOs are, in some ways, "better" than government. Rather, NGOs and governments often exist in symbiotic relationships that complement and, indeed, reinforce each other. Recognizing this mutual dependence and bridging the private–public divide may help NGOs become more credible and, in turn, more effective.

Governments are already very much present in the work of NGOs. Government regulations oblige firms to provide information which then allows NGOs to evaluate and assess others. Companies have to release data on the composition of food items, for example, which then makes it possible to evaluate safety, health, and environmental issues. Various safety standards require information on products, which can be used for other purposes. NGOs take this information and use it in various ways. It may become the basis of a public relations campaign, putting pressure on firms or on governments to enforce the public standards – the vigilante role discussed in Chapter 1 (see Elliott and Freeman 2003). It may also be used to evaluate and enforce private standards. In both cases, the government can enhance the role of NGOs by demanding more disclosure and more reporting. The UK has a number of "comply or explain rules" through which firms are obligated to report information on their activities concerning the environment or human rights: if they don't conform to a rule, they must provide reasons.[7] This is voluntarism in a formal way. The pressure to comply comes from bad publicity that would arise if NGOs took up the alarm in response to information the firms were forced to divulge. Even when governments are themselves the targets of social change, other governments support NGOs in their attempts to track and report on their behaviors; election monitoring, for instance, could not happen without the backing and, in many cases, the financial support of established democratic states seeking to reduce electoral fraud in new democracies.

Similarly, humanitarian NGOs are often dependent on governments for funds and, indeed, for protection for their workers in war-torn areas. Without minimizing the tensions that can arise between donor and developed country governments and humanitarian organizations, it would simply be impossible for such organizations to work in some parts of the world without explicit or implicit backing from these governments.

The NGO specialists working on labor standards seem to be especially attentive to the interaction of government and NGOs. They have been among the most vocal critics of the ability of NGOs to monitor effectively. Some researchers have shifted their attention from monitoring to redesigning the production system so as to reduce firm incentives to employ child labor (Baccaro 2001; Fung *et al.* 2001; Locke *et al.* 2007). These authors stress the necessity for NGOs to embrace the need for more regulation from national governments and more international agreements and enforcement from international institutions. This is a challenge for many NGOs as it would draw them into politics more directly, forcing them to engage in the processes of elections, testimony, and lobbying that create government engagement, rather than limit their activities to being "vigilantes" who complain from the outside.

Governments also need NGOs. In a large, complex world, with many issues, government agencies cannot possibly track down all abuses and errors. Independent groups can do valuable work, tracking down what is happening elsewhere. Governments are now dependent on NGO monitoring in a host of issue areas (Raustiala

---

[7] British commissions have explored these concepts. See Bullock 1977 and Cadbury 1992 on corporate governance generally. See also Turnbull 1999 and Walker 2009.

1997). Governments also rely on humanitarian NGOs to deliver aid in natural disasters and lead long-term development projects. The ties between NGOs and governments are both sometimes antagonistic and deep and binding. This symbiotic relationship between governments and NGOs is real and should be acknowledged.

Most important, for our purposes, is the ability of governments to actually enhance the credibility of NGOs. There is often a degree of antagonism between NGOs and governments. Because they are virtuous, and desire to be seen as such, NGOs often resent government interference with their activities, which they believe may divert them from their goals of social change shared with other audiences. Thus, NGOs seek to maintain an arm's-length relationship with governments and may even actively cultivate an anti-government stance. Yet, this antagonism may be counter-productive. By standardizing reporting requirements, writing rules governing conflicts of interest within organizations, and demanding greater financial transparency, governments could enhance the credibility of NGOs and help disseminate norms of best practice. For skeptical audiences, more information is always better, even when it forces NGOs to reveal their failures as well as their successes. Trustworthy NGOs should not be afraid of such reporting requirements and rules of organizational oversight, especially if it is required of all NGOs similarly. Such oversight of NGOs would reveal the virtue of the virtuous, and allow skeptical audiences to reach independent judgments of their credibility. In the long run, this improved credibility will enhance the prospects for social change.

References

Abbott, Kenneth W. and Snidal, Duncan 2000. "Hard and Soft Law in International Governance," *International Organization* 54 (3): 421–56.

Adams, Jerry 2001. "NGOs and Impact Assessment," INTRAC NGO Policy Briefing Paper No. 3.

Allison, Graham T. 1971. *Essence of Decision: Explaining the Cuban Missile Crisis*. Boston: Little, Brown.

Alterman, Jon B. with Hunter, Shireen and Phillips, Ann L. 2005. "The Idea and Practice of Philanthropy in the Muslim World," PPC Issue Paper No. 5, Bureau of Policy and Program Coordination, the Muslim World Series, USAID, Washington, DC.

Anheier, Helmut K. and Ben-Ner, Avner 2003. *The Study of Non Profit Enterprise*. New York: Kluwer Academic/Plenum Publishers.

Aspers, Patrik 2006. "Ethics in Global Garment Market Chains," in Nico Stehr, Christoph Henning, and Bernd Weiler (eds.) *The Moralization of the Markets*. London: Transaction Press, 287–307.

Auld, Graeme, Gulbrandsen, Lars H. and McDermott, Constance 2008. "Certification Schemes and the Impacts on Forests and Forestry," *Annual Review of Environment and Resources* 33: 187–211.

Baccaro, Lucio 2001. *Civil Society, NGOs, and Decent Work Policies: Sorting out the Issues*. Geneva: International Institute for Labor Studies.

Bachman, S. L. 2000. "The Political Economy of Child Labor and Its Impacts on International Business," *Business Economics* (July): 30–41.

Baland, Jean-Marie and Duprez, Cedric 2009. "Are Labels Effective against Child Labor?" *Journal of Public Economics* 93 (December): 1125–30.

Banerjee, A., Duflo, E., Glennerster, R., and Kinnan, C. 2009. "The Miracle of Microfinance? Evidence from a Randomized Evaluation," working paper, Massachusetts Institute of Technology, available at http://econ-www.mit.edu/files/4162.

Barnett, Michael 2005. "Humanitarianism Transformed," *Perspectives on Politics* 3 (4): 723–40.

2008. "Humanitarianism as a Scholarly Vocation," in Michael Barnett and Thomas Weiss (eds.) *Humanitarianism in Question: Politics, Power, and Ethics*. New York: Cornell University Press, 235–63.

2009. "Evolution without Progress? Humanitarianism in a World of Hurt," *International Organization* 63: 621–63.

Barnett, Michael and Finnemore, Martha 2004. *Rules for the World: International Organizations in Global Politics*. Ithaca, NY: Cornell University Press.

Barnett, Michael and Weiss, Thomas G. 2008. "Humanitarianism: A Brief History of the Present," in Michael Barnett and Thomas Weiss (eds.) *Humanitarianism in Question: Politics, Power, and Ethics*. New York: Cornell University Press, 1–48.

Baron, David 2001. "Private Politics, Corporate Social Responsibility, and Integrated Strategy," *Journal of Economics and Management Strategy* 10 (1): 7–45.

Basu, Arnab K., Chau, Nancy H., and Grote, Ulrike 2006. "Guaranteed Manufactured without Child Labor: The Economics of Consumer Boycotts, Social Labeling, and Trade Sanctions," *Review of Development Economics* 10 (3): 466–91.

Beckert, Jens and Aspers, Patrik 2011. *The Worth of Goods: Valuation and Pricing in the Economy*. Oxford University Press.

Bellion-Jourdan, Jérôme 2000. "Islamic Organizations: Between 'Islamism' and 'Humanitarianism'," *International Institute for the Study of Islam in the Modern World (ISIM), Newsletter* (July): 15.

Benthall, Jonathan 1999. "Financial Worship: The Qu'ranic Injunction to Almsgiving," *Journal of the Royal Anthropological Institute* 5 (1): 27–42.

2003. "Humanitarianism and Islam after 11 September," in Joanna Macrae and Adele Harmer (eds.) *Humanitarian Action and the "Global War Terror": A Review of Trends and Issues*, HPG Report 14: 37–47. London: ODI. Available at www.odi.org.uk/hpg/papers/hpgreport14.pdf.

2007. "The Overreaction against Islamic Charities," *ISIM Review* 20: 6–7. Available at www.isim.nl/files/Review_20/Review_20–6.pdf.

Besley, T. and Coate, S. 1995. "Group Lending, Repayment Incentives, and Social Collateral," *Journal of Development Economics* 46: 1–18.

Bjornlund, Eric 2004. *Beyond Free and Fair: Monitoring Elections and Building Democracy*. Washington, DC: Woodrow Wilson Center Press.

Bob, Clifford 2002a. "Globalization and the Social Construction of Human Rights Campaigns," in Alison Brysk (ed.) *Globalization and Human Rights*. Berkeley: University of California Press, 133–47.

2002b. "Merchants of Morality," *Foreign Policy* (March–April): 36–45.

2005. *The Marketing of Rebellion: Insurgents, Media, and International Activism.* Cambridge University Press.

Boje, David M. and Khan, Farzad R. 2009. "Story-branding by Empire Entrepreneurs: Nike, Child Labor, and Pakistan's Soccer Ball Industry," *Journal of Small Business and Entrepreneurship* 22 (1): 9–24.

Brewington, David V., Davis, David R., and Murdie, Amanda 2009. "The Ties that Bind: A Network Analysis of Human Rights INGOs." Paper presented at the International Studies Association annual meeting, New York.

Broukhim, Michael and Hiscox, Michael J. 2009. "Consumer Support for Fair Trade: Evidence from eBay Auctions of Fresh Roasted Coffee," unpublished ms., Harvard University.

Bruett, Tilman 2007. "Cows, Kiva, and Prosper.com: How Disintermediation and the Internet are Changing Microfinance," *Community Development Investment Review* 3 (2), Federal Reserve Bank of San Francisco.

Buckmaster, N. 1999. "Associations between Outcome Measurement, Accountability, and Learning for Non-profit Organizations," *International Journal of Public Sector Management* 12 (2): 186–97.

Bullock, Alan 1977. *Report of the Committee of Inquiry on Industrial Democracy.* London: Her Majesty's Stationary Office.

Burra, Neera. 1995. *Born to Work: Child Labor in India.* Oxford University Press.

Cadbury, A. 1992. *Financial Aspects of Corporate Governance.* London: Gee Publishing.

Carothers, Thomas 1997. "The Observers Observed," *Journal of Democracy* 8 (3): 17–31.

Carter Center 2006. *Building Consensus on Principles for International Election Observation.* Atlanta, GA: The Carter Center. Available at www.cartercenter.org/documents/CC%20Elec%20Standards%20G_final.pdf.

CBS 1995. "Children at Work; Pakistani Child Labor Prominent in Manufacture of Goods for US Sports Companies and UNICEF," April 6, news transcript (accessed through Lexis-Nexis).

Charlish, D., David, R., Foresti, M., Knight, L.-A., and Newens, M. 2003. "Towards Organizational Performance Assessment: Experiences of Strengthening Learning, Accountability, and Understanding Social Change," available at www.dgtpe.bercy.gouv.fr/fonds_documentaire/TRESOR/cicid/atelier/contrib/14.pdf.

Chowdry, Geeta and Beeman, Mark 2001. "Challenging Child Labor: Transnational Activism and India's Carpet Industry," *Annals of the American Academy of Political and Social Science* 575: 158–75.

Cingranelli, David L. and Richards, David L. 2001. "Measuring the Impact of Human Rights Organizations," in Claude E. Welch, Jr. (ed.) *NGOs and Human Rights: Promise and Performance*. Philadelphia: University of Pennsylvania Press, 225–37.

Clark, Ann Marie 2001. *Diplomacy of Conscience: Amnesty International and Changing Human Rights Norms*. Princeton University Press.

Clark, Roger S. 1981. "The International League for Human Rights and South West Africa 1947–1957: The Human Rights NGO as Catalyst in the International Legal Process," *Human Rights Quarterly* 3: 101–36.

Cmiel, Kenneth 1999. "The Emergence of Human Rights Politics in the United States," *Journal of American History* 86: 1231–50.

Compa, Lance and Hinchcliffe-Darricarrère, Tashia 1995. "Enforcing International Labor Rights through Corporate Codes of Conduct," *Journal of Transnational Law* 33: 663–89.

Conroy, Michael 2007. *Branded: How the Certification Revolution is Transforming Global Corporations*. Gabriola Island, BC: New Society Publishers.

Cooley, Alexander and Ron, James 2002. "The NGO Scramble: Organizational Insecurity and the Political Economy of Transnational Action," *International Security* 27 (1): 5–39.

Cooper, Andrew F. and Legler, Thomas 2006. *Intervention without Intervening? The OAS Defense and Promotion of Democracy in the Americas*. New York: Palgrave Macmillan.

Cutler, A. Claire, Haufler, Virginia and Porter, Tony 1999. *Private Authority and International Affairs*. Albany: State University of New York Press.

Daviron, Benoit and Ponte, Stefano 2005. *The Coffee Paradox: Global Markets, Commodity Trade, and the Elusive Promise of Development*. London: Zed Books.

de Cordier, Bruno 2009. "Faith-based Aid, Globalization and the Western-based Muslim Aid Organizations," *Journal of Disaster Studies, Policy, and Management* 33 (4): 608–28.

de Janvry, Alain, McIntosh, C., and Sadoulet, E. 2010. "The Supply and Demand Side Impacts of Credit Market Information," *Journal of Development Economics* 93 (2): 173–88.

de Waal, Alex 1997. *Famine Crimes: Politics and the Disaster Relief Industry in Africa*. Bloomington: Indiana University Press.

Des Forges, Alison 1999. *Leave None to Tell the Story: Genocide in Rwanda.* New York: Human Rights Watch.

Easterly, William 2002. "The Cartel of Good Intentions: The Problem of Bureaucracy in Foreign Aid," *Journal of Policy Reform* 5: 223.

2006. *The White Man's Burden: Why the West's Efforts to Aid the Rest Have Done So Much Ill and So Little Good.* New York: Penguin.

Ebrahim, Alnoor 2003. "Accountability in Practice: Mechanisms for NGOs," *World Development* 31 (5): 813–29.

Elliott, Kimberly Ann and Freeman, Richard Barry 2003. *Can Labor Standards Improve Under Globalization?* Washington, DC: Institute for International Economics.

Epstein, David and O'Halloran, Sharyn 1999. *Delegating Powers: A Transaction Cost Politics Approach to Policy Making under Separate Powers.* Cambridge University Press.

Finnemore, Martha and Sikkink, Kathryn 1998. "International Norm Dynamics and Political Change," *International Organization* 52 (4): 887–917.

Fisher, Ronald J. 1995. "Pacific, Impartial Third-Party Intervention in International Conflict: A Review and Analysis," in John A. Vasquez, James Turner Johnson, Sanford Jaffe, and Linda Stamato (eds.) *Beyond Confrontation: Learning Conflict Resolution in the Post-Cold War Era.* Ann Arbor: University of Michigan Press, 39–59.

Flanigan, Shawn 2006. "Charity as Resistance: Connections between Charity, Contentious Politics, and Terror," *Studies in Conflict and Terrorism* 29: 641–55.

Flannery, M. 2007. "Kiva and the Birth of Person-to-Person Microfinance," *Innovations: Technology, Governance, Globalization* 2 (1–2): 31–56.

Fowler, Alan 2002. "Assessing NGO Performance: Difficulties, Dilemmas, and a Way Ahead," in Alan Fowler and Michael Edwards (eds.) *NGO Management.* London: Earthscan, 293–307.

Francois, Patrick 2003. "Not-for-Profit Provision of Public Services," *The Economic Journal* 113 (486): C53–C61.

Fung, Archon, O'Rourke, Dara, and Sabel, Charles 2001. *Can We Put an End to Sweatshops? A New Democracy Forum on Raising Global Labor Standards.* Boston: Beacon Press.

Gandhi, Jennifer and Przeworski, Adam 2009. "Holding onto Power by Any Means? The Origins of Competitive Elections," unpublished ms., Emory University.

Geisler, Gisela 1993. "Fair? What Has Fairness Got to Do with It? Vagaries of Election Observations and Democratic Standards," *The Journal of Modern African Studies* 31 (4): 613–37.

Gereffi, Gary, Humphrey, John, and Sturgeon, Timothy 2005. "The Governance of Global Value Chains," *Review of International Political Economy* 12 (1): 78–104.

Ghatak, M. 1999. "Group Lending, Local Information, and Peer Selection," *Journal of Development Economics* 60: 27–50.

Ghatak, M. and Guinnane, T. 1999. "The Economics of Lending with Joint Liability: Theory and Practice," *Journal of Development Economics* 60 (1): 195–228.

Gibelman, Margaret and Gelman, Sheldon R. 2004. "A Loss of Credibility: Patterns of Wrongdoing among Nongovernment Organizations," *Voluntas: International Journal of Voluntary and Nonprofit Organizations* 15 (4): 355–81.

Gibney, Mark and Dalton, Matthew 1996. "The Political Terror Scale," *Policy Studies and Developing Nations* 4: 73–84.

Gleditsch, Kristian Skrede 2002. *All International Politics Is Local: The Diffusion of Conflict, Integration, and Democratization* (Ann Arbor: University of Michigan Press).

Gugerty, Mary Kay 2009. "Signaling Virtue: Voluntary Accountability Programs among Nonprofit Organizations," *Policy Sciences* 42 (3): 243–73.

Gugerty, Mary Kay and Prakash, Aseem (eds.) 2010. *Voluntary Regulation of NGOs and Nonprofits: An Accountability Club Framework*. Cambridge University Press.

Habyarimana, James, Humphreys, Macartan, Posner, Daniel, and Weinstein, Jeremy 2009. "Coethnicity and Trust," in Karen S. Cook, Margaret Levi, and Russell Hardin (eds.) *Whom Can We Trust? How Groups, Networks, and Institutions Make Trust Possible*. New York: Russell Sage Foundation, 42–64.

Hafner-Burton, Emilie M. 2008. "Sticks and Stones: Naming and Shaming the Human Rights Enforcement Problem," *International Organization* 62: 689–716.

Hall, Rodney Bruce and Biersteker, Thomas J. (eds.) 2002. *The Emergence of Private Authority in Global Governance*. Cambridge University Press.

Hammond, Laura 2008. "The Power of Holding Humanitarianism Hostage and the Myth of Protective Principles," in Michael Barnett and Thomas Weiss (eds.) *Humanitarianism in Question: Politics, Power, and Ethics*. Ithaca, NY: Cornell University Press, 172–95.

Hansen, Hans Krause and Salskov-Iversen, Dorte (eds.) 2008. *Critical Perspectives on Private Authority in Global Politics*. New York: Palgrave Macmillan.

Hansmann, Henry B. 1980. "The Role of Nonprofit Enterprise," *Yale Law Journal* 89: 835–901.

Harlow, Rachel Martin 2006. "Agency and Agent in George Bush's Gulf War Rhetoric," in Martin J. Medhurst (ed.) *The Rhetorical Presidency of George H. W. Bush*. Texas A&M Press, 56–80.

Haufler, Virginia 2001. *A Public Role for the Private Sector: Industry Self-Regulation in a Global Economy*. Washington, DC: Carnegie Endowment for International Peace.

Held, David and McGrew, Anthony (eds.) 2002. *Governing Globalization: Power, Authority, and Global Governance*. New York: Polity.

Henderson, Sarah 2002. "Selling Civil Society," *Comparative Political Studies* 35: 139–67.

Henderson, Sarah L. 2003. *Building Democracy in Contemporary Russia: Western Support for Grassroots Organizations*. Ithaca, NY: Cornell University Press.

Hilhorst, D. 2002. "Being Good at Doing Good? Quality and Accountability of Humanitarian NGOs," *Disasters* 26: 193–212.

Hiscox, Michael and Smyth, Nicholas F. B. 2009. "Is There Consumer Demand for Improved Labor Standards? Evidence from Field Experiments in Social Product Labeling." Paper prepared for the conference "Beyond Virtue," UC San Diego, La Jolla, CA, March.

Hopgood, Stephen 2006. *Keepers of the Flame: Understanding Amnesty International*. Ithaca, NY: Cornell University Press.

Howell, Jude and Pearce, Jenny 2002. *Civil Society and Development: A Critical Exploration*. Boulder: Lynne Rienner.

Husselbee, David 2000. "NGOS as Development Partners to the Corporates: Child Football Stitchers in Pakistan," *Development in Practice* 10 (3/4): 377–89.

Hyde, Susan D. 2007. "The Observer Effect in International Politics: Evidence from a Natural Experiment," *World Politics* 60 (1): 37–63.

2011a. "Catch Us if You Can: Election Monitoring and International Norm Diffusion," *American Journal of Political Science* 55 (2): 356–69.

2011b. *The Pseudo-Democrat's Dilemma: Why Election Observation Became an International Norm*. Ithaca, NY: Cornell University Press.

International Monitoring Association for Child Labour (IMAC) 2004. "Fact Sheet of the Sialkot Soccer Ball Program," July 31.

2007. "Fact Sheet of the Sialkot Soccer Ball Program," November 30.

Islamic Relief 2006. Annual Report and Financial Statements. IR, http://www.islamic-relief.com/Whoweare/FinancialReportsMain.aspx?depID=2 (accessed January 14, 2009).

Jappelli, Tullio and Pagano, Marco 1993. "Information Sharing in Credit Markets," *Journal of Finance* 48 (5): 1693–718.

Kahler, Miles and Lake, David A. (eds.) 2003. *Governance in a Global Economy: Political Authority in Transition.* Princeton University Press.

Karlan, D. and Zinman, J. 2009. "Expanding Microenterprise Credit Access: Using Randomized Supply Decisions to Estimate the Impacts in Manila," working paper, Dartmouth University, available at www.dartmouth.edu/~jzinman/Papers/expandingaccess_manila_jul09.pdf.

Karpik, Lucien 2007. *L'economie des Singularités.* Paris: Galliamard.

Keck, Margaret E. and Sikkink, Kathryn 1998. *Activists beyond Borders: Advocacy Networks in International Politics.* Ithaca, NY: Cornell University Press.

Kelley, Judith 2008. "Assessing the Complex Evolution of Norms: The Rise of International Election Monitoring," *International Organization* 62 (2): 221–55.

2009. "D-Minus Elections: The Politics and Norms of International Election Observation," *International Organization* 63 (4): 765–87.

Kendall, Jeremy and Knapp, Martin 1999. "Evaluation and the Voluntary (Nonprofit) Sector: Emerging Issues," in David Lewis (ed.) *International Perspectives on Voluntary Action: Reshaping the Third Sector.* London: Earthscan.

Kennedy, David 2004. *The Dark Sides of Virtue: Reassessing International Humanitarianism.* Princeton University Press.

Khan, Ajaz Ahmed. 2012. "The Impulse to Give: The Motivations of Giving to Muslim Charities," in Michael Barnett and Janice Stein, eds., Sacred Aid (NY: Oxford University Press).

Khan, Ajaz Ahmed and van Eekelen, Willem 2008. "Humanitarian Aid, Independence, and Innovation," available at www.islamic-relief.com/InDepth/humanitarianaid.aspx (accessed February 15, 2009).

Khan, Ajaz Ahmed, Tahmazov, Ismayil, and Abuarqub, Mamoun 2009. "Translating Faith into Development," available at www.islamic-relief.com/Indepth/translating-faith.aspx (accessed August 14, 2009).

Khan, Farzad R., Munir, Kamal A., and Willmott, Hugh 2007. "A Dark Side of Institutional Entrepreneurship: Soccer Balls, Child Labor, and Postcolonial Impoverishment," *Organization Studies* 28 (7): 1055–77.

Kiewiet, D. Roderick and McCubbins, Mathew D. 1991. *The Logic of Delegation: Congressional Parties and the Appropriation Process.* University of Chicago Press.

Kirmani, Nida and Khan, Ajaz Ahmed 2008. "Does Faith Matter: An Examination of IR's Work with Refugees and Internally Displaced Persons," *Refugee Survey Quarterly* 27: 41–50.

Kydd, Andrew 2003. "Which Side Are You On? Bias, Credibility, and Mediation," *American Journal of Political Science* 47 (4): 597–611.

Laber, Jeri 2002. *The Courage of Strangers*. New York: Public Affairs.

Lake, David A. and McCubbins, Mathew D. 2006. "The Logic of Delegation to International Organizations," in Darren Hawkins, David A. Lake, Daniel L. Nielson, and Michael J. Tierney (eds.) *Delegation and Agency in International Organizations*. Cambridge University Press, 341–68.

Locke, Richard and Romis, Monica 2007. "Improving Work Conditions in a Global Supply Chain," *MIT Sloan Management Review* 48 (2): 54–62.

Locke, Richard, Amengual, Matthew and Mangla, Akshay 2009. "Virtue out of Necessity? Compliance, Commitment, and the Improvement of Labor Conditions in Global Supply Chains," MIT Sloan Working Paper No. 4719–08.

Locke, Richard, Qin, Fei and Brause, Alberto 2007. "Does Monitoring Improve Labor Standards? Lessons from Nike," *Industrial and Labor Relations Review* 61 (1): 3–31.

Luoto, J., McIntosh, C., and Wydick, B. 2007. "Credit Information Systems in Less-Developed Countries: Recent History and a Test," *Economic Development and Cultural Change* 55 (2): 313–34.

Lupia, Arthur 1994. "Shortcuts Versus Encyclopedias: Information and Voting Behavior in California Insurance Reform Elections," *American Political Science Review* 88 (1): 63–76.

Lupia, Arthur and McCubbins, Mathew D. 1998. *The Democratic Dilemma: Can Citizens Learn What They Need to Know?* Cambridge University Press.

Lyne, Mona, Nielson, Daniel L. and Tierney, Michael J. 2006. "Who Delegates? Alternative Models of Principals in Development Aid," in Darren Hawkins, David A. Lake, Daniel L. Nielson, and Michael J. Tierney (eds.) *Delegation and Agency in International Organizations*. Cambridge University Press, 41–76.

Macrae, Joanna (ed.) 2002. *The New Humanitarianism: A Review of Trends in Global Humanitarian Action*. London: Overseas Development Institute.

McClintock, Brent 2001. "Trade as if Children Mattered," *International Journal of Social Economics* 28 (10/11/12): 899–910.

McDonagh, Pierre 2002. "Communicative Campaigns to Effect Anti-Slavery and Fair Trade: The Cases of Rugmark and Cafédirect," *European Journal of Marketing* 36 (5/6): 642–66.

McFaul, Michael 2004. "Democracy Promotion as a World Value," *Washington Quarterly* 28 (1): 147–63.

McIntosh, C. and Wydick, B. 2005. "Competition and Microfinance," *Journal of Development Economics* 78: 271–98.

McNollgast 1987. "Administrative Procedures as Instruments of Political Control," *Journal of Law, Economics, and Organization* 3 (2): 243–79.

Meyer, Carrie A. 1995. "Northern Donors for Southern NGOs: Consequences for Local Participation and Production," *Journal of Economic Development* 20: 7–22.

Morduch, J. 1999. "The Microfinance Promise," *Journal of Economic Literature* 37: 1569–614.

Myers, Marissa 1998. "When Biased Advice is a Good Thing: Information and Foreign Policy Decision-making," *International Interaction* 24: 379–403.

Naidoo, Kumi 2004. "The End of Blind Faith? Civil Society and the Challenges of Accountability, Transparency, and Legitimacy," *Accountability Forum* 2: 14–25.

Navajas, Sergio, Conning, J., and Gonzalez-Vega, C. 2003. "Lending Technologies, Competition, and Consolidation in the Market for Microfinance in Bolivia," *Journal of International Development* 15 (6): 747–70.

Neier, Aryeh 2003. *Taking Liberties: Four Decades in the Struggle for Rights*. New York: Public Affairs.

O'Neill, Michael 2009. "Public Confidence in Charitable Nonprofits," *Nonprofit and Voluntary Sector Quarterly* 38 (2): 237–69.

Orbinski, James 1999. Nobel Prize Acceptance Speech, Oslo, Norway, December 10.

Ostrom, Elinor and Walker, James (eds.) 2003. *Trust and Reciprocity: Interdisciplinary Lessons from Experimental Research*. New York: Russell Sage Foundation.

Padilla, Jorge A. and Pagano, Marco 1997. "Endogenous Communication among Lenders and Entrepreneurial Incentives," *Review of Financial Studies* 10 (1): 205–36.

2000. "Sharing Default Information as a Borrower Discipline Device," *European Economic Review* 44 (10): 1951–80.

Pearce, Jenny 2000. "Development, NGOs, and Civil Society: The Debate and Its Future," in Deborah Eade (ed.) *Development, NGOs, and Civil Society*. London: Oxfam GB, 15–43.

Poe, Steven C., Carey, Sabine C., and Vasquez, Tanya C. 2001. "How Are These Pictures Different? A Quantitative Comparison of the US State Department and Amnesty International Human Rights Reports, 1976–1995," *Human Rights Quarterly* 23: 650–77.

Polman, Linda 2010. *The Crisis Caravan: What's Wrong with Humanitarian Aid?* New York: Metropolitan Books.

Power, Samantha 2001. "Bystanders to Genocide," *Atlantic Monthly* 288: 84–108.

Prakash, Aseem and Gugerty, Mary Kay 2010a. "Trust but Verify: Voluntary Regulation Programs in the Nonprofit Sector," *Regulation and Governance* 4 (1): 22–47.

Prakash, Aseem and Gugerty, Mary Kay (eds.) 2010b. *Advocacy Organizations and Collective Action.* Cambridge University Press.

Quelch, John A. and Laidler-Kylander, Nathalie 2006. *The New Global Brands: Managing Non-Government Organizations in the 21st Century.* Mason, OH: Thomson South-Western.

Rabben, Linda 2002. *Fierce Legion of Friends: A History of Human Rights Campaigns and Campaigners.* Hyattsville, MD: The Quixote Center.

Randel, Judith and German, Tony 2002. "Trends in the Financing of Humanitarian Assistance," in Joanna Macrae (ed.), *The New Humanitarianism: A Review of Trends in Global Humanitarian Action.* London: Overseas Development Institute, 19–28.

Raustiala, Kal 1997. "States, NGOs, and International Environmental Institutions," *International Studies Quarterly* 41 (4): 719–40.

Ravi, Aparna 2001. "Combating Child Labor with Labels: Case of Rugmark," *Economic and Political Weekly* 36 (13): 1141–47.

Ray, Philip L. Jr. and Taylor, J. Sherrod 1977. "The Role of Nongovernmental Organizations in Implementing Human Rights in Latin America," *Georgia Journal of International and Comparative Law* 7: 477–506.

Riddell, Roger 1999. "Evaluating NGO Development Interventions," in David Lewis (ed.) *International Perspectives on Voluntary Action: Reshaping the Third Sector.* London: Earthscan, 222–41.

Ron, James, Ramos, Howard, and Rodgers, Kathleen 2005. "Transnational Information Politics: NGO Human Rights Reporting, 1986–2000," *International Studies Quarterly* 49: 557–88.

Rosenau, James 2002. "The Drama of Human Rights in a Turbulent, Globalized World," in Alison Brysk (ed.) *Globalization and Human Rights.* University of California Press, 148–70.

Rugmark 2008. "White Paper: Learning from the Rugmark Model to End Child Labor," available at www.rugmark.org/uploads/WhitePaper0409.pdf.

Salih, M. A. Mohamed 2002. "Islamic NGOs in Africa: The Promise and Peril of Islamic Voluntarism," in Alex de Waal (ed.) *Islamism and Its Enemies in the Horn of Africa.* London: Hurst & Company, 146–81.

Schanberg, Sydney and Dorigny, Marie 1996. "Six Cents an Hour," *Life* (June): 38.

Schlesinger, Mark, Mitchell, Shannon and Gray, Bradford H. 2004. "Restoring Public Legitimacy to the Nonprofit Sector: A Survey Experiment Using Descriptions of Nonprofit Ownership," *Nonprofit and Voluntary Sector Quarterly* 33 (4): 673–710.

Seidman, Gay W. 2005. "'Stateless' Regulation and Consumer Pressure: Historical Experiences of Transnational Corporate Monitoring," in

Frederick H. Buttel and Philip McMichael (eds.) *New Directions in the Sociology of Global Development* (Research in Rural Sociology and Development, Volume 11). Bingley: Emerald Group Publishing, 175–207.

2007. *Beyond the Boycott: Labor Rights, Human Rights, and Transnational Activism*. New York: Russell Sage Foundation.

2009. "Social Labeling in Export Supply Chains: Can Voluntary Certification Programs End Child Labor?" *India in Transition*. Available at http://casi.ssc.upenn.edu/iit/seidman.

2010. "Slender Threads: Social Labeling in the Indian Carpet Industry since the Mid-1990s," *Management and Organizational History* 5 (2): 145–64.

Sell, Susan K. and Prakash, Aseem 2004. "Using Ideas Strategically: The Contest between Business and NGO Networks in Intellectual Property Rights," *International Studies Quarterly* 48 (1): 143–75.

Sharma, Alakh 2002–2003. "Impact of Social Labeling on Child Labor in Carpet Industry," *Economic and Political Weekly* 37 (52): 5196–204.

Siegman, Karin Astrid 2008. "Soccer Ball Production for Nike in Pakistan," *Economic and Political Weekly* 43 (22): 57–64.

Simmons, P. J. 1998. "Learning to Live with NGOs," *Foreign Policy* 112 (3): 82–96.

Simon, Herbert A. 1976. *Administrative Behavior: A Study of Decision-Making Processes in Administrative Organization*. New York: Free Press.

Singer, Peter 2010. *The Life You Can Save*. New York: Norton.

Sives, Amanda 2001. "A Review of Commonwealth Election Observation," *Commonwealth and Comparative Politics* 39 (3): 132–49.

Slim, Hugo 2002. "By What Authority? The Legitimacy and Accountability of Non-Governmental Organizations," *Journal of Humanitarian Assistance*. March 10. Available at www.jha.ac/articles/a082.htm.

Smilie, Ian and Minear, Larry 2004. *The Charity of Nations*. Bloomfield: Kumarian Press.

Spar, Debora L. 1998. "The Spotlight and the Bottom Line: How Multinationals Export Human Rights," *Foreign Affairs* 77 (2): 1–12.

Stein, Janice Gross 2008. "Humanitarian Organizations: Accountable Why, to Whom, for What, and How?" in Michael Barnett and Thomas Weiss (eds.) *Contemporary Humanitarianism in Global and Theoretical Perspective*. Ithaca, NY: Cornell University Press, 124–43.

2009. "The Politics and Power of Networks: The Accountability of Humanitarian Organizations," in Miles Kahler (ed.) *Networked*

Politics: Agency, Power, and Governance. Ithaca, NY: Cornell University Press, 151–72.

Stiglitz, J. 1990. "Peer Monitoring and Credit Markets," *World Bank Economic Review* 4: 351–66.

Terry, Fiona. 2003. *Condemned to Repeat?* Ithaca, NY: Cornell University Press.

Turnbull, N. 1999. *Internal Control: Guidance for Directors on the Combined Code.* London: The Institute of Chartered Accountants in England and Wales.

VIPFE 2006. *Directorio Nacional de ONGs en Bolivia, 2005–2006: Registro Unico Nacional de ONGs.* La Paz: Viceministerio de Inversión Pública y Financiamiento Externo, Republica de Bolivia, Ministerio de Hacienda. Available at www.vipfe.gov.bo/ryp/ongs/.

Vogel, David 2005. *The Market for Virtue: The Potential and Limits of Corporate Social Responsibility.* Washington, DC: Brookings Institution Press.

Walker, S. D. 2009. *Review of Corporate Governance in UK Banks and Other Financial Industry Executives.* London: Paradigm Risk, Ltd.

Walter, Barbara F. 1997. "The Critical Barrier to Civil War Settlement," *International Organization* 51 (3): 335–64.

2002. *Committing to Peace: The Successful Settlement of Civil Wars.* Princeton University Press.

Weiner, Myron 1991. *The Child and the State in India.* Princeton University Press.

Werker, Eric and Ahmed, Faisal Z. 2008. "What Do Nongovernmental Organizations Do?" *The Journal of Economic Perspectives* 22: 73–92.

Willcox, David 2005. *Propaganda, the Press, and Conflict: The Gulf War and Kosovo.* New York: Routledge.

Wilson, Richard A. 1997. "Human Rights, Culture and Context: An Introduction," in Richard A. Wilson (ed.) *Human Rights, Culture, and Context: Anthropological Perspectives.* London: Pluto Press.

Winston, Morton E. 2001. "Assessing the Effectiveness of International Human Rights NGOs," in Claude E. Welch, Jr. (ed.) *NGOs and Human Rights: Promise and Performance.* Philadelphia: University of Pennsylvania Press.

Wiseberg, Laurie S. and Scoble, Harry M. 1977. "The International League for Human Rights: The Strategy of a Human Rights NGO," *Georgia Journal of International and Comparative Law* 7: 289–313.

Wong, Wendy 2008. "Centralizing Principles: How Amnesty International Shaped Human Rights Politics Through Its Transnational Network." Ph.D. diss., University of California, San Diego.

2009. "Becoming a Household Name: Establishing the Credibility of Human Rights NGOs." Paper prepared for presentation at the 2009 Annual Meeting of the American Political Science Association, Toronto, Canada, September 2–6.

Wydick, B. 1999. The Effect of Microenterprise Lending on Child Schooling in Guatemala. *Economic Development and Cultural Change* 47 (4): 853–69.

Young, O. R. 1967. *The Intermediaries: Third Parties in International Crises*. Princeton University Press.

Zutshi, Bupinder 2008. "Globalisation and Child Labour Linkages in India: A Case Study of Carpet and the Garment/Apparel Industry," in Bupinder Zutshi and Kailash Satyarthi (eds.) *Globalisation, Development, and Child Labour*. Delhi: Shipra Publications.

Index